PHILANTHROPY, HIDDEN STRATEGY, AND COLLECTIVE RESISTANCE

PHILANTHROPY, HIDDEN STRATEGY, AND COLLECTIVE RESISTANCE

A PRIMER FOR CONCERNED EDUCATORS

KATHLEEN deMARRAIS,
T. JAMESON BREWER,
BRIGETTE HERRON,
JAMIE C. ATKINSON,
AND
JAMIE B. LEWIS

Gorham, Maine

Myers Education Press

Copyright © 2019 | Myers Education Press, LLC

Published by Myers Education Press, LLC
P.O. Box 424
Gorham, ME 04038

All rights reserved. No part of this book may be reprinted or reproduced in any form or by any electronic, mechanical, or other means, now known or hereafter invented, including photocopying, recording, and information storage and retrieval, without permission in writing from the publisher.

> **Myers Education Press** is an academic publisher specializing in books, e-books and digital content in the field of education. All of our books are subjected to a rigorous peer review process and produced in compliance with the standards of the Council on Library and Information Resources.

Library of Congress Cataloging-in-Publication Data available from Library of Congress.

13-digit ISBN 978-1-9755-0071-9 (paperback)
13-digit ISBN 978-1-9755--0070-2 (hardcover)
13-digit ISBN 978-1-9755-0072-6 (library networkable e-edition)
13-digit ISBN 978-1-9755-0073-3 (consumer e-edition)

Printed in the United States of America.

All first editions printed on acid-free paper that meets the American National Standards Institute Z39-48 standard.

Books published by Myers Education Press may be purchased at special quantity discount rates for groups, workshops, training organizations and classroom usage. Please call our customer service department at 1-800-232-0223 for details.

Cover design by Sophie Appel
Interior composition by Rachel Reiss

Visit us on the web at **www.myersedpress.com** to browse our complete list of titles.

CONTENTS

List of Tables and Figures ... vii
Preface ... ix

1. Ideology and Education: An Introduction ... 3
2. "The Haves and the Have Mores:" Fueling a Conservative Ideological War on Public Education (or Tracking the Money)" [reprinted] ... 31
3. The Haves and the Have Mores": An Update, 2005–2018 ... 91
4. Citizens United and the Disuniting of the United States ... 115
   BY JOHN DAYTON, J.D., ED.D., & JAMIE B. LEWIS, J.D., PH.D.
5. Hidden Strategies State by State: The History and Work of the American Legislative Exchange Council (ALEC), 1973–2018 ... 139
6. Philanthropy Goes to College: Tracking the Money ... 173
7. Ideological and Philanthropic Bedfellows: Elevating the Individual over the Collective Good in Education ... 237
8. The Megaphone Behind the Myth: The Media's Role in Shaping Public Discourse about Education Reform ... 261
9. Foundry10: A Case of Philanthropy Building School and Community Partnerships ... 283
   BY LISA CASTANEDA
10. Collective Resistance: Resources for Change ... 297

About the Authors ... 305
Index ... 309

LIST OF TABLES AND FIGURES

Tables

Table 1.1　Education and the Republican Party Platform 2016 (RPP) 18-19

Table 1.2　Education and the Democratic Party Platform 2016 (DPP) 24-27

Table 3.2　Conservative Philanthropists: Where are they now................................. 107-108

Table 5.1　Donations to American Legislative Exchange Council, $100K and Above, 2003–2016 145-146

Table 5.2　Non-Leader ALEC Members and Their Roles Reported July 2018 153-159

Table 5.3　Alumni List July 2018 160-161

Table 6.1　Contributions over $1 Million to U.S. Universities from Charles Koch 2005-2016.... 179-180

Table 6.2　Total Funding to GMU, FSU, and WCU from Charles Koch Foundation, 2003–2016 181

Table 6.3　Annual and Total Funding for George Mason University from Koch, 2003–2016 183

Table 6.4　Total Funding to FSU from Charles Koch Foundation, 2003–2016...................... 196

Table 6.5　Funding to WCU from Charles Koch Foundation, 2009–2016.................... 208

Table 6.6　Examples of BB&T Program of Free Enterprise 214-215

Table 6.7 Koch-Funded Universities and Colleges with
          Total Funding over $1 Million, 2003–2016.... 218-219

Table 6.8 Koch-Funded Universities and Colleges with
          Total Funding over $100K but under $1
          Million, 2003-2016 221-228

Table 8.1 Where People Get Their News 269

Table 8.2 Least and Most Trusted Sources of News 273

Table 8.3 Types of Misleading News.................. 276

Figures

Figure 2.1 Conservative Labyrinth..................... 53
Figure 5.1 ALEC's Leadership Structure 150
Figure 5.2 Task Force on Education and Workforce
           Development 151

PREFACE

Conservative ideologues have sought to shift the focus from the collective good to the individual good and to redirect the purposes and aims of education away from public benefit and in favor of private enterprise. As such, market-oriented, privatized, and standardized approaches to education reform have worked toward achieving that goal. This book is a primer on how the political right is utilizing various aspects of philanthropy and the political process to influence educational policymaking. Chapter One provides an overview of the political and cultural ideologies currently influencing educational policymaking, primarily at the state level, while acknowledging that ideological motivations are formulated and conveyed through the national party system.

Chapter Two is a reprint of Kathleen deMarrais's 2006 essay that articulated a structure of activities developed by the right from the late 1970s through the early 2000s and the philanthropic funding underlying those efforts. These efforts on the part of wealthy philanthropists serve as a tool for policy manipulation and the utilization of dark money as a means to influence policymakers and to propagate educational initiatives that support privatization, decentralization, and the economization of education.

Chapter Three brings the history explored in Chapter Two up to the present and illustrates the ways in which these efforts have both changed and remained the same. Chapter Three also provides readers with a clear understanding of the U.S. IRS tax regulations related to nonprofit organizations and what they can and cannot do, followed by details of the development of the Philanthropy Roundtable, Donors Trust, Donors Capital Fund, and how these nonprofit organizations have worked to shape our current political context. We examine the IRS tax codes that enable philanthropic organizations to operate, the types of nonprofit organizations eligible for 501(c)(3) status—primarily charitable, educational, and religious organizations—and for 501(c)(4) status, which provides tax exemptions for organizations that operate primarily to promote "the common good and general welfare of the people of the community" (Chick and Henchey, 1995). While 501(c)(3) organizations are prohibited from engaging in political activities, a 501(c)(4) may engage in political activities if it is not the organization's primary activity. We conclude the chapter with a short summary of the early organizers of this conservative philanthropic movement and describe their activities up to the present time, followed by an in-depth discussion of the current policy implications for educators.

Chapter Four provides an in-depth look at the case of *Citizens United*, a Supreme Court decision that opened the floodgates for corporate giving to political campaigns. It includes a brief review of the relevant history of campaign reform law, the political context of the case, the majority opinion in *Citizens United*, the dissenting opinion, and a discussion of related issues and subsequent effects on the current political context.

In Chapter Five we examine the history and philanthropic funding of the 501(c)(3) nonprofit organization the American Legislative Exchange Council (ALEC) since its founding in 1973. We provide a comprehensive examination of how ALEC has developed model bills and then worked strategically with state-level legislators to turn those bills into law. In the tradition of the Philanthropy Roundtable's strategy of funding educational initiatives to win the radical right's "war of ideas" (deMarrais, 2006), ALEC employs a new spin on these strategies. In order to promote its mission of advancing the creation of free-market supporting policies, ALEC has created spaces, materials, and opportunities for individuals representing corporate interests to have direct access and influence over the development of model policies brought back to the state level. This paper looks specifically at ALEC's development of model bills related to education and the organization's plans to continue to bolster these efforts.

In Chapter Six, the authors focus on the Charles G. Koch Foundation's funding of specific conservative initiatives on college campuses, with case studies of George Mason University, the Florida State University, and Western Carolina University. We examine the resistance of faculty and students on these campuses to strings-attached funding by this foundation.

Chapter Seven examines the role of venture philanthropy and intermediary organizations in developing a national network of education reformers.

Chapter Eight includes the role of the media and philanthropy in perpetuating the idea of failed schools and the promotion of school choice.

Chapter Nine is devoted to a case study examining the work of an educational organization that highlights a different approach to community-centered philanthropy, and Chapter Ten is designed to help activists and public education advocates resist the current direction of school choice, privatization, and the economization of education.

This book is meant to function in two ways: as an instrument for heightening awareness and as a tool for resistance. Our hope is that it will be utilized as such.

References

Chick, R. & Henchey, A. (1995). M. political organizations and IRC 501(c)(4). Retrieved from https://www.irs.gov/pub/irs-tege/eotopicm95.pdf

deMarrais, K. (2006). "The haves and the have mores": Fueling a conservative ideological war on public education (or tracking the money). *Educational Studies, 39*(3), 201–240.

PHILANTHROPY, HIDDEN STRATEGY, AND COLLECTIVE RESISTANCE

Chapter One

IDEOLOGY AND EDUCATION:
AN INTRODUCTION

Neoliberalism is the dominant ideology that has impacted education in the United States over the last two decades. David Hursh (2008) states "neoliberal theory and practices have become so embedded within our economic and political decision-making that neoliberalism is rarely explicitly invoked as a rationale" (p. 35). Hursh further adds that "neoliberalism has become ingrained as the rationale for social and economic policies and, as such, is rarely challenged" (p. 44). Under neoliberal power, education is seen in economic and individualistic terms, and language influenced by capitalism prevails. Terms such as choice, competition, markets, productivity, return-on-investment, deregulation, standardization, accountability, and efficiency are used as attacks against public and democratic institutions and challenge movements for collectivism and social justice. Productivity, competition, efficiency, and marketization have become "the ultimate and sole goal of human actions" (Bourdieu, 1998, p. 30). Under neoliberalism, capitalism defines all aspects of everyday life, including education.

As an ideology, neoliberalism has become so entrenched that it is taken for granted as a foundational ideological position in the United States. In fact, any critique of the neoliberal agenda is often positioned as anti-American or anti-patriotic. Neoliberalism includes a spectrum of social, political, and economic phenomena at different levels ranging from highly abstract to concrete examples, but all are committed to the idea that the market should organize all political, social, and economic decisions (Down, 2009;

Saad-Filho & Johnston, 2005). In terms of education, the prevailing neoliberal discourse produces new subject positions and social relations framed by "an overbearing, economic, and political context of international competitiveness" (Ball, 2007, p. 2). According to neoliberal ideology, educational institutions should be modeled after capitalist economies and the free market.

The term neoliberalism is often used without a clear explanation of what it means. One definition comes from David Harvey (2005), who defines neoliberalism as a "theory of political-economic practices which proposes human well-being can best be advanced by liberating entrepreneurial freedoms and skills within an institutional framework characterized by strong private property rights, free markets, and free trade" (p. 2). Furthermore, neoliberal ideology favors state action to enable and preserve governmental and private networks and institutions that will further neoliberal practices. While Harvey's definition applies to both American and European neoliberal thought, American neoliberalism applies an additional aspect. What makes American neoliberal thought and the American form of capitalism different are its roots in the "doctrines of competition and entrepreneurship," combined with the "rejection of advancing socialist ideas" (Mirowski & Plehwe, 2009, p. 22; Walpen, 2004). This "neoliberal thought collective" traces back to multiple locations around the world, yet is rooted in a unifying political-economic philosophy, or "market-political" philosophy (Mirowski & Plehwe, 2009, p. 22; Brown, 2006, p. 698). Some scholars utilize Foucault's idea of governmentality to speak of neoliberalism as a form of governmental reason and a way of governing the world through market ideology and disciplining the masses to embody market fundamentalism (Brown, 2006, 2015; Foucault, 2008; Olssen, Codd, & O'Neill, 2004). While Harvey's (2005) explanation of neoliberalism gives a brief, concise, and generalized history of it, Mirowski and Plehwe (2009) offer a more nuanced history. Their analysis traces neoliberalism back to the Walter Lippman Colloquium held in Paris in 1938 and the Mont Pèlerin Society founded in 1947.

The Walter Lippman Colloquium was organized by French philosopher Louis Rougier and consisted of 26 prominent individuals in business and economic studies. This original neoliberal network created a model for the establishment of the Mont Pèlerin Society (MPS) by Friedrich Hayek and Wilhelm Ropke. However, the beginnings of the MPS were not without disagreement, and the future direction of neoliberal thought was debated. The MPS met in 1947 to develop a set of statements, or aims, to target threats to classic liberalism and capitalism. While not unanimously agreed upon, an initial statement of ideas called "the neoliberal ten commandments" was drafted on April 7, 1947, and serves as an indication of MPS philosophy (Mirowski & Plehwe, 2009, p. 24). The statement argued that "individual freedom can be preserved only in a society in which an effective competitive market is the main agency for the direction of economic activity," and thus can only be fostered through "decentralization of control" and the use of a privatized means of production (p. 23).

Other language we have come to associate with neoliberal ideological thought include (a) the freedom of the consumer and the freedom of the worker to choose is essential to maximize output, internal satisfactions, and efficiency; (b) individuals must have the right to plan through initiative and freedom and not be required to adhere to some centralizing use of economic resources; (c) a belief that a decline in competition and free markets would lead to totalitarianism, and thus there should be legal and institutional frameworks in place to preserve the competitive market order and decentralize control; (d) there should be limited government involvement in the life of individuals; however, if the government must be involved, its primary role is to secure individual liberty and protect capitalism; and (e) a free society should accept a moral codification that values private action and freedom of choice equal to or more valued than collective action (Mirowski & Plehwe, 2009). Ultimately, neoliberalism is an amalgamation of ideas stemming from the Austrian School of Economics, the Chicago School of Economics, Germany's Freiburg School of Ordoliberalism, and the American social and economic order focused primarily on industrialized, privatized, and standardized mass production and mass consumption called Fordism. I turn now to a discussion of neoconservativism.

Neoconservatism

Neoconservatism is a complex ideology that "has no electoral, economic, or religious base; it has never had an uncontested leader; and it has never been represented by any clearly defined organization," and it in no way can be defined as a political party (Vaïse, 2010, p. 4). Though neoconservatism is not a political party, the Republican Party is made up of a strong contingent of neoconservative thinkers and strategists. It is "a school of thought, an intellectual outlook, or perhaps a tendency or persuasion, as its godfathers Norman Podhoretz and Irving Kristol sometimes describe it" (Vaïse, 2010, p. 4). Neoconservatives "yield great power and influence over the broad conservative intellectual movement, and in turn, the Republican Party" (Thompson & Brook, 2010, p. 2). Naming the philosophical or ideological premises that neoconservatives admire is challenging because it has changed over the years. Neoconservatives, or the neocons, "wish to guide America from the top down," yet they are prone to "discontinuity, heterogeneity, and contradiction," and the word itself is "constantly in danger of losing any precise meaning" (Thompson & Brook, 2010, p. 3; Vaïse, 2010, pp. 5–6).

Fukuyama (2006) states that "the neoconservative legacy is complex and diverse, tracing its roots back to the early 1940s" (p. 4). The history of neoconservatism, however interesting, is too long and complex for this chapter, so we choose to concentrate on the current form of neoconservatism, which finds its roots in the 1960s as a reactionary counter-movement to the New Left. These neocons are considered second- and third-generation ideological adherents. From the 1970s and into Ronald Reagan's first term in the White House in the early 1980s, "the neocons have systematically taken over the conservative intellectual movement with remarkable speed, their ideas have come to dominate the Republican Party, and their policies have influenced the administrations" of each Republican president since Reagan (Thompson & Brook, 2010, p. 17). Second-generation neoconservatism figured prominently from 1968 and the end of the Johnson administration to roughly 1995, when a "new age of neoconservatism was born," becoming "a full-fledged element of the Republican Party" (Vaïse, 2010, p. 11). Third- generation neocons form the current ideological configuration, although neoconservatism may be in a period of transition marked by upheavals further to the right from groups such as the Tea Party and the Religious Right. Thus, a fourth generation marked by internal struggles is emerging and is a tenuous amalgamation of the Religious Right, Libertarians, the Tea Party, and mainstream neocons, who do not always agree.

Today, mainstream neocons blend second- and third-generation neoconservative thought and do not mind state intervention as long as it serves their ideals of economic nationalism. They tend to have a hawkish stance on the use of military force and interventionist foreign policy. They have attached "great importance to military superiority and to the democratic principle: America must be strong and ready to act in the world according to its political, [economic,] and security interests, which sometimes includes spreading democracy" (Vaïse, 2010, pp. 11–12) and an American form of imperialism called "state building." State building occurs when an external actor, usually another country, attempts to prop up or turn around an economically or politically failed state following an economic collapse or other catastrophic event such as a war or other conflict. This usually entails the desire to have this support favor the country that provides the aid. Unlike other forms of conservatism, "neoconservatives are guided by a vision of a strong state. This is especially true surrounding issues of knowledge, values, and the body" (Apple, 2006, p. 67; Brown, 2006, Saltman, 2000). Saltman argues that the neoconservative form of conservative ideology "is dangerous to public democracy as it demonstrates a deep distrust of public governance [collectivism and social programs] and public deliberation and its demands that citizens pledge their allegiance to unquestionable dogma framed through jingoistic nationalism" (Saltman, 2006, p. 348). The current conceptualization of neoconservatism seems to be united around militarism, corporatism, and pro-Israel sentiments with a belief that American power can be used for moral purposes domestically and abroad (Brown, 2006).

Brown (2006) describes neoconservatism as a "moral-political rationality" that combines elements of paleoconservatism and neoconservatism (Apple, 2000, 2006; Buras, 2008; Dorrien, 1993; Gerson, 1997; Saltman, 2014). This becomes problematic when defining the impact of conservatism on various social, political, and cultural issues. There are five fundamental principles to which contemporary neoconservatives adhere. The first is the belief in the need for the United States to play an active role in the world and to assert and defend an American-led world order that utilizes a neo-Reagan formulation of foreign policy and military supremacy supported by moral confidence in the rightness of this goal. The second principle emphasizes a connection to Straussian philosophy and the importance of promoting a political realism. According to this principle, democracy should be installed in other countries through regime change in order to protect U.S. interests in neighboring countries. While the United States is portrayed in this scenario as offering a fig leaf of democracy, it may actually serve as a mask for imperialism, economic colonialism, and militarism (in other words, hard-line Wilsonianism) (Thompson & Brook, 2010; Vaïse, 2010). The third principle promotes the idea of *Pax Americana*, a benevolent empire where Americans help bring peace and order to the rest of the world by seeking their own security. The fourth principle is the belief that global organizations such as the United Nations are ineffective and illegitimate and that America should be free to act unilaterally without their approval. The final principle argues for a massive U.S. military to maintain security for the United States and its allies and to influence regime change in other nations to maintain world order. Neocons view Europe as weak and usually promote hardline Zionism (Vaïse, 2010). Although there is no explicit mention of education in these principles, neocons have become interested in education because it can provide a training ground for future neoconservatives. Neocons believe that education reforms should be centered on ideas of patriotism, cloaked in religious elements and morality, and produce a subservient citizenry that is willing to let the experts and the elite determine the future of America. Neocons believe the citizenry must be educated to become docile, patriotic, and obedient workers whose sense of loyalty and nationalism will preclude criticism of the government and the capitalist system. Neoconservatives and paleoconservatives both work within the cultural realm to influence society; however, it is the paleoconservatives who aim for a historical form of conservatism—a traditionalism.

Paleoconservatism: What Is Old Is New Again

Conservatism is witnessing a revival in the form of conservative traditionalism. Much of the current conservative ideology is influenced by paleoconservative thought. Earlier in this chapter we mentioned how neoconservativism and paleoconservatism are often conflated by some political theorists. It is important to delineate the two ideologies when examining their impacts on education. We have already examined neoconservatism and its history, so it is important to now shift to paleoconservatism, as its ideological agenda seems to be receiving more attention lately, especially in light of Donald Trump's presidency. Paleoconservatism represents conservative traditionalists (referred to hereafter as paleocons). The term paleoconservative can be traced back to the 1980s, when Pat Buchanan and other leading conservative traditionalists began to critique the new conservatives (the neocons) in the Republican Party. Paleocons feel that the neocons have hijacked true conservatism and transformed it into something markedly different from true conservatism (Francis, 2002). Paleocons are socially and culturally conservative and signify "a brand of conservatism whose roots reach back to before the Cold War and even WWII... [they] readily accept the much-used label Old Right," and they "represent a conservatism that arose in opposition to the New Deal" (Scotchie, 1999, p. 1). However, Francis argues that "paleoconservatism is as new as neoconservatism" and "is an invention of the magazine *Chronicles*" (Francis, 2002, p. 25).

Paleoconservatism arose as a reaction against several trends in the American Right, including (a) the bid for dominance by the neocons (the dynamics regarding this battle are too protracted to explain here), (b) the perceived collapse of intellectual, moral, and political thought in the mainstream conservative movement, and (c) the growth of secularism, hedonism, and the carnal and material self-indulgence of the dominant culture, as well as the "proclivity of culture to be manipulated by media and the political elites" (pp. 25–26). Philosophically, paleocons are influenced by Edmund Burke and value rural America, old Southern Agrarian ideas, states' rights, hierarchical order, non-materialism, and traditional cultural and religious groundings embedded within a traditional nuclear family. Economically speaking, paleoconservatives abide by the Austrian school of economics, with influences from Friedrich Hayek and Ludwig von Mises (Scotchie, 1999, p. 2).

Paleocons have a special affinity with the South and admire the "decentralizing tenets of Thomas Jefferson, John Randolph, and John C. Calhoun," and they generally disagree with large-scale industrialization (p. 2). Many of the paleocons' views began to creep into the Republican Party during the presidency of George H.W. Bush. Some of their "positions and ideas were smack in the conservative mainstream: privatizing Social Security; eliminating numerous cabinet positions, including the Departments of Education, Commerce, Energy, and Transportation; a pro-life stance on abortion; and opposition to affirmative action and quotas" (p. 6). Major areas of disagreement between the Old Right and the New Right relate to issues of immigration, trade, religion, and foreign policy. Paleoconservatives distrust the degree to which the country has generated a huge debt for the purpose of military expenditures, as well as the declining moral values of big business, the destruction of small businesses and local commerce in favor of conglomerates, the outsourcing of jobs, and the gutting of state-funded infrastructure that supports institutions such as education, transportation, and emergency services (Brown, 2006).

Paleocons look at the neocons as American imperialistic empire builders, while they see themselves as keepers of the republic who honor the intentions and institutions of the founders. One can look back on the documentary *The Revisionaries* (Thurman, 2012) for examples of how paleocons see themselves in this light. Paleocons are scrambling to take back conservatism from the neocons and the neoliberals and feel as though they are the "righteous bulwarks" of conservatism. This phenomenon can be seen in the recent rise of the Alt-Right, the Tea Party, the Christian Right, and libertarianism (Brown, 2006, p. 698). Their voices are often swallowed up in the conservative cacophony, but their desire to "re-articulate and police cultural and national borders, the sacred, and the singular through discourses of patriotism, religiosity, and the West" have not been as successful in becoming part of modern conservatism (p. 699). However, a new form of conservative populism is beginning to change conservatism and push paleoconservative ideology into the mainstream. We refer to this movement as the post-neoconservative turn in American conservatism and rightist ideology.

It is sometimes difficult to decipher conservative rhetoric. The best way to discern differences between the Old Right (paleocons) and the New Right (neocons) is to examine the writings of major figures from both variants. Russell Kirk (1918–1994) wrote about paleo thought and ideology, which led to the development of his Ten Conservative Principles (Kirk, 1993, 1999). These principles state the following:

1. The conservative believes that there is an enduring moral order;

2. The conservative adheres to custom, convention, and continuity;
3. Conservatives believe in what may be called the principle of prescription, or things established by immemorial usage, so that the mind of man runneth not to the contrary.
4. Conservatives are guided by the principle of prudence.
5. Conservatives pay attention to the principle of variety.
6. Conservatives are chastened by their principle of imperfectability.
7. Conservatives are persuaded that freedom and property are closely linked.
8. Even though they oppose involuntary collectivism, conservatives uphold voluntary community.
9. Conservatives perceive the need for prudent restraints upon power and human passions.
10 The conservative understands that permanence and change must be recognized and reconciled in a vigorous society.

Paleoconservative thinking has been absorbed into the mainstream conservative movement, which is why it is often difficult to distinguish. Mainstream conservatism has taken many of the traditionalist views of the paleocons and manipulated those views for the overall rightist ideology of the Republican Party. Examples of paleocon views that have been co-opted by the conservative mainstream are the support of the nuclear family, opposition to abortion, opposition to gun control, Christian fundamentalism (the Christian Right), opposition to LGBTQIA rights, capital punishment, the war on drugs (especially marijuana), ideas regarding the original intent of the Constitution, an over-celebratory regard of history and national identity, and a reaffirmation of states' rights as the dominant political idea. Paleocons differ in that they are often slightly more sympathetic to environmental concerns than neocons and neoliberals, though this has obviously not transmitted to mainstream rightist thinking. They are more attuned to rural and poor issues because of the strong lineage of southern agrarianism, more anti-consumerist and anti-materialistic, and have slightly different motives when it comes to education. The paleocons include a majority of the Christian Right in their ranks, and their views are often borrowed for strategic and tactical purposes by the Republican Party, leading to a populist strain within conservative circles. Regardless, it is important to discuss the Christian Right separately, since they are growing in influence as they battle a war against growing secularism and Christian belief that they fear is steering the country away from its Western Christian traditions.

Conservatism has embraced a new Christian fundamentalism that has been steadily growing since the Reagan Era. "Reagan campaigned on 'values' issues such as restricting access to abortion, anti-federalism, tax credits for private schooling, and welfare reform" (Myers & Cibulka, 2015, p. 270). The Christian Right, as part of the paleo variant of conservatism, has extended these ideas, and thus "is animated by two central themes: (1) the attempt to restore to American life some nostalgic form of the sanctity of family and religion [and] (2) appropriate rules of sexual conduct and belief, both of which are rooted in the conviction that Christian morality has been replaced by secular values" (Myers & Cibulka, 2015, p. 271).

Beyond the issues of the nuclear family and issues of sexuality and abortion, the Christian Right is less unified as it ventures into other peripheral issues. Those issues include such things as economics, foreign policy, education, the environment, and taxes. Regardless, the Christian Right remains part of the larger conservative movement and tends to align most readily with the paleocons. The Christian Right and the paleocon ideology are aligned when it comes to schooling, specifically in terms of curriculum reform (especially in history and science courses), prayer in school, and Christian-based homeschooling. What our society is witnessing in the broader conservative movement is a post-neoconservative turn that includes elements of neoliberal, neoconservative, and paleoconservative thought.

The Post-Neoconservative Turn

As we write this chapter, we must acknowledge the change occurring within rightist ideology and a twenty-first-century version of conservatism. Until roughly 2008, neoconservative and neoliberal ideology dominated the politically conservative landscape. However, beginning with President Barack Obama's first term in office, the United States witnessed a fundamental change in American conservatism. Many conservatives, having become dissatisfied with the direction of the Republican Party, recognized a new sense of urgency that began to sweep conservatism, much like that witnessed during the late 1960s. The culmination of this populist uprising has recently been realized with the 2016 election of Donald Trump as president. The Alt-Right, as it is often referred to, represents a disruption of the neoconservative dominance within the National Republican Party and the national conservative movement. In reality, this populist shake-up in conservative politics is actually a resurgence and a radicalization of many paleoconservative ideals. In an August 2015 headline in the *Orlando Sentinel*, Trump was regarded as "the new face of paleoconservatism" (Murray, 2015). It has further been discussed that the election of President Trump represents the rise of White identity politics, a reaction to globalization, a pushback against liberal immigration policies, and the rise of Christian fundamentalism (Leithart, 2017). In a recent *New York Times* article, Thomas Edsall noted that "it is no secret that the President has capitalized on the increasing salience of race and ethnicity in recent years." He states that the populist and "furious reaction to many different historical and cultural developments...has created a political environment ripe for the growth of White identity [and Christian] politics" (Edsall, 2017). Regardless of the descriptors, this new conservative turn, a post-neoconservative turn, is a direct response to the sociopolitical and cultural progressiveness that characterized the two terms of President Obama.

In its broadest sense, we are witnessing reactionary politics and an increased polarization of ideological positioning. A new ideological merger has to be discussed in terms of goals, ideas, and efforts rather than in terms of any particular political party's ethos. It differs in degree from state to state and from region to region. The mixture of neoliberal, neoconservative, and paleoconservative ideas often creates paradoxes between rhetoric and actions. For example, many neoliberals believe that the capitalist system and market fundamentalism represent the best means of preserving freedom and liberty while at the same time utilizing Christian moral codification to defend the economic nationalism of the United States. Capitalism often breeds inequities and injustices that would seem to run counter to many ideas in Christianity, yet conservatives continue to link the two. Conservative crusaders target education through legislation, philanthropic work, and philosophical espionage. How will this new conservatism impact education in the future? Will it be more of the same, or something inherently different?

The answers to these questions may require some speculation. However, when examined through a critical and historical lens, it may be safe to say that neoliberal ideological goals will continue to dominate public K–16 education. The bulwark of education, curriculum and instruction, will continue to become more standardized, less critical, and under pressure from the right to move away from secular and scientific ideas (unless there is profit). Progressive ideas about immigration rights, LGBTQIA rights, integrated schooling, separation of church and state, and a host of other sociocultural issues often considered peripheral to the main issues in education are likely to become more prominent in ideological discussions if educators continue to raise them as important issues. The consolidation of goals and ideas embedded in the rightist agenda for schooling is difficult to separate from the overarching rhetoric in conservative politics. Exactly how this post-neoconservative turn will impact education in the long term is up for debate. We, as educators, political theorists, sociologists, philosophers, and so on, must be attuned to the fundamental changes occurring within educational politics and policymaking. This in itself is a full-time job, because changes are taking place much more quickly than they did in the past. For example, one only needs to examine how President Trump's administration has rapidly changed many policies and programs to include education in the short time he has been in office. While the states continue to be the dominant drivers in education policy, they often take their cues from federal policy due to their dependence on grants-in-aid. As President Trump's Secretary of Education, Betsy DeVos, imposes her own agenda on national educational policy, state-level educational policy is sure to continue its march toward privatization, economization, decentralization, charter schools, and charter systems. What follows is an attempt to glean the goals of education from ideological and party narratives.

Party, Politics, and the Ideological Agenda for Education

As suggested by Bourdieu (1998), productivity, competition, and efficiency have become an incessant drumbeat to which humans must march, and this can be seen ever so clearly in our nation's schools and education policy. The move to privatize education by way of marketization for the sake of competition and efficiency has manifested in three overarching arenas: (a) school organization; (b) teacher preparation; and (c) testing and test-prep pedagogy. While for the better part of the last century public education has been conceptualized as a public good that benefits all individuals in a society at individual and collective levels, the reform agenda of the last few decades has sought to elevate the individual over the collective good in terms of students and teachers. While there remains a conception of the public in the mantra "a rising tide lifts all boats," the focus here on the common good is a by-product of individualization. The education reforms that found an ideological impetus in the work of Milton Friedman in the 1950s found political footing within the neoliberal policies of the 1980s and reimagined the role of the public and governments, instead focusing on individuals competing in a hyper-market with the key understanding that efforts and rewards are individualized based on one's merit (meritocracy). Within capitalism, competition is a foundational component in which winners and losers are a foundational, functional, and necessary outcome. The ascendance of Donald Trump to the presidency and Betsy DeVos's subsequent nomination and confirmation as Secretary of Education have cemented this ideological disposition, which elevates the importance of markets and individualized conceptions of education for the foreseeable future. As such, federal policies are likely to continue to reinforce market-oriented approaches to school organization, teacher preparation, and the importance of testing and accountability.

Education reform is significantly influenced by rightist ideology, ideologues, and other neoliberal and conservative actors who believe that all aspects of education should reflect American exceptionalism, traditional values, norms, and beliefs, while acknowledging fundamental ideas associated with capitalism and free-market nationalism. In the last several decades, education has increasingly become a major campaign issue at both the national and state levels. It has served as an easy target of campaign rhetoric and ideologically framed discourse, often making use of the narrative of failure. Narratives within the parties differ in regard to the notions of individualism, competition, and choice, and the idea of collectivism and the common good. What follows in Table 1.1 below is a foray into the ideological narrative regarding education within the major party platforms.

If you were to continue to read through the 2016 Republican Party platform (RPP), you would see the continuation of many of the ideas discussed in Table 1 and its specific strategies. The Republican Party, home to neoconservatives, paleoconservatives, and neoliberals, has called for more options for learning, including homeschooling, career and technical education, private and/or parochial schools, increasing the number of charter schools, and online learning. Educational Savings Accounts (ESAs), vouchers, and tax credits are offered as ways for children to attend the school of their choice. As the reader will see throughout this book, philanthropies and non-governmental actors,

Table 1.1. Education and the Republican Party Platform 2016 (RPP, pp. 33–34).

LANGUAGE FROM REPUBLICAN PARTY:	COMMENTS REGARDING PARTY LANGUAGE:
"Education is much more than schooling. It is the whole range of activities by which families and communities **transmit to a younger generation**, *not just knowledge and skills, but* **ethical and behavioral norms and traditions**. *It is the handing over of a personal and cultural identity."*	This language includes the cultural conservative notions of ethical and behavioral norms, as well as nostalgic ideas that they have deemed lost or trampled upon by progressive-minded educators. It also contains the idea of transmitting to students, harkening back to the notion of students as empty vessels that must be properly filled.
"…American education has, for the last several decades, been the focus of **constant controversy**, *as* **centralizing forces** *from outside the family and community have sought* **to remake education in order to remake America."**	This language is pro-decentralization and hints at the constant narrative of failing public schools. This language attacks progressive schooling and/or social reconstruction.
"The federal government should not be a partner in that [education] effort, *as the Constitution gives it no role in education."*	This language is pro-decentralization.

Table 1.1 continued on p. 19

Table 1.1 continued from p. 18

LANGUAGE FROM REPUBLICAN PARTY:	COMMENTS REGARDING PARTY LANGUAGE:
"**Parents are a child's first and foremost educators**, *and have primary responsibility for the education of their children.* **Parents have a right to direct their children's education**, *care, and upbringing.* **We support a constitutional amendment to protect that right from interference from the state, the federal government, or international bodies such as the United Nations.**"	More language to promote decentralization while pivoting to the parents' role as primary education providers. This language is utilized to support choice in education as well.
"*We reject a one-size-fits-all approach to education and support* **a broad range of choices** *for parents and children at the state and local level.*"	The language to support school choice begins with the prior critique of centralized (public) education and toward a consumer version of schooling.
"…their education reform movement calls for **choice-based, parent-driven, accountability** at every stage of schooling…it recognizes the wisdom of local control of our schools and it wisely sees **consumer rights in education—choice—as the most important driving force** for renewing education."	Speaking to states and groups who have resisted national standards and the Common Core and positioning them as the model.
"*Administrators need* **flexibility** *to* **innovate** *and to* **hold accountable** *those responsible for student performance.*"	Language of performance and accountability rooted in innovative solutions, which is by and large the language of business.

Table 1.1 continued on p. 20

Table 1.1 continued from p. 19	
LANGUAGE FROM REPUBLICAN PARTY:	**COMMENTS REGARDING PARTY LANGUAGE:**
"**A good understanding of the Bible being indispensable for the development of an educated citizenry**, *we encourage state legislatures to offer the* **Bible in a literature curriculum** *as an elective in America's high schools.*"	Obviously a nod to the Christian Right, which also seems to direct schools to utilize a course literature coding to teach the Bible. This is a strategy utilized to keep Christian themes in the public despite the Establishment Clause.
"**Rigid tenure systems should be replaced with a merit-based approach** *in order to attract the best talent to the classroom.*"	Meritocratic, individualized, and competitive ideas of merit, performance, and achievement, combined with a lack of protections for critical educators who may choose to teach in ways not conducive to standardization and testing.
"*More money alone does not necessarily equal better performance. After years of trial and error, we know the policies and methods that have actually made a difference in student advancement:* **choice in education; building on the basics; STEM subjects and phonics;** *career and technical education; ending social promotions;* **merit-pay** *for good teachers;* **classroom discipline;** *parental involvement; and strong leadership by principals, superintendents, and local elected school boards.*"	A focus on choice, the back-to-basics movement (the classics), STEM over the humanities, merit pay, and tougher discipline policies (policing). Once again, the move away from progressive schooling that may encourage social reforms. Merit pay potentially stymies critical voices in the classroom.

coalitions and policy networks, are pushing state legislatures to include many of these ideas in state education policies.

In addition, Republicans take on an "English first" approach, which often disenfranchises new citizens and immigrants. Cultural conservatives want to see an end to family planning, a return to an abstinence-only policy for sex education, and an endorsement of the Christian ideal of marriage as between one man and one woman. Conservative ideologues are attacking current understandings of Title IX designed to protect all individuals regardless of gender, sexual orientation, and so forth, stating that it has gone too far, and that the original intent had nothing to do with protecting all forms of sexual/gender identity. This debate has moved beyond athletics and extracurricular activities to everyday issues in education such as the "bathroom bills" proposed in many southern states—for example, North Carolina. As Spring (2011) states, "In the framework of American Exceptionalism, conservative [actors] are particularly concerned with the values imparted by...instruction"—in other words, through both the stated and hidden curriculums (p. 121). In terms of curriculum, conservatives desire a return to traditionalism and celebratory history, which promotes American exceptionalism, and an end to the teaching of evolutionary theory or the requirement that intelligent design be taught as a competing theory. Conservative ideological pressures are focused on the promotion of patriotism, unbridled nationalism, non-critical/celebratory perspectives of American history, traditional religious-based morality, and a unified American culture, one centered on competition and rugged individualism, which is then incorporated and infused into the curriculum and the pedagogical practices of teachers.

In terms of higher education, there is a general distrust of academics and a push to promote online education and the origination and management of student loans as a privatized venture. The Libertarian Party, which primarily adheres to neoliberal policies and a general notion of extreme freedoms, holds beliefs that are similar to those of the Republican Party, yet melds them together into one broad statement that declares:

> Education is best provided by the free market, achieving greater quality, accountability and efficiency with more diversity of choice. Recognizing that the education of children is a parental responsibility, we would restore authority to parents to determine the education of their children, without interference from government. Parents should have control of and responsibility for all funds expended for their children's education. (Libertarian Party Platform, 2016)

Promoted within this platform are the same notions of free market, accountability, efficiency, and the emphasis on choice. The current danger is the degree to which neoliberal ideas have been attached to notions of a White, Christian identity. In this regard, with conservatives "linking American Exceptionalism to Christianity, religious-oriented conservatives believe that any attack on the role of religion in government [especially in schools] is an attack on the very foundations of American life" (Spring, 2011). Several issues come to mind, including (a) prayer in school; (b) limits on multicultural programs; (c) a push for immigrants to adapt to American culture; (d) an effort to eliminate the discussion of evolution in science and/or replace it with Young Earth creationism, intelligent design, or similar ideas; (e) the teaching of civics and American history in a positive, non-critical, celebratory manner that promotes American Judeo-Christian values and American exceptionalism and limits discussion of atrocities committed by our government; (f) opposition to the teaching of birth control in favor of abstinence-only sex education; (g) opposition to the recognition of the LGBTQIA communities; (h) a belief that character education should be a formalized process in schools; and (i) an increase in heavily authoritarian models of disciplinary tactics in school.

Saltman (2014) states that "cultural conservatives tend to emphasize curriculum and pedagogical approaches heavy on respect for, and oftentimes obedience to, authority and dominant traditions and respect for the government or at least the authoritarian parts of it" (p. xxiii). Conservatives make moral values the measure of quality education, thus constituting a moral-political formulaic of education policy reforms (Brown, 2006; Saltman, 2014). To cultural conservatives, capitalism should take a back seat to moral and religious values. Cultural conservatism provides the pedagogical content, the obedient citizen, and the patriotic consumer that fuel the neoliberal conservative's ideological educational agenda. Schooling, therefore, should be focused on character, traditional values, localized control, and morality centered on "choice" and the market. This is, by and large, undemocratic and anti-intellectual, though conservatives would argue that they believe schooling is not rigorous enough.

So how do the competitive ideas of choice, individualism, and competition differ from the language found in the Democratic Party platform (DDP) in 2016? While there are progressive ideas and fundamental notions of collectivism, one can identify paradoxes. Language within the Democratic Party platform, much like the Republican Party platform, indicates the notion of an education system that is struggling to keep up with the rest of the world (a neoliberal idea), as noted in Table 1.2 below.

The Democratic Party platform goes further in discussing the notion that education policies should motivate rather than demoralize and de-professionalize educators. The platform argues that education should provide a means to uplift society, as opposed to a competitive Social Darwinism. Unfortunately, we also see the language of choice in the Democratic platform. For example, the 2016 platform states:

> Democrats are committed to providing parents with high-quality public school options and expanding these options for low-income youth. We support democratically governed, great neighborhood public schools and high-quality public charter schools, and we will help them disseminate best practices to other leaders and educators. Democrats oppose for-profit charter schools focused on making a profit off of public resources. We believe that high-quality public charter schools should provide options for parents but should not replace or destabilize traditional public schools. (p. 34)

Table 1.2. Education and the Democratic Party Platform 2016 (DPP, pp. 30–33).

LANGUAGE FROM DEMOCRATIC PARTY:	COMMENTS REGARDING PARTY LANGUAGE:
"Democrats know that every child, no matter who they are, how much their families earn, or where they live, should have access to a high-quality education, from pre-school through high school and beyond. **But the United States still lags behind other advanced economies in providing high-quality, universal preschool programs to help all of our kids…"**	While this language seems to be more inclusive and positive, it still contains deficit language utilized to describe public education. While primarily referring to preschool programs, it implies a broad deficit.
"Our schools are more segregated today than they were when Brown v. Board of Education was decided, and we see **wide disparities in education outcomes across racial and socioeconomic lines."**	Discusses disparities among educational outcomes, but fails to address how those outcomes are measured and the social issues that may lead to problems in schools, which may not be solved in the schools.
"…the high cost of college has required too many Americans to take out **staggering student loans** *or put a degree out of reach entirely."*	Language that speaks to the growing crisis of student debt, yet the Democratic Party has been somewhat complicit in this crisis. One could argue about more progressive causes now taking up the mantle in the Democratic Party and how this may impact discussions in the growing student loan crisis.

Table 1.2 continued on p. 25

Table 1.2 continued from p. 24 LANGUAGE FROM DEMOCRATIC PARTY:	COMMENTS REGARDING PARTY LANGUAGE:
"We are selling our children and our young people short. Democrats are committed to making good public schools available to every child, no matter what zip code they live in, and at last making debt-free college a reality for all Americans."	Throughout much of the language by those on the political left is the notion of "our" children—a collectivist stance. Yet within the DPP, there is often contradictory language.
"Bold new investments by the federal government, coupled with states reinvesting in higher education **and colleges holding the line on costs***, will ensure Americans of all backgrounds will be* **prepared for the jobs and economy of the future."**	This notion, while countering the decentralization of schooling and the removal of the federal government from college tuition financing practices espoused by conservatives, seems to support the idea that jobs and the economy seem to take priority, or precedence, over other ideas in our country (a neoliberal idea).
"The federal government will push more colleges and universities to take quantifiable, affirmative steps in increasing the percentage of racial and ethnic minority, low-income, and first-generation students they enroll and graduate."	Progressive language, though lacking in specifics.
"Provide relief from crushing student loan debt."	See comments above.
"Supporting historically Black colleges and universities and minority-serving institutions."	Language that promotes the importance of maintaining viable Black colleges and universities, which serve important functions in our communities.

Table 1.2 continued on p. 26

Table 1.2 continued from p. 25

LANGUAGE FROM DEMOCRATIC PARTY:	COMMENTS REGARDING PARTY LANGUAGE:
"*Cracking down on* **predatory for-profit schools.**"	This language is meant to challenge for-profit school systems, including for-profit charters and other for-profit educational systems, such as alternative teacher preparation programs.
"*Democrats believe* **we must have the best-educated population and workforce in the world.**"	Once again, back to the neoliberal language of competition, a productive workforce, and economic indicators utilized to prove the merit of an educational system.
"*Democrats know the federal government must play a critical role in making sure every child has access to a world-class education. We believe that* **a strong public education system is an anchor of our democracy**, *a propeller of the economy, and the vehicle through which we help all children achieve their dreams.* **Public education must engage students to be critical thinkers and civic participants while addressing the well-being of the whole child**" (2016).	This statement needs a little unpacking: (1) large federal government role; (2) supports public education; (3) education is connected with democracy and the economy (neoliberal idea); and (4) public education as a means to develop critical thinkers as a product of holistic processes.
"*Democrats believe that* **all students should be taught to high academic standards.** *Schools should have adequate resources to provide programs and support to help meet the needs of every child.* **We will hold schools, districts,**	The political left utilizes the language of accountability and standards, just as the political right does.

Table 1.2 continued on p. 27

IDEOLOGY AND EDUCATION

Table 1.2 continued from p. 26

LANGUAGE FROM DEMOCRATIC PARTY:	COMMENTS REGARDING PARTY LANGUAGE:
communities, and states accountable for raising achievement levels *for all students—particularly low-income students, students of color, English Language Learners, and students with disabilities."*	
"We are deeply **committed to ensuring that we strike a better balance on testing so that it informs, but does not drive, instruction.** *To that end, we encourage states to develop a* **multiple measures approach to assessment***, and we believe that* **standardized tests must be reliable and valid.** *We oppose high-stakes standardized tests that falsely and unfairly label students of color, students with disabilities, and English Language Learners as failing; the use of standardized test scores as the basis for refusing to fund schools or to close schools; and the use of student test scores in teacher and principal evaluations, a practice which has been repeatedly rejected by researchers."*	This seems to go against merit-based approaches espoused by the right, and it directly contradicts many of the state charter districts designed to capture so-called failing schools as punishment for failing to meet adequate performance. One could argue whether any standardized testing could be reliable or valid. One could also potentially argue whether high-stakes testing disenfranchises most students while favoring only those from upper-middle-class households.
"We will support the use of **restorative justice practices** *that help students and staff resolve conflicts peacefully and respectfully while helping to improve the teaching and learning community."*	A softer form of justice (school discipline policies) than espoused by the right.

This statement sends a mixed signal that promotes school choice and charter schools while continuing to criticize some forms of school choice options. What is missing in the national discourse as a result of its absence from the Democratic party's political narrative is the forwarding of a truly progressive message of a democratic education that resists the perpetuation of neoliberal and conservative educational policies guided by neoliberal and conservative ideologues. This book is meant to elucidate the many actors—both government and non-government—who are working through meso-level institutional networks, or coalitions, to shape education in their image and for their benefit.

References

Apple, M. (2000). Between neoliberalism and neoconservatism: Education and conservatism in a global context. In N. Burbules & C. Torres (Eds.), *Globalization and education: Critical perspectives* (pp. 57–78). New York: Routledge.

Apple, M. (2006). Understanding and interrupting neoliberalism and neoconservatism in education. *Pedagogies: An International Journal, 1*(1), 21–26.

Ball, S. (2007). Education plc: Understanding private sector participation in public sector education. New York: Routledge

Bourdieu, P. (1998). Act of resistance: Against the tyranny of the market. New York: The New Press.

Brown, W. (2006). American nightmare: Neoliberalism, neoconservatism, and de-democratization. *Political Theory, 34*(6), 690–714.

Brown W. (2015). *Undoing the demos: Neoliberalism's stealth revolution*. Brooklyn, NY: Zone Books.

Buras, K. (2008). *Rightist multiculturalism: Core lessons on neoconservative school reform.* New York: Routledge.

Democratic Party Platform Committee (2016). *2016 Democratic Party platform*. Retrieved from http://www.presidency.ucsb.edu/papers_pdf/117717.pdf

Dorrien, G. (1993). *The neoconservative mind: Politics, culture, and the war of ideology.* Philadelphia, PA: Temple University Press.

Down, B. (2009). Schooling, productivity, and the enterprising self: Beyond market values. *Critical Studies in Education, 50*(1), 51–64.

Edsall, T.B. (2017, August 24). *Donald Trump's identity politics.* Retrieved from https://www.nytimes.com/2017/08/24/opinion/donald-trump-identity-politics.html

Foucault, M. (2008). *The birth of biopolitics: Lectures at the Collège de France, 1978–1979.* New York: Palgrave Macmillan.

Francis, S. (2002, December 16). The paleo persuasion. *The American Conservative.* Retrieved July 4, 2016, from http://www.theamericanconservative.com/articles/the-paleo- persuasion

Fukuyama, F. (2006). *America at the crossroads: Democracy, power, and the neoconservative legacy.* New Haven, CT: Yale University Press.

Gerson, M. (1997). *The neoconservative vision: From the Cold War to the culture wars.* New York: Madison Books.

Harvey, D. (2005). *A brief history of neoliberalism.* New York: Oxford University Press.

Hursh, D. (2008). Neoliberalism. In D. Gabbard (Ed.), *Knowledge and power in the global economy: The effects of school reform in a neoliberal/neoconservative age* (2nd ed., pp. 35–44). New York: Lawrence Erlbaum Associates.

Kirk, R. (1993). *Ten conservative principles.* Retrieved June 30, 2016, from http://www.kirkcenter.org/index.php/detail/ten-conservative-principles

Kirk, R. (1999). The question of tradition. In J. Scotchie (Ed.), *The paleoconservatives: New voices of the old right* (pp. 59–78). New Brunswick, NJ: Transaction Publishers.

Leithart, P.J. (2017, January 13). *Trumpism and paleoconservatism.* Retrieved from https://www.firstthings.com/blogs/leithart/2017/01/trumpism-and-paleoconservatism

Libertarian Party Convention. (2016). *Libertarian Party 2016 platform.* Retrieved from http://www.presidency.ucsb.edu/papers_pdf/117717.pdf

Mirowski, P., & Plehwe, D. (2009). *The road from Mont Pèlerin: The making of the neoliberal thought collective.* Cambridge, MA: Harvard University Press.

Murray, J.R. II. (2015, August 12). *Paleo-conservative 2.0: Trump honest, turns flubs into feats.* Retrieved from http://www.orlandosentinel.com/opinion/os-ed-trump-campaign-081215- 20150811-story.html

Myers, N., & Cibulka, J. (2015). Religious faith and policy in public education: A political and historical analysis of the Christian Right in American schooling. In B. Cooper, J. Cibulka, & L. Fusarelli (Eds.), *Handbook of education politics and policy* (2nd ed., pp. 267–283). New York: Routledge

Olssen, M., Codd, J., & O'Neill, A. (2004). *Education policy: Globalization, citizenship and democracy.* Thousand Oaks, CA: Sage.

Republican National Committee on Arrangements. (2016). *Republican Party platform.* Retrieved from https://prod-cdn-static.gop.com/media/documents/DRAFT_12_FINAL[1]- ben_1468872234.pdf

Saad-Filho, A., & Johnston, D. (2005). Introduction. In A. Saad-Filho & D. Johnston (Eds.), *Neoliberalism: A critical reader* (pp. 1–6). Ann Arbor, MI: Pluto Press

Saltman, K. (2000). *Collateral damage: Corporatizing public schools—A threat to democracy.* Lanham, MD: Rowman and Littlefield.

Saltman, K. (2006). The right-wing attack on critical and public education in the United States: From neoliberalism to neoconservatism. *Cultural Politics, 2*(3), 339–358.

Saltman, K. (2014). *The politics of education: A critical introduction.* Boulder, CO: Paradigm Publishers.

Scotchie, J. (1999). Introduction: Paleoconservatism as the opposition party. In J. Scotchie (Ed.), *The paleoconservatives: New voices of the old right* (pp. 1–18). New Brunswick, NJ: Transaction Publishers.

Spring, J. (2011). *The politics of education.* New York: Routledge.

Thompson, C., & Brook, Y. (2010). *Neoconservatism: An obituary of an idea.* Boulder, CO: Paradigm Publishers.

Thurman, S. (Director). (2012). *The Revisionaries.*

Vaïse, J. (2010). *Neoconservatism: The biography of a movement.* Cambridge, MA: Harvard University Press.

Walpen, B. (2004). *Die offenen Feinde und ihre Gesellschaft.* Hamburg: VSA.

Chapter Two

"THE HAVES AND THE HAVE MORES":
FUELING A CONSERVATIVE IDEOLOGICAL WAR ON PUBLIC EDUCATION (OR TRACKING THE MONEY)

This article outlines the landscape of the conservative right, in particular a core group of conservative philanthropists and their foundations as they have shaped educational ideology, policy, and practice over the last few decades. It details four interconnected strategies these philanthropists use to parlay their agendas into public policies: (1) the development of a cadre of conservative youth on college campuses, (2) scholars who can produce ideologically conservative research in clear accessible prose who then "graduate" into government service, (3) the development of a network of conservative regional and state policy centers to promote policy supportive of their views, and (4) the development of a conservative media to carry this "knowledge" forward. Specific cases from the state of Georgia are provided to illustrate each of these strategies.

The first phrase in this article's title is from a scene in Michael Moore's film *Fahrenheit 911* in which President George Bush is participating in a social event with his supporters. Standing in front of the group, he smiles broadly and states, "*This is an impressive crowd. The haves and the have mores! Some people call you the elite. I call you my base!*" (G.W. Bush, quoted in Moore, 2004, p. 112). As I watched that film, I dreamed that Moore would create a documentary where he focused on the Bush administration's educational policies. Not wanting to wait for a film that may never exist beyond my desires, I began to explore the conservative right. My strategy was to approach the task like a detective working a murder case, by tracking the money. This article shares the story of how a handful of wealthy families, fueled with conservative ideology, worked relentlessly over the past five decades to build a structure that shaped the policies we live with in P–16 education today.

My experience of this work has been that of living in a labyrinth,[1] "an intricate structure of interconnecting passages through which it is difficult to find one's way" (*American Heritage Dictionary*, 1982, p. 709). One can enter at any place in the structure, and the pathways lead to the same people in multiple organizations, institutes, and arms of the government. At the same time, it is very easy to run into new paths that lead to intriguing terrain drawing one deeper and deeper into this web of conservative power. While one may seem lost, by following the money and the web of people, the path once again becomes clear. I must admit, it took me quite a while to move from being angry at what I was finding to seeing the strategic brilliance of the conservative right as they have orchestrated their work over time. My research into this labyrinth is still in its first phase even after most of a year, so the story is partial and based solely on publicly available records. My hope is that you, too, will become engaged in this tale with me as we track the gifts of these family foundations.

In the first portion of this article I describe the landscape of the conservative right,[2] in particular a core group of conservative philanthropists and their foundations as they have shaped educational ideology, policy, and practice over the last few decades. The second portion of the article outlines the specific strategies these philanthropists have used to parlay their agendas into public policies. I illustrate each of the strategies with examples from cases in my own state of Georgia to demonstrate how close to all of our homes their impact can be felt. With few exceptions you will find similar cases on your campus, in your educational bureaucracies, and in your state government. I conclude the article with a challenge to the left, or even the center, as we move toward the next presidential campaign.

A Manifesto to Counter the Attack on the American Free Enterprise System

We enter this story with Associate Supreme Court Justice Lewis F. Powell, Jr. (1907–1998), Richard M. Nixon's appointee to the Supreme Court, who took the Oath of Office on January 7, 1972, along with William H. Rehnquist. In a eulogy delivered at Powell's funeral service in Richmond, Virginia, in 1998, Rehnquist described him as

> the very embodiment of "judicial temperament"; receptive to the ideas of his colleagues, fair to the parties to the case, but ultimately relying on his seasoned judgment. His years of diverse experience that he brought to the bench gave him a fund of common sense essential to the make-up of every great judge. He was also the epitome of a Virginia Gentleman in the very best sense of the phrase. I know that all of us who served with him will miss him. ("The Lawyer's Skill")

While these kind words of the late Chief Justice Rehnquist provide us with a view of the justice as fair and open, Justice Powell is also known for his memorandum dated August 23, 1971, just months prior to his nomination by President Nixon to the Supreme Court, in which he articulates a clear, philosophical architecture for the next four decades of conservative strategy to fight against what he perceived to be a leftist attack on democracy and the "free" enterprise system. This memo, known as the "Powell Manifesto" (Reclaim Democracy, 2005), written to Eugene B. Sydner, Jr., then Chair of the U.S. Chamber of Commerce Education Committee, was entitled *Confidential Memorandum: Attack of American Free Enterprise System*. The memo describes the sources of this attack as the Communists, New Leftists, and other revolutionaries who would destroy the entire system, both political and economic. Powell's argument is worth quoting at length as it provides the framework for the set of strategies that were then adopted and implemented by conservative philanthropists:

> No thoughtful person can question that the American economic system is under broad attack. This varies in scope, intensity, in the techniques employed, and in the level of visibility.... These extremists of the left are far more numerous, better financed, and increasingly are more welcomed and encouraged by other elements of society, than ever before in our history. But they remain a small minority, and are not yet the principal cause for concern. The most disquieting voices joining the chorus of criticism come from perfectly respectable elements of society: from the college campus, the pulpit, the media, the intellectual and literary journals, the arts and sciences, and from politicians. In most of these groups the movement against the system is participated in only by minorities. Yet, these often are the most articulate, the most vocal, the most prolific in their writing and speaking. (The Powell Memo, 1971, pp. 1–2)

The memo cites examples of ways liberal and Marxist social science faculty on college campuses (e.g., Hebert Marcuse, University of California San Diego; Yale professor Charles Reich, author of *The Greening of America*; and other public figures such as attorney William Kunstler and activist Ralph Nader) were able to attract students to their anti-free-enterprise views. He stated, "They are often personally attractive, and magnetic; they are stimulating teachers, and their controversy attracts student following. They are prolific writers and lecturers; they author many of the textbooks, and they exert enormous influence—far out of proportion to their numbers—on their colleagues and in the academic world" (The Powell Memo, 1971, p. 4). Powell further argued that the National Chamber of Commerce and other organizations in the corporate sector have the responsibility to counter this attack on the free enterprise system through engaging in "organization, in careful long-range planning and implementation, in consistency of action over an indefinite period of years, in the scale of financing available only through joint effort, and in the political power available through united action and national organizations" (The Powell Memo, 1971, p. 4).

The remainder of Powell's memo details the following methods to accomplish these goals: the establishment of a staff of "highly qualified scholars in the social sciences who do believe in the system," a staff of speakers and a speakers bureau, a staff of scholars to evaluate social science textbooks, insistence of equal time on the college campus speaking circuit, efforts to correct the imbalance of leftists on college faculties, action programs tailored to high schools, and surveillance of and equal time on media. This media includes television news, "forum-type shows," and other media, including scholarly journals, books, paperbacks, pamphlets, and paid advertisements. He suggested that "incentives might be devised to induce more 'publishing' by independent scholars who do believe in the system" (The Powell Memo, 1971, p. 6). He argued for a more aggressive role in the political arena to counter his belief that "few elements of American society today have as little influence in government as the American businessman, the corporation, or even millions of corporate stockholders...the American business executive is truly the 'forgotten man'" (The Powell Memo, 1971, p. 7). That statement is a little hard to believe from where we sit today—a testimony to what was to come. A final strategy offered in the memo called for the American business and enterprise system to encourage a "highly competent staff of lawyers" to use the judiciary, particularly the Supreme Court, to fight against this attack on the system. He noted, "Under our constitutional system, especially with an activist-minded Supreme Court, the judiciary may be the most important instrument for social economic and political change" (The Powell Memo, 1971, p. 8). In his closing statement, Powell argued, "The threat to the enterprise system is not merely a matter of economics. It also is a threat to individual freedom. It is this great truth—now so submerged by the rhetoric of the New Left and of many liberals—that must be reaffirmed if this program is to be meaningful" (The Powell Memo, 1971, p. 8).

Powell's clarion call was heard by those most willing and able to take up the challenge—the conservative philanthropists whose wealth was won or inherited through a "free" enterprise system. Powell's work articulated a systematic framework that, over the next three decades, was carefully and strategically implemented by a network of philanthropists who contributed the base for this effective war machine. It has been so effective that it has been virtually invisible to mainstream Americans. Landay (2002, p. 3) noted:

> This [conservative campaign] has amounted to the greatest organized power grab in American political history. Astonishingly, it goes largely unreported on television, radio, and most newspapers because of the applied political muscle of what Sidney Blumenthal, in his important history of the movement, has dubbed the "counter-establishment." Its media-attack tactics have largely silenced the critical attention of the mainstream press. Americans, therefore, remain largely unaware of the sweeping changes movement conservatism has wrought.

"Movement conservatism" (Kuttner, 2002) as it has come to be called, has at its core the principle that "ideas have consequences" (Chodorov, 1950/1980) with the key ideas being individual gain over public good, deregulation, big tax cuts, and privatization (Landay, 2002) in all areas of society, including education, health, and human services. I turn next to the particular philanthropists who fueled the engines of this radical right-wing movement.

The Philanthropy Roundtable and Its Members: Funding a Conservative Agenda

One of the key organizations formed following the Powell Memo was the Philanthropy Roundtable, a consortium of conservative foundations that strategically focuses the funding of these key donors. Its website states:

> Philanthropy Roundtable began in the late 1970s as an informal network of grantmakers who were troubled by an increasing lack of political and intellectual diversity within parts of the philanthropic community, and who wanted to promote greater respect for private, voluntary approaches to individual and community betterment. The goal of the Roundtable's founders was to provide a forum where donors could discuss the principles and practices that inform the best of America's charitable tradition.
>
> The Roundtable initially operated under the aegis of the Institute for Educational Affairs, gradually growing into a nationwide organization of donors supporting a formal program of conferences and publications. In 1991, the Roundtable became a free-standing organization with an independent board of directors, a small staff, and an expanded agenda of services and activities. Currently, there are more than 600 Roundtable Associates. (Philanthropy Roundtable, 2005)

To understand the context for the creation of the Philanthropy Roundtable, one must be aware of the Institute for Educational Affairs (IEA), a neoconservative organization founded in 1978 by William Simon, Secretary of the Treasury under Nixon, and Irving Kristol, the "godfather" of the neoconservatives (Irving Kristol Person Profile, Media Transparency, 2005).

Kristol was founder and editor of *The Public Interest*, "one of the first conservative publications to actively address issues of culture, religion and 'values,' as opposed to simple reactive hostility to the New Deal liberal politics of the 30s" (Irving Kristol Person Profile, 2005). IEA's stated interest was to identify "promising PhD candidates and undergraduate leaders, help them establish themselves through grants and fellowships and then help them get jobs with activist organizations, research projects, student publications, federal agencies or leading periodicals" (Media Transparency, 2005). IEA was started with $100,000 in grants from the Olin, Scaife, J.M., and Smith Richardson foundations as well as "substantial" contributions from Coca-Cola, Dow Chemical, Ford Motor, General Electric, K-Mart, Mobil and Nestle corporations. From 1985 to 1992 IEA received $1,677,293 to support its programs and general operations. IEA served to connect the funds of the donors within the Philanthropy Roundtable to the implementation of the activities consistent with the ideologies shares by both the IEA and the philanthropists. The board of directors includes Daniel S. Peters (Ruth & Lovett Peters Foundation), Heather Richardson Higgins (The Randolph Foundation), Joseph S. Dolan (Achelis & Bodman Foundations), Kimberly O. Dennis (D & D Foundation), Chester E. Finn, Jr. (Thomas B. Fordham Foundation), Michael W. Grebe (Lynde & Harry Bradley Foundation), and James Piereson (John M. Olin Foundation).

The Roundtable hosts leadership seminars as well as annual meetings where associates and an interested public focus on the role of philanthropy in programs and policy. For example, at the November 10–12, 2005, meeting at the Biltmore Resort in Phoenix, participants were able to visit the Tempe Preparatory Academy, a charter school accredited by the American Academy for Liberal Education. Other sessions at this meeting focused on education, such as: "Should Donors give to University Endowments?," "Who Will Save Catholic Schools?," "Bolstering Math and Science Education," "Can Urban School Districts be Reformed?," "School Choice: The Good, the Bard and the Ugly," and "No Shortcuts, No Excuses: A Salute to Don Fisher and the Amazing Network of KIPP Schools." The Philanthropy Roundtable's recent education-related guidebooks, free to associates of the Roundtable and individual donors, include *A Donor's Guide to School Choice* and *Jump-Starting the Charter School Movement: A Guide for Donors*.

Because these foundations are prohibited from political lobbying, the meeting is an example of education programming. Internal Revenue codes state that "section 501(c)(3) organizations are restricted in the amount of political and legislative (lobbying) activities they may conduct" (Internal Revenue Service, 2005). The IRS guidelines explain these limitations clearly:

> In general, no organization may qualify for section 501(c)(3) status if a substantial part of its activities is attempting to influence legislation (commonly known as lobbying). A 501(c)(3) organization may engage in some lobbying, but too much lobbying activity risks loss of tax-exempt status.
>
> Legislation includes action by Congress, any state legislature, any local council, or similar governing body, with respect to acts, bills, resolutions, or similar items (such as legislative confirmation of appointive office), or by the public in referendum, ballot initiative, constitutional amendment, or similar procedure. It does not include actions by executive, judicial, or administrative bodies.
>
> An organization will be regarded as attempting to influence legislation if it contacts, or urges the public to contact, members or employees of a legislative body for the purpose of proposing, supporting, or opposing legislation, or if the organization advocates the adoption or rejection of legislation.
>
> Organizations may, however, involve themselves in issues of public policy without the activity being considered as lobbying. For example, organizations may conduct educational meetings, prepare and distribute educational materials, or otherwise consider public policy issues in an educational manner without jeopardizing their tax-exempt status. (Internal Revenue Service, 2005)

While the foundations are careful to stay within the required educational activities described here, conservative foundations have actively engaged in funding aimed at shaping the political process. Rich (2005, p. 18) argued:

> a notable portion of foundation spending—a growing portion for some foundations—is targeted almost directly at the political process. This spending is intended to win the "war of ideas" under way in American politics. It supports research and advocacy that aims to influence how elected officials and the public think about a broad range of policies. This "war of ideas" is fundamentally a battle between liberals and conservatives, progressive and libertarians, over the appropriate role for government.

Rich's central argument is that while the centrist and liberal foundations such as Gates, Lilly, Ford, Robert Wood Johnson, Getty, Packard, Hewlett, Kellogg, Starr, Pew, MacArthur, Mellon, Rockefeller, and Annie E. Casey outspend the conservatives on public policy institutes ($136,485,001 to $29,447,610 by the top twelve conservative foundations), the conservatives "consistently make funding policy institutes one of their top three priorities, while the liberal and mainline foundations rarely treat it this way" (Rich 2005, p. 20). He argued that the think tanks on the left tend to be organized by issues reflective of their funders with these philanthropists supporting specific projects (e.g., Bill Gates high school reform programs) rather than the general operating support of institutes. An examination of the conservative support for the Heritage Foundation, one of the oldest and most effective conservative think tanks, reveals that a total of 295 grants in the amount of $57,497,537 between 1985 and 2003, many of which were earmarked for general support, general funding, undesignated, charitable, or "no purpose available." This high level of funding targeted to general operations enables think tanks to create a strong infrastructure. Rich supports his argument with John M. Olin Foundation's executive director

James S. Piereson's statement, "The liberal foundations became too project oriented—they support projects but not institutions. They flip from project to project.... We, on the other hand, support institutions. We provide the infrastructure for institutions." (quoting Piereson, p. 23)

Using Media Transparency's[3] website that uses publicly available IRS records to track the donations for thirty-six conservative philanthropies, I selected sixteen major foundations that were consistently named in directing funds toward pro-voucher efforts, parochial schools, conservative university programs, right-wing think tanks, and lobbying groups. The total funding provided by these sixteen foundations between 1998 and 2004 was $1,517,117,306. Seven of these foundations awarded gifts of $100,000,000 or more: Walton Family Foundation ($392,101,702), Lynde and Harry Bradley ($205,779,945), Richard and Helen DeVos (Amway) Foundation ($142,842,452), Scaife Foundations ($133,803,485), Smith Richardson ($111,543,102), F.M. Kirby Foundation ($129,738,959), and John M. Olin Foundation ($108,472,817).

While all of the conservative philanthropists tracked by Media Transparency are part of the labyrinth, there are four key conservative philanthropic foundations at its center known as the "The Four Sisters," or BOSS, for Bradley, Olin, Scaife, and Smith Richardson (The Lynde and Harry Bradley Foundation, Inc., 2005). Walmart, Earhart, Koch, Carthage, Lambe, and others provide substantial support, but I focus here on the history, purpose, and funding patterns of the "Four Sisters" as illustrative of the whole conservative philanthropic movement.

John M. Olin Foundation

I begin with the John M. Olin Foundation. Olin was founded on the family's fortune made through its Western Cartridge Company, later known as Olin Industries, then the Olin Mathieson chemical corporation. Established in 1953, the Foundation aimed to "strengthen the economic, political and cultural institutions upon which the American heritage of constitutional government and private enterprise is based.... By 1977, the Foundation was giving away more than $1 million annually" (Miller, 2003, p. 11). Olin appointed Frank O'Connell, the company's vice president for employee relations, as the first executive director with the charge to "use this fortune to help to preserve the system which made its accumulation possible in only two lifetimes, my father's and mine" (p. 11). After studying pro-market thinkers, O'Connell wrote a long memo that set forth ideas for the Foundation's mission. O'Connell remembered that "It [the memo] basically outlined the need for supporting scholars and think tanks that favor limited government, individual responsibility and a free society" (p. 11).

In January 1977, when William Simon left his post as Secretary of Treasury at the end of Gerald Ford's presidency, he joined the Foundation. Two years later, when O'Connell retired as Olin's director in 1979, he agreed with Simon and Olin that Michael S. Joyce, then director of the Institute for Educational Affairs funded by Olin, should be named Olin's executive director. Joyce provided the leadership for the Foundation's funding program until 1985 when he left to assume the presidency of the newly formed Bradley Foundation.

After John M. Olin's death in 1982, the Foundation received an additional $50 million from his estate that subsequently doubled to $105 million in the stock market boom of the 1980s. As a result of aggressive spending to comply with Olin's wish to spend the Foundation out, the Foundation was depleted to $40 million in 1993. The death of Olin's widow that year left an additional $95 million to this foundation. "During the 1990s the Foundation awarded about $20 million in grants annually" to "have a big impact over a short period of time," said James Piereson, the Foundation's executive director (p. 15). In an interview with Andrew Rich (2005), James Piereson, executive director of the John M. Olin Foundation, explained the strategy of the Olin Foundation:

> I think our role has been to promote ideas. The tax laws don't permit you to lobby or anything like that. So what

we try to do is to get behind some people or some institutions that can have some influence in promoting a set of ideas in a lot of different areas. We provide the infrastructure for these sorts of institutions. (Rich, 2005, p. 22)

Olin is different from its sisters in two respects: (1) its founder decided early to give aggressively to have a greater impact conservative initiatives more quickly and to spend itself out; and (2) it funded named programs and fellowships for scholars in prestigious institutions rather than general support for operations more typical of other conservative foundations. As an example of this aggressive spending, between 1985 and 2003, Olin gave in excess of $24 million to the American Enterprise Institute, the Heritage Foundation, the Manhattan Institute for Public Policy Research, the Hoover Institute of War, Revolution and Peace, the Intercollegiate Studies Institute and its affiliate, Collegiate Network. Harvard received $21.3 million, Washington University, $20.6 million, the University of Chicago, $19.9 million, and Yale University, $15.2 million. Olin has reached into major universities across the country in an effort to build a conservative presence in the academy. For example, at the University of Georgia, Dwight Lee, a conservative economist, received grants of $30,325 from the Olin Foundation for his work supporting a free-market economy. Lee also serves as adjunct scholar and speaker for the Cato Institute (recipient of $18.1 million from conservative foundations); a fellow at the Independent Institute, a think tank in Oakland, California (recipient of over a half million from the conservative philanthropists); and the founder of the Ramsey Center for Private Enterprise at UGA. Its mission is

> the fostering of a better understanding and appreciation of the principles and performance of private enterprise. The center engages in teaching, research and writing that demonstrate the widely dispersed benefits from decentralized decisions coordinated through competitive markets. In addition to its teaching and research functions, the

center carries on an active service program involving public lectures and programs on the private enterprise system. (Ramsey Center for Private Enterprise at UGA, 2005)

In 2005 the John M. Olin Foundation closed its doors, leaving a legacy of neoconservative influence that shapes public policies today. However, Piereson, its executive director, continues to sit on the board of the Philanthropy Roundtable.

Lynde and Harry Bradley

The next of the four sisters is the Lynde and Harry Bradley Foundation, identified by Media Transparency as "the country's largest and most influential right-wing foundation" with over $700 million in assets and awards of more than $30 million a year (Wilayto, 1997). This foundation was created from the wealth amassed in the Allen-Bradley electronic manufacturing company, founded in 1903 by brothers Lynde and Harry Bradley, sons of a prominent Milwaukee family. Allen-Bradley, a major industry in this city, was so profitable that the brothers were able to establish the Allen-Bradley Foundation in 1942. The website dkosopedia (2005) described Harry as "the more political of the two brothers and a man with extreme right-wing views." As a financial supporter and believer in Robert Welsh's John Birch Society based in Appleton, Wisconsin, Harry distributed Birch literature and invited Welsh to speak at Allen-Bradley sales meetings. According to this source, "Harry's main political targets were 'World Communism' and the U.S. federal government, not necessarily in that order. His political philosophy was laissez-faire capitalism, and he was strongly opposed to anything that might restrict his freedom to conduct his business as he saw fit" (dkosopedia, 2005).

His commitment to freedom and individualism did not, however, extend to the women workers at Allen-Bradley who, in 1966, successfully sued the company for wage discrimination. In 1970, with a workforce of 7,000, only 32 African Americans and 14 Latinos were employed by Bradley, which led to another discrimination suit that was backed by the federal government. The company was then forced to adopt an affirmative action plan (dkosopedia, 2005).

In 1985, the brothers sold Allen-Bradley to Rockwell International, a defense and aerospace corporation, resulting in a "significant" portion of these proceeds dedicated to establishing the Lynde and Harry Bradley Foundation. The Foundation became one of the largest in the country with assets of over $290 million (dkosopedia, 2005), funding programs focused on a free and independent citizenry, traditional values, local institutions, and a decentralized government. Its core principles include "limited, competent government, a dynamic marketplace of economic, intellectual and cultural activity, and a vigorous defense at home and abroad of American ideas and institutions" (Bradley Foundation, 2005).

The Foundation hired Michael S. Joyce, former president of the John M. Olin Foundation, to head its new organization. One of his first tasks was to write the Foundation's philosophy statement to guide its funding efforts:

> The Bradley brothers were committed to preserving and defending the tradition of free representative government and private enterprise that has enabled the American nation and, in a larger sense, the entire Western world to flourish intellectually and economically. The Bradleys believed that the good society is a free society. The Lynde and Harry Bradley Foundation is likewise devoted to strengthening American democratic capitalism and the institutions, principles and values that sustain and nurture it. Its programs support limited, competent government; a dynamic marketplace for economic, intellectual, and cultural activity; and a vigorous defense at home and abroad of American ideas and institutions. In addition, recognizing that responsible self-government depends on enlightened citizens and informed public opinion, the Foundation supports scholarly studies and academic achievement. (Bradley Foundation, 2005)

As a short detour off the main path here, Michael S. Joyce's story is intriguing, particularly to those of us in education. Born to an Irish Catholic, Democratic family in Cleveland, he began his career as a social studies teacher. He became active in the 1972 Nixon campaign and then went to New York City to join William Simon and Irving Kristol at the Institute for Educational Affairs, where he served as the organization's director until he moved to the Olin Foundation.

Between 1998 and 2004 the Bradley Foundation donated $250,812,909 to parochial schools, pro-voucher groups, the Heritage Foundation, and other right-wing think tanks and lobbying groups. The Bradley Foundation identifies a broad purpose for each of its programs: to improve education, economic growth, revitalize civil society, strengthen private initiative, defense and advance freedom, intellectual infrastructure, and the Bradley Legacy programs (local Milwaukee programs such as historic preservation). On its website, the Bradley Foundation lists 2003 recipients who received support to improve education with a total funding of $4,738,768. These recipients include the following:

- Partners Advancing Values in Education, a Milwaukee program to support development of a loan program for community schools ($3,041.610).
- Milwaukee's American Education Reform Council for general support ($225,000).
- Stanford's Hoover Institution on War, Revolution and Peace to support the American Public Education Initiative including the *Education Next* magazine ($225,000).
- Black Alliance for Educational Options, Washington, D.C., for general support ($200,000).
- Institute for Justice for general operations ($140,000).
- Foundation for Education Reform & Accountability, Clifton Park, New York, for general support ($100,000).
- The Thomas B. Fordham Institute, Washington, D.C. (Chester Finn and Diane Ravitch's think tank) to support

two research projects focused on the state of history in American schools ($150,000).
- Grants of less than $100,000 to school choice and charter school efforts include the Alexis de Tocqueville Institution, Center for Education Reform (Washington, D.C.), Children First America (Austin), Excellent Education for Everyone (Moorestown, N.J.), Heartland Institute (Chicago) to support publication and distribution of *School Reform News*, and the Pacific Research Institute for Public Policy (San Francisco) to support its Center for School Reform.

This sampling of funding initiatives illustrates the extent to which the Bradley Foundation focuses its educational funding on institutions promoting privatization of schooling through vouchers, charter schools, and other school reform efforts.

After 15 years of service as Bradley's CEO and planning to retire in 2001, Michael Joyce founded the Americans for Community and Faith-Centered Enterprise at the behest of George W. Bush's political advisor, Karl Rove (Rightweb, 2005). Mike Allen, a *Washington Post* staff writer, described how this organization would further Bush's "faith-based" funding initiatives:

> The administration has also been working behind the scenes to build support for the plan. Michael S. Joyce, a proponent of school choice who has been developing the intellectual framework for faith-based efforts for 12 years, said Bush asked him at a Rose Garden ceremony May 10, "Did Karl call you yet?" Joyce said Karl Rove, Bush's senior adviser, phoned later that day and asked Joyce "to undertake a private initiative to help get this legislation through." Joyce said that he insisted on independence from the White House and that the specifics were left up to him. On June 1, Joyce opened Americans for Community and Faith-Centered Enterprise with a stable of consultants and lobbyists and an office on Pennsylvania Avenue. He hopes to raise $500,000. (2001)

Joyce's "first-name based relationships" are not limited to the Bush White House. In 1980 he served as a member of Ronald Reagan's transition team. "Coach Joyce" (Media Transparency, 2005), as William Bennett referred to him, was influential in having Bennett installed as Reagan's Secretary of Education. Joyce has worked closely with Republican administrations since the Reagan administration.

Scaife Foundations

The next of the four sisters is the Scaife family of foundations (Scaife Foundations, 2005). Media Transparency describes the history of the Scaife family of foundations and its Chair, Richard Mellon Scaife:

> Financed by the Mellon industrial, oil and banking fortune. At one time its largest single holding was stock in the Gulf Oil Corporation. Became active in funding conservative causes in 1973, when Richard Mellon Scaife became chairman of the foundation. In the 1960s, Richard had inherited an estimated $200 million from his mother, Sarah. *Forbes* magazine has estimated his personal net worth at $800 million, making him the 138th richest person in the U.S. He controls the Scaife, Carthage and Allegheny foundations. In 1993, Scaife and Carthage reportedly gave more than $17.6 million to 150 conservative think tanks. (Sarah Scaife Foundations funder profile, 2005)

The Scaife Foundations family includes the Allegheny Foundation, the Carthage Foundation, and the Sarah Scaife Foundation. Between 1998 and 2004 these foundations donated $133,803,485 to the Intercollegiate Studies Institute, the Heritage Foundation, conservative foreign policy think tanks, and other right-wing lobbying and publishing groups. While the Allegheny Foundation is primarily focused on funding programs for historic preservation, civic development, and education in Western Pennsylvania, it has donated $2,668,500 to the Intercollegiate Studies Institute, an organization I detail later in this chapter. The Scaife website is sparse compared to that of Bradley, but it does provides a 2004 annual report and IRS 990 forms that report donations for last year.

The 2004 Carthage Foundation grants totaling $5.6 million supported programs to address "public policy questions concerned with national and international issues" (Carthage Foundation Annual Report, 2004) at 53 institutions including the following recipients of $100,000 or more related to educational issues: Allegheny Institute for Public Policy ($110,000), American Civil Rights Union ($100,000), American Enterprise for Public Policy Research ($300,000), Center for Media and Public Affairs ($150,000), The Federalist Society for Law & Public Policy Studies ($100,000), Federation for American Immigration Reform ($250,000), Free Congress Research and Education Foundation ($200,000), George Mason University Foundation's Center for Study of Public Choice ($145,000), and the Intercollegiate Studies Institute ($350,000). Between 1985 and 2003, the Carthage Foundation gave over $10.5 million to the Free Congress Foundation (now called the American Opportunity Foundation), an ultra-conservative group led by Paul Weyrich that describes itself as follows:

> Free Congress Foundation is politically conservative, but it is more than that: it is also culturally conservative. Most think tanks talk about tax rates or the environment or welfare policy and occasionally we do also. But our main focus is on the Culture War. Will America return to the culture that made it great, our traditional, Judeo-Christian, Western culture? Or will we continue the long slide into the cultural and moral decay of political correctness? If we do, America, once the greatest nation on earth, will become no less than a third world country. (Free Congress Foundation, 2005)

In 2004 the Sarah Scaife Foundation, another of the Scaife family foundations, supported eighty "public policy programs that address major domestic and international issues" (Sarah Scaife Foundation Annual Report, 2004). Those most substantially funded include Accuracy in Media, Inc. ($425,000), a group that publicizes accounts that illustrate "the use of classroom and/or university resources to indoctrinate students, discrimination against students, faculty or administrators based on political or academic beliefs, and campus violations of free speech" (Accuracy in Media, 2005). Its website describes these efforts:

> Every month, *Accuracy in Academia's Campus Report* goes on the air to take you behind the scenes in higher education. Dissident conservative professors and students get to tell the stories that they cannot share on their own campuses.

This Campus Report is aired on Rightalk (2005). Scaife also funded the American Enterprise Institute for Public Policy Research ($225,000), a major think tank shaping educational policy. Other recipients include the Center for Strategic and International Studies ($420,000), Claremont Institute for the Study of Statesmanship and Political Philosophy ($450,000), the Federalist Society for Law and Public Policy Studies ($200.000), Free Congress Research and Education Foundation ($450,000), the Heritage Foundation ($800,000), Institute for Foreign Policy Analysis ($610,000), Media Research Center ($350,000), National Association of Scholars ($250,000), Social Philosophy and Policy Foundation ($625,000), Stanford University Hoover Institution on War, Revolution and Peace ($725,000), and the University of Virginia Law School Foundation ($325,000). The Intercollegiate Studies Institute (ISI) given $100,000 in 2004, while funded to a lesser extent than other organizations by the Sarah Scaife Foundation, realized a total of $450,000 from all the Scaife family foundations in that year. The Collegiate Network, administered by ISI, realized an additional $230,000 in 2004 support. These two organizations together were funded by Scaife Foundations in the amount of $680,000 in one year.

Smith Richardson Foundation

The Smith Richardson fortune came from Lunsford Richardson's development of what we now know as Vicks VapoRub in his small drugstore in North Carolina. He founded a wholesale drug company and, seven years later, the Vick Family Remedies Company. Son H. Smith Richardson changed the name of Vicks Salve to Vicks VapoRub, now a household name, and the family business name to the Vick Chemical Company. These focused sales efforts supported by an aggressive advertising campaign that culminated in the creation of a "world wide medical empire" (Smith Richardson Foundation, 2005). Merrell Company acquired Vicks and was renamed Richardson Merrell, Inc. In 1935, H. Smith and his wife, Grace Jones Richardson, established the H. Smith Richardson Foundation, whose mission is:

> to contribute to important public debates and to help address serious public policy challenges facing the United States. The Foundation seeks to help ensure the vitality of our social, economic, and governmental institutions. It also seeks to assist with the development of effective policies to compete internationally and to advance U.S. interests and values abroad. This mission is embodied in our international and domestic grant programs. (Smith Richardson Foundation, 2005)

One of the wealthiest families in the United States, Forbes estimates its worth at $870 million. In addition to funding specific projects, the Foundation awards research grants ($60,000 each) to individuals with the purpose of supporting the work of the "next generation of public policy researchers and analysts...who are interested in conducting research and writing on domestic public policy issues. Grantees are expected to produce a book or an article suitable for publication in a peer-reviewed journal."

Between 1996 and 2003, Smith Richardson awarded grants totaling over $1 million to the American Enterprise Institute for Public Policy Research ($4,566,713), Brookings Institution ($2,979,432), Hudson Institute ($1,635,479), Hoover Institution on War, Revolution and Peace ($1,456,612), Manhattan Institute for Policy Research ($1,165,981), Potomac Institute for Policy Studies ($1,165,981), as well numerous prestigious universities, with the top recipients being Yale ($6,591,120), Harvard ($6,036,919), Columbia ($2,666,334), and Stanford ($2,0097,067). Others funded between $1 million and $1.6 were Georgetown University, George Washington University, Duke University, University of North Carolina, University of Chicago, University of California Berkeley, The Johns Hopkins University, and Princeton University.

You have noticed by now the common names among think tanks named as recipients of grants from all four sisters, particularly Heritage, American Enterprise Institute for Public Policy, and the Hoover Institution. This deliberate, focused, and substantial funding over many years given to a small number of conservative think tanks has enabled those institutes to grow in their capacity to produce "scholarship" that is fed in the form of highly accessible research and policy briefs to the media as well as federal and state legislators to shape the dialogue, and then support and promote policies around particular issues with education at the top of the list. In the National Committee for Responsive Philanthropy's March 2004 Report, a breakdown of conservative grant dollars (1999–2001) listed policy at the top of the list with 46% of the total and education with 10% of the total (tied with legal issues).[4] The conservative philanthropic community, with its belief in a competitive, free market has spent years and millions of dollars to promote school choice in the form of charter schools, tuition vouchers, and publicly funded religious education. This shaping of public discourse and policy was accomplished through four core strategies (see Figure 2.1): (1) the development of a cadre of conservative youth on college campuses, (2) scholars who can produce ideologically conservative research in clear accessible prose who then "graduate" into government service,

Figure 2.1. Conservative Labyrinth

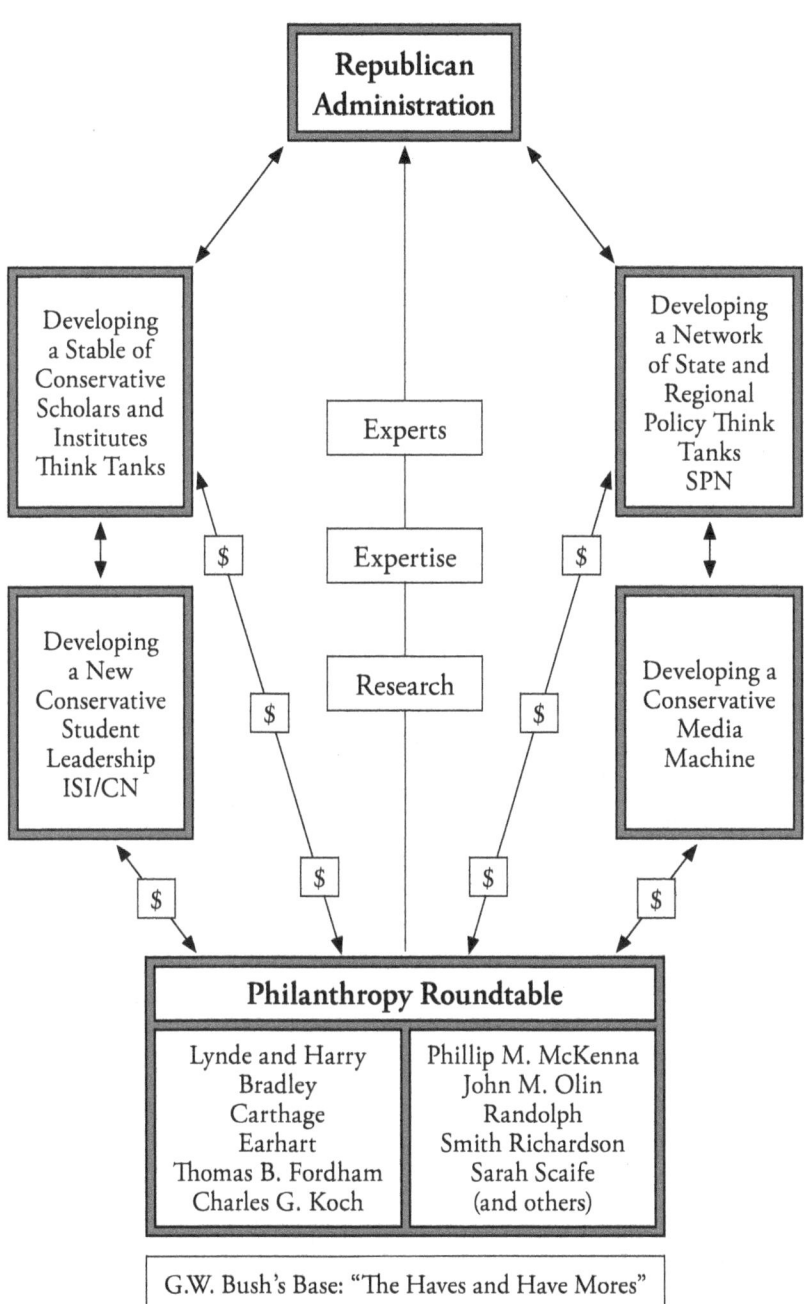

(3) the development of a network of conservative regional and state policy centers to promote policy supportive of their views, and (4) the development of a conservative media to carry this "knowledge" forward. Next, I examine each of these strategies with specific examples from my own state of Georgia. A fifth, but perhaps less successful, strategy is the development of a conservative Black leadership that I do not address in this article.

Strategy #1: Developing a New Young Conservative Leadership

Conservatives realized early that in order to develop a new stable of participants in the movement, they needed to reach out to college-age youth. As early as 1950, Frank Chodorov, with "a passionate commitment to individualism and to the free market" (Hamilton 1980, p. 13), wrote a brief essay entitled "A Fifty-Year Project," first published in pamphlet form by the National Council for American Education. Chodorov argued that during the first half of the twentieth century, the "American character moved from individualist to collectivist" (Chodorov, 1950/1980a, p. 151) through what Chodorov called the socialist movement that took hold largely on college campuses. He argued that "the possibility of winning over the faculty to the individualistic idea might as well be dismissed aforehand, simply because the professorial mind is by and large beyond redemption" (p. 160). The plan Chodorov proposed in this essay consisted of

> A lecture bureau, manned by a secretariat and a corps of lecturers. The business of the bureau would be to arrange for lectures on or near the selected campuses. The lecturers—probably difficult to find these days—would have to be acquainted with socialistic theory as well as the literature of individualism, for since the purpose is to uproot the trend of thought, the student would have to be impressed with

its inadequacies. Whatever the subject matter of the lecture, the doctrine of the primacy of the individual, as against the supremacy of the social order, must be emphasized; thus, the student will learn to recognize in the classroom or textbook the insidious implication that the social order and its political establishment take precedence over the individual. Every lecture must contain a challenge. (p. 161)

Chodorov believed that once these youth had access to this alternative view, "the project would develop a momentum of its own" (p. 161). He suggested the formation of Individualistic Clubs with an intercollegiate affiliation that would encourage student writing with prizes given for essays that would then require a publication outlet. Chodorov reworked the essay with a new title, "For Our Children's Children," published in *Human Events*, calling for a beginning to his project. The essay received attention as well as a $1,000 donation from J. Howard Pew, and with assistance from the Foundation for Economics, Chodorov, established the Intercollegiate Society of Individualists (ISI). ISI was the "first large free-market organization to focus its efforts on influencing college students. Its goal was to be an effective antidote to the well-organized Intercollegiate Society of Socialists" (Steelman, 1996, p. 6). William F. Buckley was mentored by Chodorov and became the first president of the ISI. He later wrote about Frank Chodorov, "Organizing anything was alien to the vaguely anarchic spirit of Frank Chodorov, and so he told me that I would be president [of ISI]" (Intercollegiate Studies Institute, 2005). ISI was a "high point" for Chodorov, an "important part of the conservative movement in the 1950s and 1960s" (Hamilton, 1980, p. 29) and remains a key component of the conservative strategy today. Buckley noted that Chodorov "deeply influenced the postwar conservative movement" (Buckley, 1962).

Chodorov is worth a bit of a trip down another path of the labyrinth to place him within the context of the larger conservative movement of the mid-twentieth century. Described as "one of the giants of the American Old Right" (Steelman, 1996, p. 1),

Chodorov was born in New York City in 1887, the eleventh child of poor Russian immigrants with a given name, Fishel Chodorowsky. After graduating from Columbia University in 1907, he worked numerous jobs while steeping himself in the literature of Henry David Thoreau, Albert Jay Nock, and Henry George. Considering himself within the classical liberal tradition, he "viewed the state as the greatest threat to individual liberty and human happiness...and feared the state's ability to conscript its citizens and use them to wage war" (Steelman, 1996, p. 2). This antistate, antiwar position in a pre–World War period led to his dismissal as director of the Henry George School of Social Science in 1937. He then turned to publishing *The Freeman* from 1944 to 1951, where he wrote essays advocating antistatist, individualist, and free market views. He was a critic of state involvement in education and in his essay "Why Free Schools are Not Free" argued:

> a free school is one that has no truck with the state, via its taxing powers. The more subsidized it is, the less free it is. What is known as "free education" is the least free of all, for it is a state-owned institution; it is socialized education—just like socialized medicine or the socialized post office—and cannot possibly be separated from political control. (Chodorov, 1948/1980c, p. 237)

He concluded this essay:

> If we would reform our educational system basically, we must desocialize it. We must put it back where it belongs, in the hands of parents. Theirs is the responsibility for the breeding of children and theirs is the responsibility for the upbringing. The first error of public schooling is the shifting of this responsibility, the transformation of the children of men into wards of the state. All the other evils follow from that. (p. 239)

His critique of public education was a precursor to the advocates of school choice and the voucher movement of the conservatives in the latter part of the twentieth century through to the present time. His essay "Private Schools: The Solution to America's Education Problem" was published in pamphlet form by the National Council for American Education, an organization founded by Allen A. Zoll, an anticommunist, to "eradicate from our schools Marxism, Socialism, Communism and all other forces that seek to destroy the liberty of the American people"[5] (Zoll, 1949, p. 23). Chodorov critiqued the "collectivist concepts" in texts that advocated social rather than individual values, progressive pedagogy, and teachers that "keep the public school in the headlines by their agitation for larger stipends" (Chodorov, ND/1980b, p. 240). He argued that "there is nothing wrong with the public school that could not be cured by putting it into active competition with the private school" (p. 241), suggesting that it "should be possible to derive a method by which they [the poor] could pay for their schools directly, rather than through the taxing powers of the government" (p. 242). He explained his plan:

> However, since federal income taxation is the largest single direct burden put on the household, and since comparatively few of us are now free of it, the simplest way of solving our school problem is by a federal exemption for tuition.... Instead of subsidization, with a consequent increase in taxation, it could more easily improve our school system by putting it on a competitive basis. Incidentally, the federal government would thus remove the widely held suspicion that its interest is not in the betterment of the child's mind through education but in the control of it through indoctrination (p. 247).... Indeed, if the proposed tuition exemption should reach the legislative stage, who would oppose it but those who are hell-bent for a regime of socialism? (p. 251)

Ironically, these same ideas resurfaced decades later, and conservatives claim Chodorov himself disdained the label conservative, regarding himself as an "individualist." He remarked, "As for me, I will punch anyone who calls me a conservative in the nose. I am a radical" (Chodorov, 1956, letter to *National Review*, p. 23; quoted by Hamilton, 1980, p. 29). After his death in 1966 at the age of 79, the name Intercollegiate Society of Individualists was changed to Intercollegiate Studies Institute and bears the slogan *Educating for Liberty* on its logo.

Chodorov's original idea to develop a cadre of young student leaders passionate about conservative beliefs is alive and well in the ISI today. This organization, now based in Wilmington, Delaware, was a regular recipient of conservative philanthropic funding totaling $17,489,600 from 1985 to 2003, with the most lucrative grants from Scaife Foundations ($10,577,800), J.M. Olin ($3,002,600), Lynde and Harry Bradley ($1,147,100), Philip M. McKenna ($1,225,500), and Earhart ($926,100) (Media Transparency, 2005). Most of these funds were targeted to general operations support or "no purpose specified." Through its support of a network of campus newspapers, the ISI promotes and develops students who are good writers with the potential to become the next generation of scholars to carry forward the conservative message to both the academic community and to the public. Outstanding alumni of ISI include Edwin J. Feulner, Jr., founder and president of the Heritage Foundation, as well as consultant on domestic policy to President Reagan from 1981 to 1989, a Hoover Institute Fellow, and a member of George Mason University's Board of Visitors, a university that has realized $15,877,278 in conservative funding from 1985 to 2003.

Today, ISI administers the Collegiate Network, an affiliate organization that shares its core philosophy and purpose. According to its website, in 1979 two University of Chicago students, Tod Lindberg, now editor of the Hoover Institution's *Policy Review*, and John Podhoretz, currently a columnist for the *New York Post*, founded the *Counterpoint*, a newspaper to "counter the one-sided reporting that dominated the principal student publication on their campus." They asked for and received grants from the Institute for Educational Affairs (IEA) to defray publishing costs. The IEA grant program that supported the University of Chicago's alternative student publications became known as the Collegiate Network, and by 1983 the Network added summer and year-long student internships to its repertoire for the development of young conservative leaders. Its mission is "aimed at training a cadre of conservative college-age youth who would eventually transform America's media landscape." In 1990, the Madison Center for Educational Affairs, headed by William Bennett, Harvey Mansfield, and Allan Bloom, merged with IEA to become simply The Madison Center. This center administered the Collegiate Network "to sustain the growing number of conservative student publications" (Collegiate Network, 2005) until it was moved to Wilmington, Delaware, in 1995, where its administration was transferred to the ISI. During the years 1985–2003, the Collegiate Network realized $4,615,000 in grants for general support from Bradley, Olin, Scaife, and, to a lesser extent, Carthage. This well-funded organization's mission is:

> to focus public awareness of the politicization of American college and university classrooms, curricula, student life, and the resulting decline of educational standards. To achieve this mission, the Network provides financial and technical assistance to student editors and writers at scores of independent publications at leading colleges and universities around the country. These publications have a combined annual distribution of more than two million copies. Assistance includes annual operating grants, annual journalistic training conferences, campus mentoring sessions, story ideas and editorial resources, a quarterly newsletter, Internet discussion groups, summer and year-long internships at leading national media outlets and extensive guidance from experienced professionals. (Intercollegiate Studies Institute, 2005)

Currently the Collegiate Network's 89 member papers include *The Dartmouth Review*, Princeton's *American Foreign Policy* and *The Princeton Tory*, *The Michigan Review*, University of California Berkeley's *The California Patriot*, *The Stanford Review*, and, at the University of Virginia, *The Virginia Advocate*. The yearlong fellowships and summer internships place students at William Kristol's *The Weekly Standard*, *USA Today*, *The Washington Examiner*, *National Review*, *The American Spectator*, *The Washington Times*, *US News & World Report*, and *Radio America*.

As a local example, in 2003, with the support of the Collegiate Network, conservative students at the University of Georgia created a newspaper called *The Georgia GuardDawg*. This paper publishes five issues a year with a distribution of 3,000 for each issue. David Kirby, student publisher of the *GuardDawg*, in a letter to the *Red & Black*, UGA's main student newspaper, argued:

> Although conservatives may constitute a majority of students on campus, in the classroom, we lose our voice. Either through active or passive repression, conservative ideas often are kept out of academics. Bradley Alexander, a copy editor for The GuardDawg, described an incident where a history professor at the University said in class that he "hated George Bush" and that various members of the Republican administration were "chickens." According to Alexander, this professor repeatedly launched into conspiracy theories involving President Bush, creating an atmosphere that certainly was not conducive to the open flow of ideas or the free expression of opinion. (2005, p. 4A)

The paper's stated mission is:

> *The Georgia GuardDawg* is an independent journal of news and opinion for the University of Georgia Community. It was founded on July 15, 2003 by a group of students dedicated to providing a forum for free expression of

conservative ideals and philosophy on campus. At a college dominated politically and intellectually by radical, outspoken, leftist organizations, we have an obligation to balance the dialogue with conservative viewpoints. Our hope is to enable UGA students to hear both sides of the story through a publication that combines humor, opinion, news and feature articles. *The Georgia GuardDawg* defends three interrelated aspects of our heritage. In these three ways we stand politically, economically and socially conservative. (2005, p. 6)

The principles referred to in this mission statement are limited government, economic freedom, and traditional family values supported by quotes from Thomas Jefferson, Milton Friedman, and Alexis de Tocqueville. The paper features advertisements encouraging students to join ISI to "Get the Education you Deserve" with benefits that include the institute's *Intercollegiate Review*, fellowship opportunities, support for alternative student newspapers, networking with leading conservatives, developing leadership and career skills, and attending conferences and seminars. In the most recent issue and located on the same page as an article entitled "www.top_ten_conservative websites roundup.com" is an advertisement directed at student readers: "Students: Do you have a wacky liberal professor teaching one of your classes? Tell us! We'll publish their crazy antics in our paper" (2005, p. 6).

From Frank Chodorov's early vision for the ISI to its current form, the ISI/Collegiate Network, a huge network of conservative students and campus newspapers, has developed to foster "conservative voices in an increasingly liberal world" (2005).

Dinesh D'Souza may be the poster child for the success of ISI and the Collegiate Network. D'Souza, author of conservative books including *The End of Racism: Principles for a Multiracial Society*, *Letters to a Young Conservative*, and *Illiberal Education: The Politics of Race and Sex on Campus*, founded and served as the editor of the *Dartmouth Review*, the first member of the Collegiate Network.

D'Souza was a John M. Olin Fellow at the American Enterprise Institute and in 2003 was the Robert and Karen Rishwain Fellow at the Hoover Institute, a think tank at Stanford that received $20,330,146 in support from 1985 to 2003 from conservative philanthropists. Hoover is also the home of fellows Chester E. Finn, Newt Gingrich, Thomas Sowell, and Diane Ravitch. D'Souza's career as a conservative scholar has been generously funded from 1985 to 2002 with $1,647,749 in grants from John M. Olin paid primarily through the American Enterprise Institute. Media Transparency notes that "He seems to be on the permanent payroll of the John M. Olin Foundation" (2005).

Strategy #2: Developing a Stable of Conservative Scholars: From Universities to Right-Wing Think Tanks and on into Government Service

Developing and supporting a network of young scholars and writers provides a ready source of new talent and labor for the conservative think tanks. In the three final decades of the twentieth century, the number of think tanks grew from fewer than seventy in 1970 to more than three hundred in 2000 and "more than half of the new think tanks that formed in this period were identifiably ideological" (Rich, 2005, p. 20). Rich's *Think Tanks, Public Policy, and the Politics of Expertise* (2004) provides a comprehensive examination of the landscape of think tanks in today's political context. He classified the ideology of these institutes based on information provided by the think tanks in their printed materials and websites, largely words and phrases describing their missions and concerns. His assessment of the ideologies of the think tanks in 1996 was that while 45% were either centrist or had no identifiable ideology, the majority of the think tanks were "avowedly ideological in character, either conservative or liberal," with 65% conservative, promoting work supportive of limited government and free market economies, with the remaining 35% think tanks as liberal. He identified the following ten largest conservative think tanks in order of their 1995 budget as follows: Heritage Foundation ($25,055,050), Hoover Institute($15,477,000), American Enterprise Institute ($12,633,796), Hudson Institute ($9,312,850), Free Congress Foundation ($7,707,180), Cato Institute ($7,077,749), American Legislative Exchange Council ($4,612,074), Rutherford Institute ($4,357,098), Reason Foundation ($3,416,412), and National Center for Policy Analysis ($3,029,444).

In 2002, twelve of the largest conservative foundations (Bradley, Smith Richardson, Sarah Scaife, Earhart, J.M. Olin, Claude R. Lambe, Charles G. Koch, JM Foundation, Carthage, Philip M. McKenna, David H. Koch, and Henry Salvatori) spent $29.4 million on public policy institutes, including those I've mentioned. While this funding is only about one-fourth of what the large mainstream foundations contribute to public policy institutes ($136,485,003), Rich (2005) argued that the mainline/progressive think tanks focus their funding on specific issues and projects, strive for "neutrality" or "unbiased research," and typically do not provide funding for general operating support of the think tanks in the way the conservatives do. Rich supported this argument with the following comment from a research director of a progressive think tank: "If you're on the left, you have to go to the foundations and say you're neutral, unbiased—not politicized. You're certainly not liberal. If you're ideological, they don't want to support you. It's frustrating—because, by contrast, if you're on the right, the foundations will only fund you if you toe the ideological line, if you want to do battle for the conservative cause" (p. 24).

While it is beyond the scope of this article to review the work of each of these think tanks, I profile the Heritage Foundation as an example of one with a strong focus on privatizing public schooling through school choice, vouchers, and related efforts, and hence a force in shaping educational policy nationwide.

The Heritage Foundation

The Heritage Foundation, the premier conservative think tank by funding and relative influence, was established in 1973 with start-up grants from conservative philanthropists shortly after the Powell Manifesto. Brewery magnate Joseph Coors gave $250,000, Richard Scaife gave $900,000, and Edward Noble provided "significant" sums for the think tank. Conservative activist Paul Weyrich, founder and first president of the institute, has a vita that includes key posts across a host of other right-wing institutes, media, and government posts including Free Congress Foundation CEO, Council for National Policy treasurer and executive committee, Empowerment Television, *Journal of Family and Culture*. A well-funded organization, between 1985 and 2003 Heritage realized $57.5 million in gifts from conservative foundations primarily to support general operations and fellowships. Its mission is:

> to formulate and promote conservative public policies based on the principles of free enterprise, limited government, individual freedom, traditional American values, and a strong national defense. (Heritage Foundation, 2005)

Holland "Holly" Coors is on Heritage's Board of Trustees as well as on the Board of the Adolph Coors Foundation and the Castle Rock Foundation. Richard Scaife has been a Heritage trustee for twenty years. In a Heritage biosketch, Scaife's connections to the media, other institutes, and universities are evident:

> Scaife's extensive involvement in the publishing industry—he is the owner and Chairman of the Board of the *Tribune-Review* as well as a number of radio stations—has brought a refreshing alternative voice to the media markets of Western Pennsylvania, including his hometown of Pittsburgh. His enduring commitment to the

free society is evident in his role as a director with the Pittsburgh World Affairs Council and his service on the boards of the Hoover Institution, Pepperdine University and other major educational institutions. (Heritage Foundation, 2005)

Heritage's staff of well over one hundred includes management and professional staff, communications specialists, policy analysts and senior fellows (Media Transparency). Its operation has four marketing divisions that include public relations for (1) marketing ideas to the media and public; (2) government relations to Congress, the Executive branch, and government agencies; (3) academic relations to the university, community, resources bank to institutions, including state think tanks, and the international conservative network; and (4) corporate relations to business and trades. The Heritage network provides a consistent, focused message to each of these constituencies through its publications and resource banks, support of conservative scholars and policy analysts, speakers bureau aimed at college campuses, and an activist role in government. "In its activist role, Heritage has been linking policy analysts, Republican party officials, conservative scholars and grassroots constituencies together for years."

Heritage demonstrates its commitment to developing college student leaders through its Young Leadership Network, Young President's Club, Heritage Congressional Fellowship, Heritage Internship Program, and Job Bank. The foundation's website is inviting to college students:

> Heritage takes great interest in young conservative minds, and we are pleased to consider you a member of this important group. Our interns work directly with research analysts and policy-makers in each of our departments. In addition, our interns attend weekly seminars with top Heritage Fellows and other outside policy think tanks. We

arrange tours to places like the United States Capitol, the Library of Congress, Mount Vernon, and the Pentagon. Our alumni can be found working in influential policy-making, legal, media, and academic positions. (Heritage Foundation, 2005)

The Heritage Congressional Fellowship and Congressional Fellowship Alumni programs provide support for Capital Hill staffers through monthly dinner programs, book clubs, and other resources. The Alumni program

> aims to provide networking opportunities in addition to a continuing education in key concepts, such as the principles of the American Founding and the leading concepts of conservative thought to enable congressional staffers to better address current legislative issues and grapple with contemporary politics and policy.

Heritage has a huge media machine in its Center for Media and Public Policy. A "Press Room" offers news releases, commentary, easily arranged interviews with Heritage experts, a 24-hour media hotline with five media contacts, and even offers its own radio studios free of charge:

> The Heritage Foundation now features two state-of-the-art radio studios capable of broadcasting your show to listeners across the country. They are available free and on Capitol Hill—allowing you to stay real close to the real action in Washington. In addition to equipment such as a 14-channel Harris Pacific Legacy On-Air Mixer and Sennheiser HD 280 Pro headphones, the studios even have Internet and cable TV access to keep you updated of breaking news while you're on the air. It's all here, just waiting for the next broadcaster to sign up at no charge—and do a great show.

To illustrate Heritage's commitment to shaping educational policies, one can examine the lengthy relationship Heritage has had with William Bennett, Reagan's secretary of education, and his numerous conservative education projects and organizations over the years. As a John M. Olin Distinguished Fellow at the Heritage Foundation, Bennett received Olin Foundation funding totaling $425,000 (1993–96) to support his Cultural Policy Studies Program. Today Bennett is the director of *Empower America*, "... a unique combination of public policy institute and political advocacy organization" (Media Transparency quoting former Empower America website, 2005). This organization was cofounded in 1999 by Bennett, Jack Kemp, Jeanne Kirkpatrick, and Vin Weber (founding members of Project for a New American Century with Bennett, advisor to the G.W. Bush campaign, former Minnesota representative). Donald Rumsfeld served as a board member for the organization. Empower America's mission statement reflects an agenda much like that of Heritage and other conservative think tanks:

> devoted to ensuring that government actions foster growth, economic well-being, freedom and individual responsibility. The ideas that have fueled America's stunning economic expansion—opportunity, competition, ownership and freedom—must be the framework for reform of century-old public systems such as K–12 education, the tax code and Social Security. Uniquely positioned in Washington, Empower America bridges the gap between the array of think tanks that produce white papers on the public-policy debate and the actual enactment of policy. In implementing our free-market, entrepreneurial principles into law, we are convinced, through actual experience, that we are the most effective "delivery" system in existence. (Empower America, 2005)

In 1994, Heritage and Bennett's Empower America co-sponsored the orientation for incoming members of Congress, an annual event that had been run by the Kennedy School of Government in Boston for twenty years. The orientation featured a presentation by right-wing radio/TV talk show host Rush Limbaugh, referred to by Bennett as "a symbol of encouragement." Limbaugh was voted an honorary member of Congress at this session (Media Transparency, 2005).

In 2000, Bennett's Empower America received $150,000 from both Olin and Bradley for the annual reedition of "The Index of Leading Cultural Indicators" that "attempts to bring a similar kind of data-based analysis to cultural issues. It is a statistical portrait (from 1960 to the present) of the moral, social and behavioral conditions of modern American society—matters that, in our time, often travel under the banner of 'values'" (Bennett, 1993). During the last decade of the 20th century, Bennett received slightly over $1 million to support his education projects including Empower America Freedom Works, a merger of Empower America ($370,000) and Citizens for a Sound Economy ($18,317,912) that boasts a website slogan of "lower taxes, less government, more freedom" with 27 state chapters, including one in Georgia.

The Heritage website offers policy briefs, suggested readings, current news on Capitol Hill, featured research, policy blogs, and many other links to resources that support its agenda. This multi-issue think tank provides both research and policy briefs to "inform" both domestic and foreign policies. The research side of the site focused on issues specific to education aimed to "build a new vision for America's twenty-first century schools in which every child has access to excellence in a competitive market of public, private, charter, and home schools." This site divides educational issues into K–12, Parental Choice, and Higher Education, and includes facts and figures, talking points, and recommendations consistent with Heritage's mission. It provides a "required reading" list that features papers such as "No Child Left Behind: Where do we go from here?" and "Refocusing higher education aid on those who need it." Heritage produces its *Education Notebook*, a "bi-monthly analysis of education news" reporting federal legislative activities. Included on this page are links to other conservative institutes such as Choices in Education, Cato Institute, Center for Education Reform, Manhattan Institute, Freedom Work, and the Thomas B. Fordham Foundation, all of which are supported by the conservative philanthropies.

The Heritage Foundation tracks school choice and the charter school movement in its state-by-state status analysis, with Ohio, Arizona, Florida, Utah, and Louisiana listed as "hot states"—those with strong charter school laws, large numbers of charter schools and numbers of students in those schools. As a local example, Heritage gave Georgia a much lower ranking with its school charter law rated as "weak," only 36 charter schools in operation, 14,952 students enrolled in those schools with no publicly funded private school choice [yet]. Each state's summary analysis describes the chronology of legislative and judicial events related to school choice, the stance of the governor for school choice, and composition of the legislature. For example, under "Georgia's 2005 developments," it reported

> that three parents filed suit against the state saying Georgia's education system should be declared unconstitutional because it does not provide equal opportunities in education for families who are not wealthy. The parents in the case suggest several solutions including statewide public school choice or publicly-funded vouchers (though the language in the suit does not use the term vouchers). (Heritage Foundation, 2005)

The site includes links to state resources supportive of school choice, including The Georgia Public Policy Foundation (GPPF), a conservative state think tank that established a Charter School Resource Center to assist parents interested in opening charter schools. I describe the work of this organization later in this chapter. You may want to view Heritage's analysis of your state's school choice law.

In an assessment of its success at its 20-year anniversary, Newt Gingrich remarked, "The Heritage Foundation is without a question the most far-reaching conservative organization in the country in the war of ideas, and one which has had a tremendous impact not just in Washington, but literally across the planet" (Rich, 2005, p. 24). Heritage is just one of over one hundred well-funded conservative think tanks producing "research" and publications that inform education policies and practices at the state and local levels. While Heritage is a premier example of how think tanks work with the media and government to influence public debates, there are others working in similar ways with funding from the same coffers to shape current educational debates, including The American Enterprise Institute, the Hudson Institute, The Cato Institute,[6] and the Hoover Institute, to name a few.

As an illustration of how conservative think tank scholars impact P–12 schooling at the local level in Georgia, I turn to a relative newcomer to the landscape, the Thomas B. Fordham Foundation and its cofounder (with Chester Finn), Diane Ravitch. Fordham is based in Dayton, Ohio, home of the Fordham family. The Thomas B. Fordham Institute within the Fordham Foundation received five grants in 2002–03 totaling $535,000, with two from the Walton Foundation ($385,000) simply identified as "charitable" and three from the Lynde and Harry Bradley Foundation ($150,000) to support projects "studying the state of history in schools."

Fordham's cofounder, Ravitch, is a right-wing success story: a faculty member at New York University, a fellow at the Hoover Institute, a nonresident senior fellow at the Brookings Institution, as well as Trustee on the Fordham Foundation Board. Earlier in her career, Diane Ravitch moved from her position as adjunct professor at Teachers College where she was well-funded by the conservative philanthropists ($2,150,150 between 1985 and 1999) to Assistant Secretary of Education and Counselor to Secretary of Education Lamar Alexander (1991–93) in President George H.W. Bush's administration. In that post, she was responsible for the Office of Educational Research and Improvement in the

U.S. Department of Education, where "she led the federal effort to promote the creation of state and national academic standards" (Ravitch, 2005).

Through her writing, government service, and work with these think tanks she is recognized as a conservative expert on state and national standards for education and an advocate of privatization of education through school choice. Last year Ravitch served as the "expert consultant" for the newly minted Georgia Performance Standards (GPS) in social studies. The process that was used for creating these new standards in reading, language, mathematics, science, and social studies began with external experts who created standards that were then approved by a team of Georgia teachers and higher education faculty. The DOE website reported that in addition to these "expert consultants," the standards of Michigan, North Carolina, and Texas were reviewed. In the case of the social studies standards, Ravitch served as Georgia's "expert consultant," wrote the standards, and submitted them to the Department of Education. Powell (2005) provided Ravitch's view of this curriculum development process gained through an e-mail exchange where Ravitch responded to his query about how she became involved in the process and her role in writing the standards. She explained that Marc Tucker's National Center for Education and the Economy was contracted by the Georgia State Department of Education to work on the new Georgia Performance Standards and then invited her to write a draft proposal of the social studies standards. A committee of teachers contributed a different draft, and the two drafts were "melded together." She reported that this version of the document was then revised by a committee of Georgia professors and returned to her for review and revision, with some of her suggestions incorporated into the final document. A member of this committee of higher education professors shared his version of the process, noting that a committee of professors met for two sessions (three days total) to discuss and approve the standards. A committee member described the first two-day session as an "editing session with little latitude for any significant additions" in which the committee was instructed not to change the content. He explained that the second one-day meeting was a "rubber stamp" approval of the social studies standards.

A webcast from the Georgia Department of Education boasts the quality of the new GPS standards in math and English/language:

> The state of Georgia is among the nation's elite when comparing the quality of each state's math and English/language arts curriculum framework. Georgia's new standards have received a letter grade of "B" in both subjects, placing it on the "honor roll."... State Superintendent of Schools Kathy Cox has led the revision of Georgia's mathematics, English/language arts, science, and social studies curriculum frameworks. "The new Georgia Performance Standards set high expectations for all students and will truly be the blueprint for both student and teacher success," Cox said. "The newly strengthened curriculum is the foundation for educational change as Georgia aims to lead the nation in improving student achievement." (Atlanta, 2/17/05)

Interestingly, the Honor Roll status received by those standards was granted in a study called "The State of State Standards 2005: Math and English," conducted by the Thomas B. Fordham Foundation, Professor Ravitch's own think tank. Ravitch's conservative "expert" influence has touched the lives of Georgia's teachers and students through both the curriculum and the mandatory testing program that will be based on those standards.

I turn to the third strategy of the conservative right—the development of an extensive, highly organized, and well-informed network of state policy think tanks that serves as a pathway through the labyrinth carrying conservative national research and policy to the states.

Strategy #3: Developing a Network of Well-Funded State Policy Centers: Dissemination of a Conservative Policy Agenda in the Guise of Neutral Public Nonprofit Efforts

Given their philosophical beliefs focused on local control, smaller federal government, and devolution of authority from the federal to the state level, it makes sense for the foundations to build policy-influencing bodies in the states. Media Transparency reports over $9 million in awards from the conservative philanthropists between 1992 and 1994, with more than sixty state or regional conservative think tanks built over the 1980s and early 1990s (2005).

The South Carolinian Roe Foundation alone, which focused its spending on these think tanks, contributed $420,00 (1998–2003) to the State Policy Network (SPN), a California-based umbrella organization, with lesser amounts awarded to particular state and regional centers. The only organization that Roe funded more was the Heritage Foundation, with $596,000 from 1998 to 2003. While the other philanthropists worked largely at the national level, Roe worked across the United States at a state level in an effort to influence local policies reflective of a conservative ideology. The State Policy Network, founded in 1992, describes itself as

> the professional service organization for America's state-based, free market think tank community. Our work advances a free society by providing leadership development, management training, and networking opportunities for think tank professionals and promoting strategic partnership among market-oriented organizations.... SPN is the only group in the country dedicated solely to improving the practical effectiveness of independent, nonprofit, market-oriented, state-based think tanks. SPN's programs enable these organizations to better educate local citizens, policy makers, and opinion

leaders about market-oriented alternatives to state and local policy challenges. (State Policy Network, 2005)

SPN focuses its programs on (1) leadership development initiatives "needed to make state-based, market-oriented think tanks more effective, respected, and successful advocates for personal and economic freedom in their respective states"; (2) a policy development and research exchange program that "maximizes the impact of cutting-edge research and new policy strategies"; (3) a state policy resource center and clearinghouse that "makes readily available in one location essential and comprehensive information necessary for launching a successful policy institute and for effectively growing and strengthening existing policy organizations"; and (4) acts as a professional association service leader that "provides professional services to its member groups in an effort to increase their competitive advantage and effectiveness in identifying, recruiting, equipping, retaining, and rewarding a highly talented and growing cadre of freedom leaders for the policy battles of the 21st century" (State Policy Network, 2005). A SPN directory and map shows over 100 regular and associate members. Conservative philanthropists supported SPN and 51 of its member organizations with total donations of $38,907,448 between 1987 and 2003. The earliest and most heavily funded was the Wisconsin Policy Research Institute (WPPI) at $7,362,975, with others such as the Capital Research Center in DC ($7,776,153), the Commonwealth Foundation, Pennsylvania ($2,973,480), and Heartland Institute in Illinois ($2,273,767) receiving substantial awards.

As an example of the way SPN works, in late September 2005 it hosted its thirteenth annual, three-day meeting in Charleston, South Carolina, where speakers from state and regional think tanks from all over the U.S. conducted sessions. A sampling of institutes present were the Mercatus Center, Evergreen Freedom Foundation, Property Rights Alliance, American Land Rights Association, Defender of Property Rights, Mackinac Center for Public Policy, Texas Public Policy Foundation, Heartland Institute,

Progress & Freedom Foundation, and the Goldwater Institute. Jay Greene, senior fellow, Manhattan Institute for Policy Research and author of *Education Myths: What Special Interest Groups Want You to Believe about Our Schools and Why It Isn't So* and Carsten Walter, Heritage Foundation's development officer, were among the presenters. At the top of the list of discussion topics was K–12 education reform, followed by health care policy reform, Medicaid reform, pre-K education, eminent domain/property rights, fundraising, marketing/media outreach, and leadership development. The last three efforts in this list are the hallmarks of conservative think tanks at all levels to both maintain themselves and to develop broader networks and are well-funded by the philanthropists. Education-focused sessions included "Emerging issues in the school choice debate," "To Pre-K or not to Pre-K: The policy and the politics," and "Pre-K: The education monopoly's next wave." Individual sessions and receptions were sponsored by the Charles G. Koch Foundation, the Milton and Rose D. Freidman Foundation, a conservative foundation devoted to funding parental choice initiatives; and Americans for Tax Reform. The last evening of the conference included "a special book signing opportunity with contributing authors" David Salisbury, Cato Institute (co-editor of *What America Can Learn from School Choice in Other Countries*, 2005) and Lewis Andrews, executive director, Yankee Institute for Public Policy (author of *The Other Good Reason for School Choice*). The evening concluded with a reception and the 2005 Roe Awards Banquet. Meetings such as this one inform and shape the agenda of the state and regional think tanks as they work with legislators in their states to shape public policy generally and education policy in particular. Books and other resources featured at these meetings are then marketed and distributed on their websites and discussed in state-level policy events.

John Hood, President of the John Locke Foundation in Raleigh, North Carolina, correlated the success of influencing the policymaking process with the quality and quantity of personal contacts. He argued that

> For state think tanks, this [using personal contacts] is good news. We face a daunting array of ideological rivals—be they tenured radicals in universities, labor unions, liberal foundations, or left-wing think tanks and activist groups. The idea that we—the few, the proud—can prevail anyway is deeply reassuring. Developing personal relationships is a costly process, however. It means committing substantial time and energy to several important tasks. They include: gathering intelligence, gaining credibility, giving face-time, and narrowcasting (keeping mailouts limited and effective). (2001, pp. 1–2)

As a local example, Georgia's SPN member, the Georgia Public Policy Foundation (GPPF), a recipient of conservative foundation funding ($182,000 from 1998 to 2003), describes itself as the "only private, nonpartisan research and education organization in Georgia that focuses on state policy issues." The foundation, founded in 1991, reports several highly successful education initiatives:

> The Foundation has been on the cutting edge of education reform for more than a decade, having the independence to propose innovative and often controversial ideas that have now become mainstream:
> - The nationally acclaimed Report Card for Parents was one of the first state report cards in the nation in 1996—now there are more than one hundred. It is also credited with spurring many other reforms. We have been retained by the Georgia Chamber of Commerce and the Metro Atlanta Chamber of Commerce to monitor the implementation of standards-based accountability throughout the state.
> - Through our early policy research and Charter School Resource Center, we have been a catalyst for charter school development and improvements in the charter school

law. Today, Georgia has nearly 40 charter schools—ten years ago there were none.
- Our annual No Excuses awards that honor high achieving, high poverty schools underscores the now common theme that all children can learn.
- Our research on alternative certification to improve teacher quality has resulted in the successful Georgia Teacher Alternative Preparation Program (Georgia Public Policy Foundation [GPPF] 2005). The GPPF, located in Atlanta and convenient to Georgia's legislators, is a multi-issue think tank focused on public policy, environment, education, health care and transportation that holds regular policy luncheons, produces the Georgia Policy Review and other policy briefs, "Friday Facts," press releases, and provides speakers for events around the state. Despite its nonpartisan claim, GPPF's website features connections to the other SPN organizations and resources consistent with SPN's conservative agenda including a resource bank for parents interested in starting charter schools. The Heritage Foundation noted that GPPF's resource center helps "groups maneuver through the daunting legal and financial challenges involved in opening a charter school" (Heritage Foundation, 2005). The GPPF also releases rankings of every public school in the state and encourages parents to learn more about their children's schools and to compare their school's performance against the performance of the schools" (Georgia Public Policy Foundation Education Agenda, 2005).

The GPPF's *Agenda 2005: A Guide to the Issues* highlights education initiatives, including (1) school choice with calls to "Strengthen the existing Charter School Act of 1998 (O.C.G.A.§20-2-2060) to clarify funding equity and encourage greater numbers of innovative "start-up" charter schools; (2) teacher quality that "shifts the focus of alternative teacher certification to demonstrated ability and content knowledge rather than specific prerequisites and encourage[s] rewards for teachers based on student performance and success"; and (3) support for the "implementation of the new Georgia Performance Standards" which are rigorous, clear and measurable and based on national and international research with efforts to "Develop and maintain challenging assessments/tests aligned to the Georgia Performance Standards."

The network of national and state level think tanks, with their stables of conservative scholars, would not be experiencing the level of influence they are now without the infrastructure of a conservative media. I turn now to this final strategy of the right.

Strategy #4: Spinning the Spin: Developing a Conservative Media to Disseminate Conservative Ideologies (or Why Our Families Watch Fox News)

The media machine is a critical strategy used by the well-funded right. Without the media in all its forms, the conservative labyrinth would not have the reach it does. Philanthropists learned early that while ideas have consequences, the ideas need to be sold. Herb Berkowist, Heritage's former vice president for communications, stated:

> Our belief is that when the research project has been printed, then the job is only half done. That is when we start marketing it to the media.... We have as part of our charge the selling of ideas, the selling of policy proposals. We are out there actively selling these things, day after day. It's our mission. (Rich, 2005, quoting a July 22, 1996, interview)

One need only go into a bookstore to see the proliferation of books and magazines published by the conservative right. These authors, supported with grants and fellowships from conservative think tanks, have inundated the mass market with their books and expert testimony on "what works." Often the "research" is published by the think tanks themselves. Side-stepping the academic peer review system, these books are "peer reviewed" by conservative magazines funded by the same conservative web. The books and their authors are then delivered via conservative talk radio, television "news" shows, the speakers' circuit, conservative websites, and other marketing outlets through a network of right-wing organizations, including the State Policy Networks.

The effective use of the Internet has served to market the right-wing agenda through dissemination of brief, clear, authoritative "facts" supported by "expert" scholars. The *Georgia GuardDawg* argued that "Any good right-winger needs to be armed with useful and up-to-date information about the world, and those Web sites offer a straightforward way to quickly catch up on what some of the utmost conservative voices are saying" (*Georgia GuardDawg*, 2005, p. 6). Among its "Top Ten" websites are www.foxnews.com, www.townhall.com, and www.cato.org. The conservative funding of this media is evident again by following the money:

- Irving Kristol's National Affairs, Inc., publisher of *The National Interest* and *The Public Interest*, in 1986 received more than $4 million alone from Bradley and eighty-five grants totaling $8,067,600 (1985–2003).
- *Commentary Magazine* was the recipient of forty-five grants totaling $2,032,500 (1990–2003).
- Senior AEI fellow Ben Wattenberg's PBS *Think Tank* received thirty-two grants totaling 2,887,500 (1992–2003)—ironically at the same time the right lobbies to stop funding for public radio and television.
- William F. Buckley's *Firing Line* received seventeen grants for a total of $3,610,000 (1985–1999) as well as his *National Review* that received nine grants for a total of $439,700 (1986–2002).

- Conservative magazine *The American Spectator* received twenty-one grants totaling $930,000 (1985–2003).
- David Horowitz's Center for the Study of Popular Culture received 136 grants totaling $13,859,000 (1989–2003), which in part funded its online *FrontPage Magazine* with 1.7 million hits per month.

Conservative marketing began early with Chodorov's attention to the creation of a network of student newspapers and has developed into a force that is so pervasive that yes, our families watch *Fox News* and really think they've entered the "no-spin zone."

How Well Is the Conservative War on Public Education Working? Implications for the Left

I find it ironic as a child of the '60s and antiwar protester to realize that conservative philanthropists learned well the lessons of the left for creating a movement that now controls the political agenda and public policy today. The very conservatives who prize individual freedom and a free enterprise system built a structure over the last four decades that is much like DeVos's Amway pyramid scheme, with marketing aimed at a wide supporting base and those with the most money and power at the top. This carefully crafted labyrinth is tremendously influential at all levels of government, the academy, and the media and results in conservative policies across domestic and global issues (Kuttner, 2002; Krehely, House, and Kerrnan, 2004). Unlike the movements of the radical left that were loud and visible, this movement is one that works below the surface, is well funded, and carefully uses the media to shape public opinion and hence public voting behavior. It is so far below the surface that most of us are unaware of its reach. Even though John Saloma warned us of this conservative labyrinth in 1984, it functions largely below public awareness.

One might argue that the left has its own funders who pump even more money into educational programs and efforts. The success of the right, however, is due to the consistent, narrow, and carefully focused funding to specific efforts over decades, including (1) development of college students to become the next generation of conservative scholars, leaders, and media personalities; (2) financial support of academics who create easily accessible scholarship consistent with a conservative ideology; (3) creation of a large network of conservative think tanks at the federal and state policy levels whose focus is to turn conservative "research" into practice through the creation and passing of public policy; and (4) a media machine that convinces the American public of the correctness of its points, through the guise of neutrality. By the time the concepts reach the policy stage in state legislatures and the U.S. Congress, they have had so much airtime through media outlets of all kinds that they are widely regarded as making "good sense" and have bipartisan support, as we saw in the case of No Child Left Behind. Across all these strategies is the passionate commitment to a clearly focused conservative agenda that has remained the same over decades and is communicated to the general public through:

1. A common and consistent message despite internal philosophical differences among the right-wing groups.
2. Clear accessible language that proclaims to be factual, neutral, nonpartisan and based on scientific research.
3. Marketing, marketing, marketing.
4. Patience.

James Piereson, executive director and trustee of the Olin Foundation, explains this last point in an essay aimed at donors who fund academic programs:

> It may take a long time to influence the academic world, or even a single college. It can take years of sustained support to establish a strong academic center. Important books can

take several years to write and then to publish. Many years are required to train students to the point where they can take up academic posts, and several years more before they begin to have an influence on their fields. This kind of work requires patience, and also requires that donors think like institutions—that is, for the long run. This can be a challenge for individual donors who are not prepared to wait a decade or more before the funds begin to have an effect. (2005, p. 1)

The success of this movement is demonstrated in the shift to right-wing public policies over the past decades and through the movement of individuals across the organizations, think tanks, and government service within the structure of this web. For example, RightWeb (2005) profiled 83 individuals in George Bush's administration with ties to conservative foundations and think tanks. Examples include the following:

- John Ashcroft, Attorney General (Federalist Society)
- Dick Cheney (PNAC, AEI, Jewish Institute for National Security)
- Linda Chavez, Bush's first choice for labor secretary (PNAC, Fox News, Manhattan Institute, Capital Research Center, Independent Women's Forum, etc.)
- Elaine Chao, Secretary of Labor (Heritage Foundation Distinguished Fellow)
- David Frum, former G.W. Bush speechwriter (AEI, Manhattan Institute, The Weekly Standard)
- Jeane Kirkpatrick, US Representative to UN Human Rights Commission and UN Ambassador under Reagan (AEI Senior Fellow, Freedom House, Empower American, etc.)
- Richard Perle, Defense Policy Board (AEI, PNAC, Hudson Institute, etc.)
- Condoleezza Rice, Secretary of State (Hoover Institution Senior Fellow)

"THE HAVES AND THE HAVE MORES" 83

In the parlance of critical theorists, that was the language of critique. Now the language of possibility. What can we as individual scholars and members of organizations like the American Educational Studies Association do in the face of this conservative web with its heavy influence on our lives in P–16 public education? I conclude with a David Letterman approach—my Top Ten Strategies for counteracting the conservative war on public education:

1. *Learn more about the conservative labyrinth and its impact on public education at all levels.* Use websites like Media Transparency, RightWeb, People for the American Way, and others to become more knowledgeable about this movement. Attend meetings and conferences of conservative think tanks sponsored by the philanthropists to see how they work. If you don't trust my analysis, do your own. And if you do, build on what I've done.
2. *Help make the network visible.* Share this information and these connections with your family, friends, and colleagues—everyone you know. Maybe if your family knew who bought Fox News they might switch to CNN.
3. *Become knowledgeable about the public policy think tanks in your state and region to keep up with the next set of initiatives on the table.* You already have at least one in your state or region and they are a step ahead of you now in influencing P–16 education policy.
4. *In addition to your scholarly audience, write clear and succinct pieces for op-ed sections of the papers, undergraduate texts, and books for a lay audience.*
5. *In your college, shape the state agenda before you have to react to it.* Volunteer for state-level committees that are linked to education policy such as new P–12 curriculum standards committees, changes in teacher education standards, etc. While these often seem like mundane meetings, this is where the work gets done and policy gets played out. A

recent example from Georgia demonstrates this point. This fall, several AESA members (Charles Jackson, Jamie Lewis, Deron Boyles, and I) participated in University System of Georgia Board of Regents committees that developed new core courses for teacher education in the state. Through leadership in these committees, we were able to align one of the courses to the Council for Social Foundations in Education (CSFE) standards and to save a required social foundations course from degenerating into a "hot topics in education" course.

6. *Create a policy center focused on educational issues* where you can create clear, accessible policy briefs that reach legislators in your state. Take a lesson from the right and produce briefs neutral and authoritative in language, focused on one issue, with clear policy recommendations. Use the Heritage toolkit to assist with the construction and management of the center.
7. *Communicate regularly with legislators* as an individual, with colleagues in professional associations, or through the growing number of Web groups (e.g., MoveOn.org).
8. *Share stories from your work in schools with policymakers.* What impact has this state and federal legislation had on students, teachers, and schools? Take a page from the right by telling a poignant story that illustrates the issue, recommend a change in policy and practice, and ask that the policy or practice be implemented.
9. *Get involved politically*—run for the school board, run for state or federal posts, work for a campaign, or send money to those candidates that reflect your views.
10. Check to see where your own money is going and align your investments and spending with your priorities. In other words, do you really want to shop at Walmart?

One final thought, if this is all public record, just think of what we don't know!

Acknowledgments

I would like to thank two University of Georgia students who provided research assistance for this project. First, a warm thanks to Kathryn Otrosina, an undergraduate student, who generously gave of her time and thoughtful insights as we uncovered the conservative labyrinth. She provided invaluable assistance for this project. Second, thanks to Brent Allison, a doctoral candidate, who scoured the Web to track the specifics of the conservative groups' spending through their IRS data.

Notes

1. John S. Saloma, *Ominous Politics: The New Conservative Labyrinth* (Hill & Wang, 1984), describes this structure as a "major new presence in American politics."
2. The conservative right movement includes ideologically diverse positions including, as Barry (2003) identified, the following: [militant] anticommunists, Christian Right, conservative internationalists, conservative mainstream, libertarians, national security militarists, neoconservatives, New Right, old guard right, paleoconservatives, and social conservatives. James Smith (1991), in *The Idea Brokers: Think Tanks and the Rise of the New Policy Elite*, argued that "despite their intellectual diversity, the conservatives, of necessity, banded together in the face of mutual enemies" (p. 170)—the Liberal Establishment of the 1960s.
3. 1985 is the earliest year available on Media Transparency databases. Unless otherwise noted, funding amounts from conservative philanthropists cited throughout this chapter are based on Media Transparency's research on publicly available IRS records from 1985 to 2003.
4. For a thorough analysis of the influence of conservative foundations on public policy, see Krehely, House, and Kerrnan, 2004.
5. For a detailed description of this organization, see Atwell (2003).
6. The Cato Institute, Washington, D.C., is a libertarian think tank with ninety staff, sixty adjunct scholars, and sixteen fellows. In 2001,

the *Washington Post* reported that Cato had spent about "$3 million in the past six years to run a virtual war room to promote Social Security privatization" (People for the American Way, 2005).

References

Accuracy in Media. (2005). Available online at http://www.academia.org

Allen, M. (2001, June 25). Bush aims to get faith initiative back on track: Stricter rules to be added for use of funds by groups. *Washington Post*, p. A01.

American Heritage Dictionary. (1982). (2nd College ed.) Boston: Houghton Mifflin.

Atwell, J. (2003). *The work of a super-patriot: Allen Zoll and the National Council for American Education.* Bachelor's thesis, University of North Carolina at Asheville.

Barry, T. (2003, December). Glossary of the right-wing sectors in U.S. foreign policy. Accessed July 7, 2005, from http://rightweb.irc-online.org/charts/glossary_body.html

Bennett, W. (1993, March 15). Quantifying America's decline. *Wall Street Journal.* Accessed August 13, 2005, from http://www.columbia.edu/cu/augustine/arch/usadecline.html

Bradley Foundation. (2005). Available online at http://www.bradleyfdn.org/

Buckley, W.F. (1962, December 4). Review of Chodorov's *Out of step. National Review, 192*, pp. 46–47.

Carthage Foundation. (2004). *Annual report, 2005.* Available online at http://www.scaife.com/sarah.html

Carthage Foundation. (2005). Available online at http://www.scaife.com/carthage.html

Chodorov, F. (1980a). A fifty-year project. In F. Chodorov, *Fugitive Essays* (pp. 151–162). Indianapolis, IN: Liberty Press. (Original work published 1950)

Chodorov, F. (1980b). Private schools: The solution to American's educational problem. In F. Chodorov, *Fugitive Essays* (pp. 240–251). Indianapolis: Liberty Press. (Original work published 1950)

Chodorov, F. (1980c). Why schools are not free. In F. Chodorov, *Fugitive Essays* (pp. 232–239). Indianapolis, IN: Liberty Press. (Original work published 1950)

Collegiate Network. (2005). Retrieved from https://www.collegiatenetwork.org/about

Council for Social Foundations of Education: CSFE News and Updates. (n.d.). Retrieved from https://csfeonline.org/

dkosopedia. (2005). Accessed June 10, 2005, from www.dkosopedia.com

Empower America. (2005). Available online at http://web.archive.org/web/20030622093625/www.empoweramerica.org/stories/story Reader$2

Free Congress Foundation. (2005). Available online at http://americanopportunity.org/

Georgia Department of Education. (2005, February 17). *Georgia Performance Standards* [Webcast]

Georgia GuardDawg. (2005, October). An alternative student newspaper at the University of Georgia supported by the Collegiate Network. Available online at http://www. guarddawg.com

Georgia Public Policy Foundation Education Agenda. (2005). Accessed June 30, 2005, from http:// www.gppf.org/default.asp?pt=news&RT=5

Hamilton, C.H. (1980). Introduction. In F. Chodorov, *Fugitive Essays* (pp. 11–30). Indianapolis, IN: Liberty Press.

Heritage Foundation. (2005). Available online at http://www.heritage.org

Hood, J. (2001, Summer). The personal touch. *SPN News*. Accessed August 29, 2005, from http:// www.spn.org/newsite/main/news.php

Intercollegiate Studies Institute. (2005). Accessed June 19, 2005, from http://www.isi.org/spotlight/awards/content/hoeflich_award.pdf

Intercollegiate Studies Institute Collegiate Network. Accessed June 19, 2005, from http;//www. isi.org/cn/

Internal Revenue Service. (2005). *Charitable organization exemption requirements*. Accessed October 5, 2005, from http://www.irs.gov/charities/charitable/article/0,,id=96099,00.html

Irving Kristol person profile. (2005). Accessed June 27, 2005, from http://www.mediatransparency.com/personprofile.php?personID=35

Kirby, D. (2005, October 13). Letter to the editor. Red & Black, p. 4A. [Official student newspaper, University of Georgia]

Klein, D., et al (2005). *State of State Math standards 2005*. Washington DC: Thomas B. Fordham Foundation. Retrieved from https://edexcellence.net/publications/sosmath05.html

Krehely, J., House, M., & Kerrnan, E. (2004, March) *Axis of ideology: Conservative foundations and public policy* (p. 237). Washington, DC: National Committee for Responsive Philanthropy.

Kuttner, R. (2002). Philanthropy and movement. *The American Prospect*, 13(13), 207, 237.

Landay, J. (2002). *The Powell Manifesto: How a prominent lawyer's attack memo changed America*. Accessed October 9, 2005, from http://www.mediatransparency.com/story.php?storyID=21

The lawyer's skill became the judge's excellence. Associate Supreme Court Justice Lewis F. Powell Jr. 1907–1998. Accessed July 7, 2005, from http://www.uscourts.gov/ttb/sept98ttb/powell.html

Lynde and Harry Bradley Foundation, Inc. *Funder profile*. (2005). Accessed June 16, 2005, from http://www.mediatransparency.com-funderprofile.php?funderID=1

Media Transparency (Now Conservative Transparency, owned by Media Matters). (2005). Available online at http://bridgeproject.com/?transparency

Miller, J.J. (2003). *Strategic investment in ideas: How two foundations reshaped America*. Washington, DC: The Philanthropy Roundtable.

Moore, M. (2004). *The official Fahrenheit 9/11 reader*. New York: Simon & Schuster.

National Committee for Responsive Philanthropy. (2004). *State of philanthropy 2004*. Washington, DC: Author.

People for the American Way. (2005). *Buying a movement*. Accessed June 10, 2005, from http://www.pfaw.org/pfaw/general/defautlt.asps?oid=9261

Piereson, J. (2005, May/June). Planting seeds of liberty. Accessed July 19, 2005, from http://www.philanthropyroundtable.org/magazines/2005/mayjune/coverstory.htm

Philanthropy Roundtable. Accessed on June 19, 2005, from http://www.philanthropyroundtable.org/.

Powell, D. (2005). "You don't need no engine to go downhill": Georgia's performance standards and the future of social studies. Unpublished paper, University of Georgia.

The Powell Memo (also known as the Powell Manifesto). (1971). Accessed July 7, 2005, from http://reclaimdemocracy.org/corporate_accountability/powell_memo_lewis.html

Ramsey Center for Private Enterprise at UGA. (2005). Accessed July 7, 2005, from http://www.terry.uga.edu/~dlee/ramsey.html

Ravitch, D. (2005). Diane Ravitch's CV. accessed July 14, 2005, from http://www.dianeravitch.com/vita.html

Reclaim Democracy. (2005). Available online at http://www.reclaimdemocracy.org

Rich, A. (2004). *Think tanks, public policy, and the politics of expertise.* New York: Cambridge University Press.

Rich, A. (2005, Spring). War of ideas: Why mainstream and liberal foundations and the think tanks they support are losing in the war of ideas in American politics. *Stanford Social Innovation Review*, pp. 18–25.

Rightalk. (2005). *Accuracy in academia.* Available online at http://academia.org/profile/123

Rightweb. (2005). *Karl Rove.* Available online at http://rightweb.irc-online.org

Saloma, J.S. (1984). *Ominous politics: The new conservative labyrinth.* New York: Hill & Wang.

The Sarah Scaife Foundations funder profile. (2005). Accessed June 13, 2005, from http://www. mediatransparency.com/funderprofile.php?funderID=3

Scaife Foundations. (2005). Available online at http://www.scaife.com

Smith, J. (1991). *The idea brokers: Think tanks and the rise of the new policy elite.* New York: Free Press.

Smith Richardson Foundation. (2005). Accessed October 9, 2005, from http://www.srf.org

State Policy Network. (2005). Accessed August 29, 2005, from http://www.spn.org

Steelman, A. (1996). Frank Chodorov: Champion of liberty. *The Freeman, 46* (12).

Stotsky, S. & Finn, C. (2005). *State of State English standards 2005.* Washington, DC: Thomas B. Fordham Foundation. Retrieved from https://edexcellence.net/publications/sosenglish05.html

Wilayto, P. (1997, June 1). The feeding trough: The Bradley Foundation, *The Bell Curve* & the real story behind W–2: Wisconsin's national model for welfare reform. Accessed June 5, 2005, from http://www.mediatransparency.org/story.php?storyID=6

Zoll, A.A. (1949). *They want your child! The real meaning of federal "aid" to education—Showing its relation to the whole Marxist movement.* New York: National Council for American Education.

Chapter Two is a reprint of the article "The Haves and the Have Mores": Fueling a Conservative Ideological War on Public Education (or Tracking the Money) *Educational Studies, 39*(3): 201-240. DOI: 10.1207/s15326993es3903_3, by Kathleen deMarrais (2006). The article has been reprinted with permission from Taylor & Francis and the original can be found at the Journal's web site: https://www.tandfonline.com

Chapter Three

"THE HAVES AND HAVE MORES":
AN UPDATE, 2005–2018

Stability, Expansion, and Newly Identified Players

As we saw in the article "The Haves and the Have Mores": Fueling a Conservative Ideological War on Public Education (or Tracking the Money)," reprinted as Chapter Two of this volume, a small group of conservative philanthropists set in place a fifty-year movement to actively infuse legislation at the state and national levels with conservative values. The article detailed the 1971 *Powell Memo*, which served as the clarion call for wealthy conservative philanthropists to pool their resources in the form of the Philanthropy Roundtable to work toward policies that placed individualism over the pubic good and promoted deregulation, tax cuts, and privatization across health, human services, and education. As we approach the fifty-year anniversary of the *Powell Memo*, these efforts have transformed what was once a democracy into an oligarchy ruled by a small group of wealthy capitalists, most of whom are the same individuals who founded the Philanthropy Roundtable. This simple but carefully crafted strategy focused on developing conservative youth on college campuses, producing ideologically conservative research within think tanks, creating a network of state-level policy centers to influence legislation at the state level, and a conservative media to sell these ideas to the general public.

The chapters in this volume highlight how each of these strategies within the conservative movement have developed and grown over this fifty-year period.

Chapter Four herein, "*Citizens United* and the Disuniting of the United States," details how the Supreme Court's *Citizens United* decision has allowed unlimited and anonymous resources to flow into political campaigns, producing a political context in the United States wherein a small number of wealthy individuals control elections and, by extension, legislation and even the composition of the Supreme Court. Powell called for the American business and enterprise system to encourage a "highly competent staff of lawyers" to use the judiciary—particularly the Supreme Court—to fight against this attack on the system. He argued: "Under our constitutional system, especially with an activist-minded Supreme Court, the judiciary may be the most important instrument for social economic and political change" (Powell Memo, 1971, p. 8). His call to action in this regard has been highly successful, as we currently see a conservative-majority Supreme Court.

Chapter Five, "Hidden Strategies State by State: The History and Work of the American Legislative Exchange Council (ALEC), 1973–2018," describes the development of the American Legislative Exchange Council and how that group has now eclipsed and informed the State Policy Network (SPN) to influence the enactment of its conservative values into policies at the state level.

Chapter Six, "Philanthropy Goes to College: Tracking the Money," provides examples of the ways in which philanthropists have used their wealth to influence university curricula through the development of professorships, right-leaning centers, and conservative student book clubs, scholarships, and fellowships. The Charles G. Koch Foundation is highlighted in this chapter.

The student-centered strategy in the 1970s was focused on the development of the Intercollegiate Studies Institute to develop a corps of conservative students through the development of conservative campus newspapers across the United States dedicated to conservative philosophies. Students involved in these early newspapers were given the opportunity to network with leading conservatives, were granted summer and year-long fellowships, and often went on to become writers and scholars at conservative think tanks. The Intercollegiate Studies Institute—a 501(c)(3)—continues to be funded by conservative philanthropies, with 520 transactions listed on IRS 990 tax filings between 1985 and 2014, for a total of $49,869,786. Key funders included the DeVos Urban Leadership Initiative ($8,225,000), the Sarah Scaife Foundation ($7,925,000), the John M. Olin Foundation ($3,702,600), the John Templeton Foundation ($3,638,950), the Lynde and Harry Bradley Foundation ($3,517,100), the F.M. Kirby Foundation ($2,240,000), and the Earhart Foundation ($2,116,100), among others. While this organization continues to access funding from the conservative right, Chapter Six illustrates philanthropic strategies that move far beyond the early student newspapers. In recent years, wealthy individuals have focused their efforts on creating a network of colleges and universities where philanthropy has purchased ideologically conservative professorships, curricula, departments, and centers with the aim of developing and expanding a cadre of conservative scholars, writers, lawyers, and politicians to further their causes.

Chapter Seven, "Ideological Bedfellows: Elevating the Individual over the Collective Good in Education," uses network analysis to show the prevalence of a growing network of education reform organizations funded by dark money that support the myth of failed public education. This chapter makes the argument that the political right and left have become "strange bedfellows" in that they are committed to promoting the same kinds of educational reforms, which are neoliberal, focused on individualism and consumerism, and have been historically supported by the ideological right in the United States. Bolstered by conservative money, narratives of educational reform in the United States rarely focus on reinvesting in public education or supporting the collective good in education. This chapter places particular network actors in historical context to challenge these taken-for-granted narratives surrounding education reform in the United States.

Chapter Eight, "The Megaphone Behind the Myth: The Media's Role in Shaping Public Discourse about Education Reform," illustrates the role of the media in shaping a conservative offensive targeted at public education, with the goal of privatizing schools, curriculum, testing, and other services. Building on the narrative of "failing" public schools discussed in Chapter Seven, this chapter conducts a social network analysis of ownership and connections across various media platforms to demonstrate how conservative philanthropic groups have propelled and supported the myth of failing public schools and other messages consistent with a neoliberal agenda for education. This powerful message, which is disseminated across media platforms ranging from television, local and national news, to social media, ultimately benefits the economic elite and further disenfranchises marginalized members of society by turning schools into potential sites for making money at the expense of the collective good. This chapter argues that the consolidation of media control into smaller and more conservative outlets has increased the promotion of market-oriented education reforms supported by wealthy philanthropists like Charles G. Koch and organizations that represent the interests of private industry, such as the American Legislative Exchange Council (ALEC). The chapter explores issues of critical digital literacy that are surfacing in an era of so-called "fake news."

Turning toward collective political action possibilities in Chapter Nine, "Foundry10: An Example of Philanthropy Building School and Community Partnerships," Lisa Castenada describes an alternative, progressive form of philanthropy in which philanthropists work at the grassroots level with teachers and administrators to support the needs of the schools and communities in which they are located. Here, rather than starting with the ideological interests of the philanthropists, Foundry10 begins with the educational experts who are familiar with the context and needs of the community. We provide this case as an alternative way to "do philanthropy."

The concluding Chapter Ten, "Collective Resistance: Resources for Change," enumerates extensive resources—including organizations, websites, and readings—to engage readers in ways to become knowledgeable and resist current conservative philanthropic practices both individually and collectively. Our goal is to create educators who are well informed of the funding and strategies used by rightist philanthropists and to further the efforts of those willing to stand up to movements aimed at dismantling democracy in the United States.

Since each of these chapters focuses on the conservative movement's strategies, the remainder of the present chapter provides an updated and concise description of the U.S. IRS tax regulations related to nonprofit organizations and what they can and cannot do, followed by details of the development of the Philanthropy Roundtable, Donors Trust, the Donors Capital Fund, and how these nonprofit organizations have worked to shape our current political context. We conclude with a short summary of the early organizers of this conservative philanthropic movement and where they are today. We turn now to a brief review of the U.S. IRS tax codes as they relate to nonprofits.

U.S. IRS Tax Rules for Nonprofit Organizations

Nonprofit organizations in the United States are governed by Internal Revenue Service tax codes as developed and passed by the legislative and administrative branches of government. The organizations that are the focus of this book have been approved as nonprofit organizations and operate within those rules, so this section provides a brief overview of the subsections of the tax codes, what organizations can and cannot do, and the reporting requirements that govern them. The U.S. tax codes define a nonprofit as an "organization [that] commonly performs some type of public or community benefit, without the purpose of making a profit" (Types of Tax Exempt Organizations, n.d.). We will focus here on those organizations that qualify for 501(c)(3) and 501(c)(4) status. IRS Publication 557 (rev. January 2018) lists 29 different types of organizations exempt from paying federal income taxes. Among those relevant to this book are 501(c)(3) and 501(c)(4) organizations. While a 501(c)(3) organization can include activities deemed to be religious, educational, charitable, scientific, literary, testing for public safety, and to foster national or international amateur sports competition or prevention of cruelty to children or animals, a 501(c)(4) organization can include civic leagues and social welfare organizations.

501(c)(3) organizations.

Those organizations described in section 501(c)(3) are commonly referred to as charitable organizations" and are "classified as either a public charity or a private foundation" (Types of Tax Exempt Organizations, n.d.). A public charity has an active fundraising program and can receive contributions from many sources, including the general public, governmental agencies, corporations, private foundations, or other charities. These organizations receive income by furthering the purposes of the organization. In contrast, a private foundation that funds activities typically has a single major source of funding (usually gifts from one family or corporation rather than funding from many sources), and most have as their primary activity the making of grants to other charitable organizations and to individuals rather than the direct operation of charitable programs."

These organizations can receive federal tax-deductible contributions from both individuals and corporations. "Like federal law, most states allow for deductibility for state income tax purposes.... [M]any states allow exempt(ion) from sales tax on purchases, as well as exemption from property taxes [and] special nonprofit, bulk rate postage discounts are available from the Post Office to qualifying organizations."[1]

501(c)(4) organizations.

Organizations established as social welfare organizations or civil leagues under Subsection 501(c)(4) "must not be organized for profit and must be operated exclusively to promote social welfare."[2] These organizations "must operate primarily to further the common good and general welfare of the people of the community (such as by bringing about civic betterment and social improvements).[3] Per the IRS, social welfare organizations fall into one of the following three categories:

1. Organizations that may be performing some type of public or community benefit but whose principal feature is lack of private benefit or profit.
2. Organizations that would qualify for exemption under section 501(c)(3) but for a defect in their organizing documents or if they were not "action organizations."
3. Nonprofit organizations that traditionally have been labeled in common parlance as social welfare organizations.

For our purposes, the primary difference between the 501(c)(3) and 501(c)(4) organizations is that a 501(c)(4) organization can engage in "some political activities, so long as that is not its primary activity." The IRS states:

> Seeking legislation germane to the organization's programs is a permissible means of attaining social welfare purposes. Thus, a section 501(c)(4) social welfare organization may further its exempt purposes through lobbying as its primary activity without jeopardizing its exempt status.[4]

"However, any expenditure it makes for political activities may be subject to tax under section 527(f)."[5] Also, "an organization that has lost its section 501(c)(3) status due to substantial attempts to influence legislation may not thereafter qualify as a section 501(c)(4) organization."[6] To this point, the legal restrictions on 501(c)(3) organizations in regard to political activity are articulated clearly on the IRS website, which mentions the following restrictions:

- ...all section 501(c)(3) organizations are absolutely prohibited from directly or indirectly participating in, or intervening in, any political campaign on behalf of (or in opposition to) any candidate for elective public office. Contributions to political campaign funds or public statements of position (verbal or written) made on behalf of the organization in favor of or in opposition to any candidate for public office clearly violate the prohibition against political campaign activity.
- Certain activities or expenditures may not be prohibited depending on the facts and circumstances. For example, certain voter education activities (including presenting public forums and publishing voter education guides) conducted in a nonpartisan manner do not constitute prohibited political campaign activity. In addition, other activities intended to encourage people to participate in the electoral process, such as voter registration and get-out-the-vote drives, would not be prohibited political campaign activity if conducted in a nonpartisan manner.
- On the other hand, voter education or registration activities with evidence of bias that (a) would favor one candidate over another; (b) oppose a candidate in some manner; or (c) have the effect of favoring a candidate or group of candidates, will constitute prohibited participation or intervention.

Reporting Requirements for 501(c)(3) Organizations

All 501(c)(3) organizations must operate with transparency so that their annual tax returns, typically using Form 990, are publicly available documents, allowing the general public, including researchers like us, access to their annual assets, resources, expenditures, names of their boards of directors, and so on. With these reporting requirements, we have been able to access various 501(c)(3) organizations' tax filings over time to observe their donations and spending patterns. Specifically, IRS tax codes require the following:

> ...must make available for public inspection certain annual returns and applications for exemption and must provide copies of such returns and applications to individuals who request them. Copies usually must be provided immediately in the case of in-person requests, and within 30 days in the case of written requests. (Internal Revenue Service, n.d.)

Exempt organizations (both private and public) must make available for publication their exemption application and their annual returns (typically a Form 990). However, "an organization is not required to provide a copy of its Form 990 if the organization has made that form publicly available (e.g., through Internet posting), but must nevertheless make the form available for in-person inspection."[7] In addition, "returns must be available for a three-year period beginning with the due date of the return (including any extension of time for filing) or, if later, the date it is actually filed."[8] Further, "an exempt organization, other than a private foundation, need not disclose the name and address of any contributor."[9] However, "contributor names and addresses listed on an exempt organization's exemption application are subject to disclosure."[10]

In summary, both 501(c)(3) and 501(c)(4) nonprofit organizations are similar in the way tax filings are reported through IRS 990 forms. The key difference between the two types of nonprofits is that 501(c)(3)s are strictly prohibited from engaging in political activity, whereas 501(c)(4)s can engage in political activity as long as it is not the primary activity of the organization. Next, we turn to a discussion of the current activities of the Philanthropy Roundtable, a key player in the conservative philanthropic movement.

The Philanthropy Roundtable: An Update

Since the 1970s, the Philanthropy Roundtable has been a consistently well-funded organization that markets itself as "America's leading network of charitable donors working to strengthen our free society, uphold donor intent, and protect the freedom to give. Our members include individual philanthropists, families, and private foundations."[11] Its website states that the organization's mission is "to foster excellence in philanthropy, to protect philanthropic freedom, to assist donors in achieving their philanthropic intent, and to help donors advance liberty, opportunity, and personal responsibility in America and abroad." The organization's "Guiding Principles" reflect a focus on generating wealth within the private sector and maintaining original donor intent as follows:

- Philanthropic freedom is essential to a free society;
- A vibrant private sector generates the wealth that makes philanthropy possible;
- Voluntary private action offers solutions for many of society's most pressing challenges;
- Excellence in philanthropy is measured by results, not good intentions;
- A respect for donor intent is essential for philanthropic integrity.

The organization reports an annual budget of $10 million, with a staff of 30 and over 660 individual and organizational members.[12] Philanthropy Roundtable has had a long history of shaping the funding of right-leaning philanthropists, their families, and private foundations toward particular causes in line with their ideologies. The organization publishes guidebooks with recommendations for channeling funding to specific efforts, including changing certification policies for teachers to link tenure and pay to student performance, support for the expansion of charter schools and policies favoring charter and private schools, policies to limit the influence of teachers' unions, as well as other efforts that align with a neoliberal agenda. This right-wing agenda can be seen in the organization's history of leadership and its connection to conservative think tanks and the State Policy Network established decades ago. The current president, Adam Meyerson, began his work at the Philanthropy Roundtable in 2001. From 1993 up to that time, he served as the vice president for educational affairs at the Heritage Foundation, and from 1983 to 1998 was editor in chief of its magazine, *Policy Review*. He serves on the board of the State Policy Network described in Chapter Two and is the board chair of Donors Capital Fund, a 501(c)(3) supporting organization that provides services to clients at the price of $1,000,000 or more who want to set up donor-advised funds. Donors Capital Fund is associated with Donors Trust, a public charity "dedicated to the ideals of limited government, personal responsibility, and free enterprise"[13] that is discussed in more detail later in this chapter.[14]

Philanthropy Roundtable relies on significant contributions from its conservative philanthropist members. Based on 13 publicly available IRS 990 tax filings from 2002 to 2014, Conservative Transparency[15] reported 530 transactions with a combined value of $18,425,610 in contributions. The organization's assets in 2014 were valued at $11,276,561. A review of the funding provided to the Philanthropy Roundtable between 1993 and 2013 (Conservative Transparency, accessed August 7, 2018), reveals many of the same right-wing contributors described in Chapter Two of this volume, including the Lynde and Harry Bradley Foundation (leading with $4,225,000), the John Templeton Foundation, the Searle Freedom Trust, the Walton Family Foundation, and the William E. Simon Foundation. The Charles Koch Foundation contributed much less ($333,454) between 1993 and 2014, but the largely Koch-funded Donors Trust and Donors Capital Fund provided Philanthropy Roundtable with a total of $2,525,940 between 2004 and 2014. Thus, rather than contributions linking the Koch Foundation directly by name, these two funds work to keep the contributions more hidden. We turn now to a fuller discussion of Donors Trust and Donors Capital Fund.

Donors Trust and Donors Capital Fund

Donors Trust, a 501(c)(3) charitable organization, is a Virginia-based donor-advised fund that dispersed almost $30 million in grants in 2011. Donors Capital Fund, whose 2011 grants totaled more than $56 million, offers its account holders a degree of anonymity unavailable to private foundations.[16] Both of these organizations have helped conservative philanthropic funders conceal what they choose to fund and have been referred to as the "Dark-Money ATM" of the Conservative Movement (Kroll, 2013).

Donors Trust was established in 1999 to "ensure the intent of the donors dedicated to the ideals of liberty."[17] According to its website, Donors Trust is "the community foundation for the liberty movement." It claims that it "was the first donor-advised fund established to safeguard the charitable intent of donors committed to the principles of limited government, personal responsibility, and free enterprise."[18] The website further explains:

> Donors Trust is the sole donor-advised fund dedicated to safeguarding the charitable intentions of donors who are committed to promoting a free society through the ideals of limited government, personal responsibility, and free enterprise. We differentiate ourselves from other community foundations and donor-advised funds by providing a safe, efficient, and *principled* philanthropic vehicle.[19]

The Donors Trust website lists key areas of interest, including "reduce your taxes, advance your principles, protect your intent, define your legacy."

In reporting its successes, the organization states: "To date, Donors Trust has received over $1 billion from these donors who are both dedicated to liberty and to the cause of perpetuating a free and prosperous society through philanthropic means. Since inception, Donors Trust has granted out over $900 million to over 1600 charities."[20]

While serving as a donor-advised fund dedicated to carrying out the wishes of the original contributor, another key advantage held by Donors Trust is its guarantee of anonymity—if reported to the IRS, names of contributors will not become public record. Charles G. Koch is among an exclusive pool of donors who have used Donors Trust as a "pass-through," says Marcus Owens, the former director of the IRS Exempt Organizations Division, now in private legal practice. "It obscures the source of the money. It becomes a grant from Donors Trust, not a grant from the Koch brothers."[21] The term "dark money" has been used to describe this phenomenon, in that the sources of money have become obscured by this process (Mayer, 2016). The Koch Foundation is the largest contributor to Donors Trust through its Knowledge and Progress Fund, as well as its Charles Koch Foundation.[22]

In addition to the Knowledge and Progress Fund and the Charles Koch Foundation, the largest backers of Donors Trust include the Richard and Helen DeVos Foundation, Farmer Family Foundation, Donald and Paula Smith Foundation, Searle Freedom Trust, Lynde and Harry Bradley Foundation, and John M. Olin Foundation, all at $1 million or more (990s obtained using the Foundation Directory Online[23]). Conservative Transparency confirms these findings in its statement that "While most of Donors Trust and Donors Capital Fund's contributors are unknown, several major conservative funders have reported contributions to them, including the Searle Freedom Trust, the Richard and Helen DeVos Foundation, the Lynde and Harry Bradley Foundation, and the Charles G. Koch Foundation."[24] According to Conservative Transparency and based on the philanthropy's 990 tax filings, Donors Trust had assets of $102,089,508 in 2013, up from $995,512 in 2002. In a report dated February 14, 2013, the Center for Public Integrity revealed that Donors Trust had "passed nearly $400 million from private donors to free-market causes since 1999."[25]

Conservative Transparency reported that Donors Trust and its linked organization, Donors Capital Fund, dispersed $86 million in grants ($30 million and $56 million, respectively) in 2011. Top recipients of those grants included the Americans for Prosperity Foundation,[26] the American Enterprise Institute,[27] the Heartland Institute,[28] the Franklin Center for Government & Public Integrity,[29] and the State Policy Network.[30, 31]

Like the Philanthropy Roundtable, the leadership of Donors Trust reflects a conservative ideology. For example, Whitney L. Ball, founder, president, and CEO of Donors Trust, served as the Director of Development at the Cato Institute, a think tank founded by the Koch Foundation; in addition, he sat on the board of the State Policy Network, served as Executive Director of the Philanthropy Roundtable and the Institute of Humane Studies, and served on the board of George Mason University[32] (see Chapter Six for more details on these institutions). We turn now to a brief discussion of Donors Capital Fund to show how these two organizations are linked, and the role that Donors Capitol Fund plays in service to Donors Trust.

Donors Capital Fund: A supporting organization for Donors Trust.

Donors Capital Fund[33] is a 501(c)(3), 509(a)(3) supporting organization associated with Donors Trust. Section 509(a)(3) covers "supporting organizations" that support other public charities, governmental units, and certain other exempt organizations. They receive public charity status based on that relationship, without regard to the source of their income.[34] Thus, as stated on its website:

> As a rule, Donors Trust refers clients to Donors Capital Fund if they expect to open donor-advised funds of over $1,000,000. In turn, the Fund provides personalized philanthropic services and specialized asset management for all clients with accounts that carry balances of $1,000,000 or more. All contributions to donor-advised funds held by

Donors Capital Fund are tax deductible under Section 170 of the IRS Code.³⁵

The tagline for Donors Capital Fund, "An Investment in Freedom," is elaborated in its missions and principles statement:

> Donors Capital Fund only supports a class of public charities firmly committed to liberty. These charities all help strengthen American civil society by promoting private initiatives rather than government programs as the solution to the most pressing issues of the day in the areas of social welfare, health, the environment, economics, governance, foreign relations, and arts and culture.³⁶

Donors Capital Fund ensures that the original donor's intent be maintained "during their lifetime and beyond."³⁷ As with Donors Trust, any donor to this fund, though reported to the IRS, can request anonymity by requesting that his or her name be excluded from the public record.

While Donors Trust and Donors Capital Fund were both founded in 1999 (much later than the Philanthropy Roundtable), knowledge of the organizations and their impact did not become widely known until journalists and researchers began to focus on them. As one example, Andy Kroll's 2013 article "Exposed: The Dark-Money ATM of the Conservative Movement," published in *Mother Jones*, described Donors Trust as funding conservative public policy in the areas of climate science, economic regulations, labor unions, and public schools. In a 2012 *Frontline* article entitled "Institutionalizing Delay: Foundation Funding and the Creation of U.S. Climate Change Counter-Movement Organizations," J.M. Breslow profiled Drexel University sociologist Robert Brulle, who tracked the conservative funding of the climate change counter-movement and found that approximately one-quarter of it came from Donors Trust and Donors Capital Fund (Breslow, 2012). This speaks to the necessity of continuing to "track the money" as much as possible, despite the increased barriers to doing so.

Conservative Philanthropists: Where Are They Now?

In Table 3.1, we provide readers with a glimpse of where some of the top conservative philanthropists are now. The following data are reported by Conservative Transparency based on each organization's 990 tax filings.

Table 3.1 details a continuous flow of conservative funding, some of it dating back to 1986, from the same nonprofit organizations mentioned in Chapter Two, which was originally published in 2005. While it does not report all funding of the conservative activities we discuss throughout this book, it provides a glimpse of fourteen key organizations, all dedicated to privatization of public education at all levels, the support of right-leaning think tanks, and the scholars within them to produce narratives to support conservative legislation then promoted through the American Legislative Exchange Council and the associated State Policy Network, and the support of political candidates willing to push the conservative agenda. The 50-year strategy developed by the conservative movement has remained firmly in place and has come to fruition in today's sociopolitical context. As Brulle argues, funding supports long-term strategic initiatives and builds and maintains institutions to this end; thus, tracking the funding helps to understand and assess institutional capacity (Breslow, 2012). The National Center for Charitable Statistics[38] is a useful site in tracking funding.

Conclusion

In this chapter we have revisited the strategies of the conservative philanthropists and their organizations in updating the findings

Table 3.1. Conservative Philanthropists: Where are they now

501(C)(3) FOUNDATIONS	TOTAL TRANSACTIONS	TOTAL CONTRIBUTIONS	YEARS OF FUNDING	WEBSITE
Castle Rock Foundation (Adolph Coors Foundation, since 2011)	699	$40,100,613	1995–2011	coorsfoundation.org
Charles Koch Foundation (Formerly the Charles G. Koch Charitable Foundation)	1,831	$169,265,685	1986–2014	www.charleskochfoundation.org
Earhart Foundation	6,282	$93,541,372	1995–2012	NA
F. M. Kirby foundation	4,841	$323,077,750	1998–2012	fmkirbyfoundation.org
John M. Olin Foundation	3,877	$341,908,798	1985–2013	web.archive.org
John Templeton Foundation	2,401	$319,279,684	1999–2011	www.templeton.org
The Lynde and Harry Bradley Foundation	16,311	$862,705,516	1985–2013	www.bradleyfdn.org

Table 3.1 cont. on p. 108

Table 3.1, cont. from p. 107

501(C)(3) FOUNDATIONS	TOTAL TRANSACTIONS	TOTAL CONTRIBUTIONS	YEARS OF FUNDING	WEBSITE
The DeVos Urban Leadership Initiative	2,682	$625,894,793	1998–2013	www.dvuli.org
Roe Foundation	1,516	$19,981,619	1986–2012	www.theroefoundation.org/grants.html
Scaife Foundations (includes Sarah Scaife, Scaife Family, Allegheny, Carthage Foundations)	6,782	$63,262,644	1985–2012	www.scaife.com
Searle Freedom Trust	793	$83,150,849	2001–2012	searlefreedomtrust.org
Smith Richards Foundation	3,821	$316,190,500	1996–2012	www.srf.org
Walton Family Foundation	10,330	$3,364,627,837	1998–2012	www.waltonfamilyfoundation.org
William E. Simon Foundation	4,559	$101,823,999	1986–2012	www.wesimonfoundation.org
TOTAL	66,725	$6,724,811,659		

of the article reprinted in this book as Chapter Two. In 2004 and 2005, when deMarrais was doing the research for that article, the dark money of the Koch brothers, as well as that of their donor-advised funds—Donors Trust and Donors Capital Fund—were still in the shadows. For a thorough history and analysis of the Koch brothers and their foundation beyond what we present in Chapter Six, see Jane Mayer's (2016) thorough and well-researched book, *Dark Money: The Hidden History of the Billionaires Behind the Rise of the Radical Right*.

In order to fully understand the changes within the current conservative philanthropic movement, we have provided a detailed explanation of the U.S. IRS tax regulations related to nonprofit organizations and what they can and cannot do. Another key change has been the development of donor-assisted funds which, as we have seen, serve to protect the identity of private foundations and their funders and at the same time ensure that the original intent of the funder is maintained even beyond the life of the donor. Organizations such as Donors Trust and Donors Capital Fund protect the original intent of the fund from changes by heirs who may not share the libertarian or conservative ideologies of the original funder. What has remained the same is the strategy to fund and support a network of interrelated institutions dedicated to building and promoting charter and private institutions at all levels of education at the cost of education as a public good, to fight to dismantle unions, deny the science of climate change, preserve the wealth of a small number of billionaire capitalists, and promote the myth that public schools are "failing." For example, the current Secretary of Education, Betsy DeVos, who has a long history of family foundation funding for educational efforts consistent with rightist ideologies, has promoted education policies that reflect similar rightist and neoliberal ideologies in their support for the privatization and commodification of public schools, as well as other policies informed by and supporting the myth that public schools are failing and would be better run by private industry.

For example, a recent article in *The New York Times* reported that DeVos was considering allowing states to take money from their school enrichment funds to purchase guns for teachers. Because the 2015 Every Student Succeeds Act (ESSA) does not explicitly prohibit the purchase of weapons, its vague language opens the door for DeVos to authorize states to use enrichment grant monies to purchase weapons (Green, 2018). DeVos's thought, however, was met with resistance. Senator Patty Murray, a Democrat from Washington, said, "When Republicans and Democrats came together to pass the bipartisan Every Student Succeeds Act, we were clear that these grants were intended to help foster safe, healthy and supportive environments that improve student learning—not prop up the N.R.A. and gun sales" (Green, 2018). DeVos's policy consideration not only supports the Trump administration's call to arm educators in the wake of school shootings, but also shows how DeVos has been willing to use her position to subvert existing legislation to represent conservative and neoliberal interests, regardless of the original intention of the legislation.

Nonprofit organizations such as Donors Trust and Donors Capital Fund were established to protect and maintain wealth within already-rich families and organizations by reducing contributions to the federal and state tax base and using these funds to promote their own ideological causes. Of course, the argument is often made that there are centrist and left-leaning, liberal nonprofit organizations that do the same thing. The key difference is in the brilliant and long-term strategies of the right. Centrist and left-leaning philanthropies are much more likely to fund specific, time-limited projects rather than build institutions in the way the right has done.

Going forward, educators and concerned citizens should think critically about the way money flows in and out of our public school systems. Tracking the money and working to understand the hidden intentions and motivations behind philanthropy in education is becoming increasingly difficult, particularly in the wake of the Supreme Court's *Citizens United* decision. For this reason, it is increasingly important for educators to become informed about the complex mechanisms at work in how public schools are funded, how educational policy is crafted, and who benefits. We encourage you to become informed and to read on.

Notes

1. www.501c3.org/what-is-a-501c3/
2. irs.gov
3. irs.gov
4. irs.gov
5. irs.gov
6. irs.gov
7. irs.gov
8. irs.gov
9. irs.gov
10. irs.gov
11. https://www.philanthropyroundtable.org/home/about/who-we-are
12. https://www.philanthropyroundtable.org/home/about/who-we-are/history-of-the-philanthropy-roundtable
13. http://donorscapitalfund.org/AboutUs/Overview.aspx
14. https://www.philanthropyroundtable.org/home/about/our-staff/detail/adam-meyerson
15. http://conservativetransparency.org/
16. http://conservativetransparency.org/org/donorstrust-donors-capital-fund/
17. https://www.donorstrust.org/who-we-are/mission-principles/
18. https://www.donorstrust.org/
19. https://www.donorstrust.org/where-to-start/understanding-donor-intent/
20. https://www.donorstrust.org/who-we-are/mission-principles/
21. https://www.publicintegrity.org/2013/02/14/12181/donors-use-charity-push-free-market-policies-states
22. https://www.publicintegrity.org/2013/02/14/12181/donors-use-charity-push-free-market-policies-states
23. https://fconline.foundationcenter.org/
24. http://conservativetransparency.org/org/donorstrust-donors-capital-fund/

25. https://www.publicintegrity.org/2013/02/14/12181/donors-use-charity-push-free-market-policies-states
26. http://conservativetransparency.org/org/americans-for-prosperity-foundation/
27. http://conservativetransparency.org/org/american-enterprise-institute/
28. http://conservativetransparency.org/org/heartland-institute/
29. http://conservativetransparency.org/org/franklin-center-for-government-public-integrity/
30. http://conservativetransparency.org/org/state-policy-network/
31. http://conservativetransparency.org/org/donorstrust-donors-capital-fund/
32. http://conservativetransparency.org/org/donorstrust-donors-capital-fund/
33. http://donorscapitalfund.org/
34. https://www.nonprofitissues.com/to-the-point/whats-difference-between-501c3-and-509a1
35. http://donorscapitalfund.org/AboutUs/Overview.aspx
36. http://donorscapitalfund.org/AboutUs/MissionPrinciples.aspx
37. http://donorscapitalfund.org/AboutUs/MissionPrinciples.aspx
38. http://nccs.urban.org/

References

Breslow, J.M. (2012, October 23). Robert Brulle: Inside the climate change "countermovement." *Frontline*. Retrieved from https://www.pbs.org/wgbh/frontline/article/robert-brulle-inside-the-climate-change-countermovement/

Conservative Transparency. (2018). Retrieved from http://conservative-transparency.org/

Green, E.L. (2018, August 23). Betsy DeVos eyes federal education grants to put guns in schools. *The New York Times*. Retrieved from https://www.nytimes.com/2018/08/23/us/politics/devos-guns-in-schools.html

Internal Revenue Service. (n.d.). *Public disclosure and availability of exempt organizations returns and applications: Public disclosure requirements in general*. Retrieved from https://www.irs.gov/charities-non-profits/

public-disclosure-and-availability-of-exempt-organizations-returns-and-applications-public-disclosure-requirements-in-general

Kroll, A. (2013, February 5). Exposed: The dark-money ATM of the conservative movement. *Mother Jones.* Retrieved from https://www.motherjones.com/politics/2013/02/donors-trust-donor-capital-fund-dark-money-koch-bradley-devos/

Mayer, J. (2016). Dark money: The hidden history of the billionaires behind the rise of the Radical Right. New York: Doubleday.

Powell memo (also known as the *Powell manifesto*). (1971.) Retrieved from http://reclaimdemocracy.org/corporate_accountability/powell_memo_lewis.html

Types of Tax-Exempt Organizations. (n.d.). Retrieved from https://www.irs.gov/charities-non-profits/types-of-tax-exempt-organizations

Chapter Four

CITIZENS UNITED AND THE DISUNITING OF THE UNITED STATES

by John Dayton, J.D., Ed.D., & Jamie B. Lewis, J.D., Ph.D.

The October 14, 1941, issue of *Labor* published a eulogy for Justice Louis Brandeis written by Raymond Longerman (the pen name often used by Edward Keating) that recalled a conversation in which Brandeis stated: "We must make our choice.... We may have democracy, or we may have wealth concentrated in the hands of a few, but we can't have both" (Campbell, 2013, pp. 255–256; Dilliard, 1941, pp. 42–45). The struggle between democracy and oligarchy in the United States is as old as the country. From the nation's beginnings, members of the wealthy classes expressed dire concerns about the dangers of popular elections and political control by the masses. Based on these concerns, they successfully embedded anti-democratic mechanisms in the U.S. governance system, including representative rather than direct democracy, restrictions on citizenship and voting rights, an Electoral College with the authority to override the popular vote, and lifetime federal judges not directly accountable to the people. In the area of campaign finance and the role of corporations in contributing to and influencing federal elections, "*Citizens United v. FEC* (2010) may prove to be the most important campaign finance decision in decades as a critical step in a transformation of campaign finance law under the Roberts court" (Kang, 2010–2011, p. 243). In this decision, the U.S. Supreme Court overturned its own precedents and ruled that corporations were entitled to the same free-speech rights as individuals under the Constitution. The resulting "corporations are people too" constitutional standard severely limited Congress's ability to regulate corporate money in politics, and instead allowed corporate money to flow into the U.S. political system virtually without restriction. To the degree that the political arena is a zero-sum game, when one group's influence is expanded, another group's influence is diminished. The *Citizens United* decision tipped the balance in favor of the wealthy power elite over ordinary citizens. In *Reynolds v. Sims* (1964), the Court articulated the "one person one vote" rule to promote general equality of representation in the political process. But what happens when one person is an average citizen and the other "person" is a wealthy multinational corporation with virtually unlimited funds? It is unlikely that the average citizen could achieve equality of representation in a political system built on competing campaign donations and the purchase of expensive, mass-market media political advertising. This begs the question: what happens to democracy under these circumstances?

This chapter reviews *Citizens United* and its role in further enabling a wealthy corporate oligarchy over citizen democracy in an increasingly divided nation. This chapter includes a brief review of the relevant history of campaign reform law, the majority opinion in *Citizens United*, the dissenting opinion, and a discussion of related issues.

Legal and Legislative History

Prior to the 2010 U.S. Supreme Court decision in the *Citizens United* case, corporations and unions were banned from funding federal campaigns by the Tillman Act (1907) and the Taft-Hartley Act (1947), respectively. One objective behind these bans was to "limit contributions to ensure that wealthy individuals and special interest groups did not have a disproportionate influence on Federal Elections."[1] Recognizing the need for an institutional structure to provide both oversight of and compliance with campaign finance laws, Congress enacted the Federal Election Campaign Act of 1971 (FECA), which granted oversight to the Clerk of the House, the Secretary of the Senate, and the Comptroller General of the United States General Accounting Office. "The FECA, effective April 7, 1972, not only required full reporting of campaign contributions and expenditures, but also limited spending on media advertisements."[2] FECA allowed corporations and unions to create Political Action Committees (PACs), which had the authority to solicit voluntary contributions and use these monies to contribute to federal political campaigns. As the Watergate scandal unfolded, it was disclosed that monies collected by the Committee to Re-elect the President (CRP) had been used to finance the individuals who broke into the Democratic National Party's headquarters in the Watergate Hotel. This discovery of campaign finance abuse led Congress to act in 1974 to create the Federal Election Commission, an independent body created to ensure compliance with campaign finance laws. The constitutionality of key provisions of the 1974 amendments were challenged by Senator James L. Buckley. However, the court's decision in *Buckley v. Valeo* (1975) upheld the provisions related to campaign finance limits concerning contributions and overturned the restrictions placed on campaign expenditures. While the Supreme Court recognized the underlying First Amendment issues with regard to both contributions and expenditures, the Court reasoned that upholding the restrictions on contributions served the important role of preserving the "integrity of our system of representative democracy by guarding against unscrupulous practices." The Court did find that restrictions on campaign expenditures had a chilling effect on the free-speech rights of candidates; therefore, the government lacked a compelling reason to place restrictions on expenditures.

The Bipartisan Campaign Reform Act (BCRA) of 2002, however, prohibited corporations from spending funds on media to directly advocate for or against a federal political candidate within 30 days of a primary or 60 days of a general election.[3] The BCRA was supported by an extensive factual record concerning campaign funding and political corruption. The BCRA sought to establish reasonable bipartisan regulations aimed at the compelling governmental interest in preventing the use of virtually unlimited corporate funding to unduly influence federal elections. Advocates of the BCRA expressed concerns about protecting against foreign influence in U.S. elections resulting from potentially massive and borderless multinational corporate funding sources if these sources were not properly regulated. The BCRA carried civil and criminal penalties for violations.

Citizens United v. Federal Election Commission.

The issue before the Supreme Court in *Citizens United* was whether the provisions of the BCRA, which restricted unions, corporations, and profitable organizations from independent political spending and prohibited the broadcast of political media funded by them within 60 days of a general election (or within 30 days of a primary election) violated the First Amendment's protection of freedom of speech. Justice Anthony Kennedy wrote the majority opinion, which held that the First Amendment protects not only individual speakers, but associations of individuals, and does not allow prohibitions of speech based on the identity of the speaker as well. Therefore, the First Amendment rights of free speech are extended to corporations, as associations of individuals. Because spending money is essential to disseminating speech, as established in *Buckley v. Valeo* (1975), limiting a corporation's ability to spend money is unconstitutional because it limits the ability of its members to associate effectively and to speak on political issues.

By way of background on the organization, Citizens United is a conservative 501(c)(4) nonprofit corporation founded in 1988 with a $12 million annual budget. The group is funded by for-profit corporations and individuals, and its mission is to restore the U.S. government to "citizens' control," seeking to "reassert the traditional American values of limited government, freedom of enterprise, strong families, and national sovereignty and security" (www.CitizensUnited.org). David Bossie was the president and chairman of Citizens United in 2000 and held that position until he took a leave of absence to serve as deputy campaign manager for Donald Trump in 2016 and introduced Trump to Steve Bannon and Kellyanne Conway. As part of its political advocacy activities, Citizens United wanted to broadcast commercials within 30 days of the 2008 presidential primary elections for *Hillary: The Movie*, a 90-minute political documentary it had produced that included interviews with Dick Morris and Ann Coulter and reviewed various scandals in which Hillary Clinton allegedly participated. Citizens United filed suit in U.S. District Court seeking to enjoin the Federal Election Commission from enforcing its regulations prohibiting the airing of political media within 30 days of a primary election because it was concerned that airing the commercials would subject the corporation to civil and criminal penalties. Citizens United argued that this regulation was unconstitutional because it infringed on its First Amendment free-speech rights. Citizens argued that BCRA's disclosure and disclaimer requirements were unconstitutional. The district court dismissed Citizens United's complaint because the movie constituted direct advocacy, as opposed to "an electioneering communication," since it had no other reasonable interpretation than an appeal to vote against Hillary Clinton. The district court relied on the legal precedents from the U.S. Supreme Court's prior decisions in *Austin v. Michigan Chamber of Commerce* (1990) (which held that the unique state-granted corporate structure, which facilitates the accumulation of massive funds, warranted reasonable regulation to prevent corruption and distortion of the political process) and *McConnell v. Federal Election Commission* (2003) (upholding bans on "soft money" in elections). Nonetheless, the Supreme Court granted Citizens United's writ of certiorari, agreeing to review the case.

Discussion of the Citizens United Decision

Section 203 of the BCRA prohibits corporations and unions from using general treasury funds to make independent expenditures for speech that constitutes "electioneering communication" or speech that expressly advocates the election or defeat of a candidate (2 U.S.C. Sec. 441b). The federal law and regulations define electioneering communications as "any broadcast, cable or satellite communication that refers to a clearly identifiable candidate for Federal office" and is made within 30 days of a primary election and that is publicly distributed" (11 CFR Sec. 100.29(a)(2)).

To avoid unwarranted judicial activism and to promote appropriate judicial restraint, it is longstanding federal judicial policy to attempt to rule narrowly and avoid broad constitutional questions when cases may be resolved on more narrow statutory grounds. Astoundingly, in *Citizens United*, the Court rejected more narrow grounds presented by both parties and instead chose to rule on the broad constitutional question of free-speech rights for corporations. Justice Kennedy wrote:

> The Court cannot resolve this case on a narrower ground without chilling political speech, speech that is central to the meaning and purpose of the First Amendment. See *Morse v. Frederick*, 551 U.S. 393, 403 (2007). It is not judicial restraint to accept an unsound, narrow argument just so the Court can avoid another argument with broader implications. Indeed, a court would be remiss in performing its duties were it to accept an unsound principle merely to avoid the necessity of making a broader ruling. Here, the lack of a valid basis for an alternative ruling requires full consideration of the continuing effect of the speech suppression upheld in *Austin*.

In a 5-to-4 opinion written by Justice Kennedy and joined by Justices Roberts, Scalia, Thomas, and Alito, a narrow majority of justices in *Citizens United* took direct aim at the Court's campaign finance law precedents in *Austin* and *McConnell*. Concerning the constitutionality of congressional regulations on campaign expenditures by corporations, the Court stated:

> [T]he *Austin* majority undertook to distinguish wealthy individuals from corporations on the ground that "[s]tate law grants corporations special advantages—such as limited liability, perpetual life, and favorable treatment of the accumulation and distribution of assets."[4] This does not suffice, however, to allow laws prohibiting speech. "It is rudimentary that the State cannot exact as the price of those special advantages the forfeiture of First Amendment rights."[5]

Concerning *Citizens United*'s free-speech claim, the Court found that the Act's "prohibition on corporate independent expenditures is thus a ban on speech.... Its purpose and effect are to silence entities whose voices the Government deems to be suspect" and to disadvantage corporations in the political system.[6] Although most persons might not view wealthy corporations as actually "disadvantaged" in the U.S. political system, according to the Court:

> By taking the right to speak from some and giving it to others, the Government deprives the disadvantaged person or class of the right to use speech to strive to establish worth, standing, and respect for the speaker's voice. The Government may not by these means deprive the public of the right and privilege to determine for itself what speech and speakers are worthy of consideration. The First Amendment protects speech and speaker, and the ideas that flow from each.[7]

The Court concluded: "We find no basis for the proposition that, in the context of political speech, the Government may impose restrictions on certain disfavored speakers. Both history and logic lead us to this conclusion."[8]

In reaching its decision, the Court reviewed campaign finance law in the United States and acknowledged that "At least since the latter part of the 19th century, the laws of some States and of the United States imposed a ban on corporate direct contributions to candidates."[9] The Court noted that "*Austin* found a compelling governmental interest in preventing 'the corrosive and distorting effects of immense aggregations of wealth that are accumulated with the help of the corporate form and that have little or no correlation to the public's support for the corporation's political ideas."[10] Nonetheless, the Court found that:

> If the First Amendment has any force, it prohibits Congress from fining or jailing citizens, or associations of citizens, for simply engaging in political speech. If [*Austin's*] antidistortion rationale were to be accepted, however, it would permit Government to ban political speech simply because the speaker is an association that has taken on the corporate form.[11]

Although the recognition of corporate campaign funding as equal to individual free-speech rights was a stunning victory for the plaintiffs in *Citizens United*, the plaintiffs did not get everything on their wish list from the Court. They objected to disclosure and disclaimer requirements, which required speakers to publicly state their identity in political ads. But the Court rejected these arguments in *Citizens United* and upheld the disclaimer and disclosure requirements as valid.[12]

The Court found that "disclosure is a less restrictive alternative to more comprehensive regulations of speech."[13] Concerning disclaimers and disclosures, the Court stated:

> In *McConnell*, the Court recognized that [disclosure requirements] would be unconstitutional as applied to an organization if there were a reasonable probability that the group's members would face threats, harassment, or reprisals if their names were disclosed.... Citizens United, however, has offered no evidence that its members may face similar threats or reprisals. To the contrary, Citizens United has been disclosing its donors for years and has identified no instance of harassment or retaliation.[14]

In *Citizens United*, the majority concluded that:

> When Congress finds that a problem exists, we must give that finding due deference; but Congress may not choose an unconstitutional remedy. If elected officials succumb to improper influences from independent expenditures; if they surrender their best judgment; and if they put expediency before principle, then surely there is cause for concern. We must give weight to attempts by Congress to seek to dispel either the appearance or the reality of these influences. The remedies enacted by law, however, must comply with the First Amendment; and, it is our law and our tradition that more speech, not less, is the governing rule. An outright ban on corporate political speech during the critical preelection period is not a permissible remedy. Here Congress has created categorical bans on speech that are asymmetrical to preventing quid pro quo corruption.[15]

Justice Stevens's dissenting opinion, joined by Justices Ginsberg, Breyer, and Sotomayor, took direct aim at the majority's conclusion that corporations must be treated like natural persons under the Constitution:

> The conceit that corporations must be treated identically to natural persons in the political sphere is not only inaccurate but also inadequate to justify the Court's disposition of this case. In the context of election to public office, the distinction between corporate and human speakers is significant. Although they make enormous contributions to our society, corporations are not actually members of it. They cannot vote or run for office. Because they may be managed and controlled by nonresidents, their interests may conflict in fundamental respects with the interests of eligible voters. The financial resources, legal structure, and instrumental orientation of corporations raise legitimate

concerns about their role in the electoral process. Our lawmakers have a compelling constitutional basis, if not also a democratic duty, to take measures designed to guard against the potentially deleterious effects of corporate spending in local and national races.[16]

The majority's decision in *Citizens United* was a stunning departure from long-established historical standards concerning campaign finance. As Justice Stevens recognized: "The majority's approach to corporate electioneering marks a dramatic break from our past. Congress has placed special limitations on campaign spending by corporations ever since the passage of the Tillman Act in 1907."[17] Concerning the relevant history of the BCRA, Justice Stevens noted: "Congress crafted BCRA in response to a virtual mountain of research on the corruption that previous legislation had failed to avert. The Court now negates Congress' efforts without a shred of evidence on how [the Act] or its state-law counterparts have been affecting any entity other than Citizens United."[18] The dissenting Justices objected that:

> The Court today rejects a century of history when it treats the distinction between corporate and individual campaign spending as an invidious novelty born of *Austin v. Michigan Chamber of Commerce*. Relying largely on individual dissenting opinions, the majority blazes through our precedents, overruling or disavowing a body of case law.[19]

As the dissenting justices recognized, the majority's decision was striking in its seeming disregard for well-established judicial principles and precedents, including a disregard for the foundational legal principle of *stare decisis*, the ancient judicial principle of respecting and following applicable legal precedents:

> *Stare decisis* protects not only personal rights involving property or contract but also the ability of the elected

branches to shape their laws in an effective and coherent fashion. Today's decision takes away a power that we have long permitted these branches to exercise. State legislatures have relied on their authority to regulate corporate electioneering, confirmed in *Austin*, for more than a century.[20]

Justice Stevens was very direct about what appeared to be the motivation for this far-reaching judicial approach in *Citizens United*: "Essentially, five Justices were unhappy with the limited nature of the case before us, so they changed the case to give themselves an opportunity to change the law."[21] The dissenting opinion accused:

> In the end, the Court's rejection of *Austin* and *McConnell* comes down to nothing more than its disagreement with their results. Virtually every one of its arguments was made and rejected in those cases, and the majority opinion is essentially an amalgamation of resuscitated dissents. The only relevant thing that has changed since *Austin* and *McConnell* is the composition of this Court.[22]

Justice Stevens expressly recognized the serious potential for harm from *Citizens United*, stating: "The Court's ruling threatens to undermine the integrity of elected institutions across the Nation. The path it has taken to reach its outcome will, I fear, do damage to this institution."[23] The dissenting opinion concluded:

> [T]he Court's opinion is thus a rejection of the common sense of the American people, who have recognized a need to prevent corporations from undermining self-government since the founding, and who have fought against the distinctive corrupting potential of corporate electioneering since the days of Theodore Roosevelt. It is a strange time to repudiate that common sense. While American democracy is imperfect, few outside the majority of this Court

would have thought its flaws included a dearth of corporate money in politics.[24]

Discussion

In *Citizens United*, dissenting justices warned that the Court's ruling may undermine the integrity of elected institutions at the state and national levels. Anything that undermines citizens' confidence in the integrity of democratic institutions poses a special threat to the continued political stability of the United States. A common history, ancestry, or religion may help to bind a nation together. But in the United States, as a nation of immigrants, these factors cannot serve as binding forces. Instead, in his *An American Dilemma* (1944), Gunnar Myrdal recognized the "American Creed" (i.e., ideals of liberty, justice, and equality) as the essential common bond for preserving the great diversity of the United States and allowing persons of all races, religions, and backgrounds to live and work together toward mutual progress.

"No justice, no peace" isn't just a political slogan. It's a historical reality. When justice is repeatedly denied, people lose faith in the political system and demand reform. To be sustainable as a unifying force, the American Creed's promise of liberty, justice, and equality must be perceived by citizens as real, or at least achievable. If people stop believing in the reality of the American Creed and the fairness of the legal/political system, the nation's social contract begins to unravel. Liberty, justice, and equality are the essential terms of the nation's social contract.

The Court's decision in *Citizens United* adds yet another layer of doubt concerning American social justice, as the social contractual terms of the American Creed came into clear conflict with the financial interests of wealthy factions in *Citizens United*, but nonetheless the Court ruled in favor of the wealthy factions. Perhaps the most shocking part of this legal/political coup in *Citizens United* was that it was achieved by using the people's Bill of Rights

(1789). The Bill of Rights was intended to protect the people from power; not to protect power from the people, as occurred in *Citizens United* when the Court prohibited the people's Congress from regulating corporate influence in the electoral process to deter political corruption and foreign interference.

The *Citizens United* majority's suggestion that "history and logic" led them to their conclusion seems contrary to both history and logic. As accomplished students of history, Jefferson and other U.S. founders were deeply concerned about establishing governance systems capable of preventing the new democracy from being hijacked by wealthy factions. As Benson (2012) recognized: "Ensuring that private interests could not seize control of the government and use its power for their private benefit was a key interest of the founding fathers."

While the corporate model is a useful vehicle for doing business, Jefferson and other founders recognized the danger that wealthy multinational corporate interests posed to citizen governance and the integrity of a democratic political system. In recognition of these concerns, governmental granting of corporate status was historically premised on the stipulation that the people and their government remained the clear sovereign, and that the rights and benefits of acting in a corporate form were granted on the condition that the corporation was subject to the reasonable regulations of the people's government and to the service of a legitimate public purpose.

Since *Citizens United*, however, the corporate servant has moved further toward becoming the master, now possessing constitutional rights of free speech equal to those of the people. But with resources to advance their interests far in excess of those held by most people, this raises serious dangers that a government of, for, and by the people is becoming the government of, for, and by the corporations. As Gilman noted:

> In an age in which money and television ads are the coin of the campaign realm, it is hardly surprising that corporations deployed these ads to curry favor with, and to gain influence over, public officials...corporations with large

war chests to deploy on electioneering may find democratically elected bodies becoming much more attuned to their interests....[25] In the real world, we have seen, corporate domination of the airwaves prior to an election may decrease the average listener's exposure to relevant viewpoints, and it may diminish citizens' willingness and capacity to participate in the democratic process.[26]

Beneath a façade of free-speech equality, the result in *Citizens United* was a decision that in practice granted a preferred legal and political status to wealthy corporations to disproportionately influence the political system. As the dissenting justices in *Citizens United* recognized:

> The Court's blinkered and aphoristic approach to the First Amendment may well promote corporate power at the cost of the individual and collective self-expression the Amendment was meant to serve. It will undoubtedly cripple the ability of ordinary citizens, Congress, and the States to adopt even limited measures to protect against corporate domination of the electoral process. Americans may be forgiven if they do not feel the Court has advanced the cause of self-government today.[27]

It is only stating the obvious to say that corporations as "persons" and individual citizens as persons do not play on a level playing field in the political arena. The average U.S. citizen, for example, lives five or six decades as an adult able to participate in the political process and earns a median net compensation of approximately $30,000 per year. Most persons make decisions based on moral conscience, and all are subject to personal sanctions for violations of the law, including imprisonment. In contrast, corporations are potentially immortal; large multinational corporations have virtually unlimited streams of funding; a non-person has no conscience; and a non-person cannot be held personally accountable or jailed.

Nonetheless, after *Citizens United*, the natural person and the paper-created corporation are now recognized by the Court as having the same rights under our First Amendment's free-speech provisions. Why did the Court twist itself into such logical knots in *Citizens United* to reach such a nonsensical conclusion? The majority's decision in *Citizens United* does not appear to be the result of the application of neutral principles of law by objective judges. On the contrary, in order to reach the result in *Citizens United*, the majority had to engage in tortured logic and directly overrule two prior U.S. Supreme Court precedents, *Austin* and *McConnell*. Karlan (2012) offered this explanation:

> Forty years ago, conservatives quite deliberately set out to change how the Constitution is interpreted and enforced. They set their sights on key doctrines undergirding the New Deal, the Second Reconstruction, and the Great Society—in particular the Supreme Court's expansive constructions of congressional authority under the power to regulate commerce, the taxing power, the spending power, and the enforcement powers in the Reconstruction Amendments. And they recognized that the success of this project was likely to be sharply influenced by the judicial philosophies of the individual justices who sit on the Court. But they presented their program as one of judicial modesty, restraint, and respect for the democratic process—as a reaction, in fact, to the Warren Court. By now, after seven terms of the Roberts Court, the curtain has risen and the revealing is well underway. A conservative majority wants to reverse or limit much of the Warren Court legacy—not just the cases at its outer boundaries, but the cases at its very core, including its ratification of the Second Reconstruction and the Great Society. (Karlan, 2012)

Courts commonly present their decisions as the products of objective application of laws and above the political fray, as they should be in order to maintain legitimacy. But according to Chafetz (2015), the reality may sometimes betray that assertion, particularly when judges are making decisions about political governance and elections:

> By any reasonable understanding of the words, the courts both govern and play a crucial role in deciding who governs. Courts govern all the time, simply because that is what it is to make decisions that control the actions and interactions of others. But the nature of election law is such as to give governance in that field a recursive quality: Reagan picks judges who pick George W. Bush, who picks judges who pick the rules governing the elections of future pickers-of-judges. (p. 111)

The American system of governance works when the foundations of the American Creed—that is, the ideals of liberty, justice, and equality—are the driving forces of our common government. The problem is that for those who seek oligarchy over democracy, their driving forces are unquestionable authority, self-serving corruption, and unchecked political domination. Tragically, history is replete with examples of oligarchy triumphing over democracy through the use of divide-and-conquer strategies, beating the drums of war, and exploiting ignorance and fear in the masses (see Klein, 2008). Although these dark strategies have commonly worked to keep a group of wealthy oligarchs in power in the short-term, ultimately, they are destructive, unsustainable, and cannot serve as the long-term foundation for a healthy, stable society.

The philosopher Plato compared the virtues and vices of democracy (i.e., rule by the governed) and oligarchy (i.e., rule by a small social or corporate elite). While democratic self- governance is certainly imperfect, the greater dangers of rule by an all-powerful few are obvious. Winston Churchill famously said that "Democracy is the worst form of government, except all those other forms that have been tried from time to time." Imperfect humans cannot create and operate a perfect government. But at least in a citizen-governed democracy, ordinary citizens have an opportunity for greater control over their own lives, a means of protecting their essential liberties, and a means of holding people with power equally accountable under the law.

In further shifting the political balance in favor of wealthy corporate interests, *Citizens United* was yet another nail in the casket of U.S. democracy. When asked about the Court's decision in *Citizens United*, former U.S. President Jimmy Carter said:

> It violates the essence of what made America a great country in its political system. Now it's just an oligarchy with unlimited political bribery being the essence of getting the nominations for president or being elected president. And the same thing applies to governors, and U.S. Senators and congress members. So, now we've just seen a subversion of our political system as a payoff to major contributors, who want and expect, and sometimes get, favors for themselves after the election is over.... At the present time the incumbents, Democrats and Republicans, look upon this unlimited money as a great benefit to themselves. Somebody that is already in Congress has a great deal more to sell. (Zuesse, 2016)

Research confirms that the U.S. is, in fact, an oligarchy and not a democracy. Gilens and Page (2014) found that:

> [E]conomic elites and organized groups representing business interests have substantial independent impacts on U.S. government policy, while average citizens and mass-based interest groups have little or no independent influence. The results provide substantial support for theories of Economic-Elite Domination and for theories of Biased Pluralism, but not for theories of Majoritarian Electoral Democracy or Majoritarian Pluralism. (p. 564)

To the extent that hope for restoring democracy still exists in the current U.S. system, it must be found in efforts to promote education in critical thinking and civic courage. Citizens must be able to clearly identify and understand governance challenges and have the civic courage and persistence necessary to work together for positive resolutions. In particular, the corrupting forces of money in the political process must be effectively addressed. As Andrias (2015) stated:

> If we want to understand our current predicament—and if we hope to have any chance of pulling ourselves out of it—we need to focus not only on partisanship but also on the problem of concentrated wealth and its organization to achieve political ends. After a period of shared prosperity following the New Deal and World War II, the United States has, over the last generation, experienced a dramatic rise in economic inequality.
>
> Disparities in income and wealth are at levels not seen since the Gilded Age. Rising inequality has been accompanied by the concentration, or re-concentration, of political power among wealthy individuals, large business firms, and organized groups representing them, as well as by a precipitous decline of countervailing organization among middle- and low-income Americans. Organized wealth has overtaken other civic and social organizations as the key driving force in American politics. (p. 421)

Although *Citizens United* received most of the media attention, the same conservative 5-to-4 majority further opened the floodgates of big money into U.S. politics in *McCutcheon v. Federal Election Commission* (2014) by removing aggregate contribution limits to candidates and parties. For decades now, there has been a seemingly relentless effort to advantage wealth in the political/legal system. As Andrias (2015) recognized: "Through a range of strategies—from campaign donations, lobbying, and regulatory comment, to the provision of expertise to government officials and the threat of litigation—wealthy individuals, large business firms, and their organizations dominate every step of the political process" (p. 422). Andrias further noted that "increasingly, corporations are investing large sums in saturating the intellectual environment in order to influence policymakers and staffers. The goal, lobbyists report, is to legitimate certain arguments, ideas, and solutions" (pp. 446–447).

Adding to the concern, U.S. citizens are now in a situation where political gerrymandering has rendered the votes of millions functionally worthless while enabling, for example, a Congress with approval ratings nearing single digits to enjoy reelection rates above 90%. Wealthy elites then financially compete for the favor of the politically untouchable "elected" officials in gerrymandered political fortress districts where the only real challenge they may face is from a primary challenger in their own party, and voters may only have one party and one choice on the ballot in the general election, which is in truth no real choice.

There are efforts to address these challenges to democracy—for example, the proposed "We the People" Democracy Reform Act of 2017, a bill to "reduce the grip of special interest and return democracy to the American people by increasing transparency and oversight of our elections and government, reforming public financing for Presidential and Congressional elections, and requiring states to conduct Congressional redistricting through independent commissions." The provisions of the act

- create a small-donor, public matching funds system for presidential and congressional races;
- close disclosure loopholes for outside spending groups, require 48-hour disclosure for large contributions to candidates and parties;
- provide accountability for campaign ads run by outside groups;
- shut down individual-candidate Super PACs and strengthen rules prohibiting coordination;

- establish a new approach for enforcing campaign finance laws; and
- strengthen lobbying and revolving-door laws.

Additionally, such legislation would establish nonpartisan redistricting commissions to draw House congressional districts; create an automatic voter registration system for citizens eligible to vote but not registered; provide for same-day voter registration; require presidents to divest assets that create potential conflicts of interest into a blind trust and to make public their tax returns; require disclosure of visitor lists to the White House and other places where the president does regular business; and strengthen Executive Branch conflict-of-interest and revolving-door rules ("We the People" Democracy Reform Act of 2017). Even though this bill was introduced on September 27, 2017, it is still in committee.

Conclusion

As Tribe (2015) recognized, "The public discourse surrounding *Citizens United* makes clear that the case is about far more than its precise holding and the analysis underlying that holding: it is about the kind of democracy our Constitution should be understood to create and the types of governing arrangements it should be understood to put in place" (p. 478). Massive demographic shifts are changing the political face of the United States and, in the process, threatening established interests. Those threatened by these changes have now spent decades creating mechanisms protecting the established oligarchy and the financial and political elite from the forces of democracy and an increasingly diverse electorate. *Citizens United* has acted as one of these anti-democratic mechanisms. The American people are going to have to decide whether they actually want citizen democracy or whether they are willing to continue tolerating the growing oligarchy of concentrated wealth dominating the legal/political process, as our circumstances are proving Justice Brandeis correct. We cannot have both.

Notes

1. https://transition.fec.gov/info/appfour.htm
2. https://transition.fec.gov/info/appfour.htm
3. Also known as the "McCain-Feingold Act," P.L. 107-155 (2002).
4. 558 U.S. 310, at 350–351, citing Austin, 494 U.S., at 658–659.
5. *Id.* at 351, *citing* Austin, 494 U.S., at 680 (Scalia, J., dissenting).
6. *Id.* at 339.
7. *Id.* at 340–341.
8. *Id.* at 341.
9. *Id.* at 343.
10. *Id.* at 348.
11. *Id.* at 349.
12. *Id.* at 367.
13. *Id.* at 369.
14. *Id.* at 370.
15. *Id.* at 361.
16. *Id.* at 394 (Stevens, J., concurring in part and dissenting in part).
17. 34 Stat. 864 (1907).
18. 558 U.S. 310, at 400 (Stevens, J., concurring in part and dissenting in part).
19. *Id.* at 395 (Stevens, J., concurring in part and dissenting in part), citing Austin v. Michigan, 494 U.S. 652 (1990).
20. *Id.* at 411 (Stevens, J., concurring in part and dissenting in part).
21. *Id.* at 398 (Stevens, J., concurring in part and dissenting in part).
22. *Id.* at 414 (Stevens, J., concurring in part and dissenting in part).
23. *Id.* at 396 (Stevens, J., concurring in part and dissenting in part).
24. *Id.* at 479 (Stevens, J., concurring in part and dissenting in part).
25. Gilman, *Id.* at 455.
26. *Id.* at 472.
27. *Id.* at 475.

References

Andrias, K. (2015). Separations of wealth: Inequality and the erosion of checks and balances. *University of Pennsylvania Journal of Constitutional Law, 8*(419), 419–447.

Austin v. Michigan Chamber of Commerce, 494 U.S. 652 (1990).

Benson, J. (2012). Saving democracy: A blueprint for reform in the post-*Citizens United* era. *Fordham Urban Law Journal, 40,* 723–725, *citing* Bradley A. Smith (2010), "The myth of campaign finance reform," *National Affairs, 2,* 75–77. Retrieved from http://www.nationalaffairs.com/doclib/20091228_ Smith.pdf

Buckley v. Valeo. (1975). *Oyez.* Retrieved January 24, 2018, from https://www.oyez.org/cases/1975/75-436

Campbell, P.S. (2013). *Democracy v. concentrated wealth: In search of a Louis D. Brandeis quote.* 16 Green Bag 2D 251.

Chafetz, J. (2015). Does election law serve the electorate? *University of Chicago Legal Forum, 73,* 111.

Citizens United v. FEC, 130 S. Ct. 876 (2010).

CitizensUnited.org. (2018). Retrieved from http://citizensunited.org/

Dilliard, I. (Ed.). (1941). *Mr. Justice Brandeis, great American: Press opinion and public appraisal.* St. Louis, MO: Modern View Press.

Gilens, M., & Page, B. (2014). Testing theories of American politics: Elites, interest groups, and average citizens. *Perspectives on Politics.* Retrieved from https://scholar.princeton.edu/sites/default/files/mgilens/files/gilens_and_page_2014_testing_theories_of_american_politics.doc.pdf

Kang, M.S. (2010–2011). After *Citizens United. Indiana Law Review, 44,* 243.

Karlan, P.S. (2012). Foreword: Democracy and disdain. *Harvard Law Review, 126*(1), 10–11.

Klein, N. (2008). *The shock doctrine.* New York: Picador.

McConnell v. Federal Election Commission, 540 U.S. 93 (2003).

McCutcheon v. Federal Election Commission, 134 S. Ct. 1434 (2014).

Myrdal, G. (1944). *An American dilemma.* London: Routledge.

Reynolds v. Sims, 377 U.S. 533 (1964).

Taft-Hartley Act of 1947, 80 H.R. 3020, Pub. L. 80-101, 61 Stat. 136, codified as amended at 80 U.S.C.

Tillman Act of 1907, 34 Stat. 864b, codified as amended at 59 U.S.C.

Tribe, L.H. (2015). Dividing *Citizens United*: The case v. the controversy. *Constitutional Comment, 30*, 463–478.

"We the People" Democracy Reform Act of 2017. (2017, October 17). Retrieved from https://www.tomudall.senate.gov/imo/media/doc/WE%20THE%20PEOPLE%20DEMO CRACY%20REFORM%20ACT%20SUMMARY.pdf

Zuesse, E. (2016, August 3). Jimmy Carter is correct that the U.S. is no longer a democracy. *Huffington Post*. Retrieved from https://www.huffingtonpost.com/eric-zuesse/jimmy- carter-is-correct-t_b_7922788.html

Chapter Five

HIDDEN STRATEGIES STATE BY STATE:
THE HISTORY AND WORK OF THE AMERICAN LEGISLATIVE EXCHANGE COUNCIL (ALEC), 1973–2018

Founded in Chicago in 1973, the American Legislative Exchange Council (ALEC) is a 501(c)(3) nonprofit that describes itself as an organization "whose mission is to increase individual liberty, prosperity and the well-being of all Americans by advancing and promoting the principles of limited government, free markets and federalism" (ALEC, 2016). In its *ALEC 2016–2018 Strategic Plan*, the organization outlined its identity and purpose as follows:

> The American Legislative Exchange Council (ALEC) is a 501(c)(3) nonprofit organization dedicated to advancing and promoting the Jeffersonian principles of limited government, free markets and federalism at the state level. ALEC accomplishes this mission by educating elected officials on making sound policy and providing them with a platform for collaboration with other elected officials and business leaders. This forum for the free exchange of ideas—along with education for elected officials—has made ALEC one of the most powerful forces in the resurgence of free-market reform at the state level. (p. 4)

ALEC holds private meetings twice a year (Barkan, 2013) where state legislators gather to view policy briefs that they can introduce as bills in their home-state legislatures. Legislators are encouraged and coached to use particular discursive strategies, repetition, and the shotgun bill techniques to ensure the passage of these bills (Anderson & Donchik, 2016). Some of ALEC's model bills related to education have focused on eliminating teachers unions (Givan, 2014) and tenure for professors in colleges and universities, and advocating for more certification measures as a way to institute a system of "accountability" over teachers across all levels (Anderson & Donchik, 2016). ALEC's bills reflect the belief that schools should be run like businesses, and the privatization and marketization of public education is supported through a strategic and tenuous alliance of neoliberal, neoconservative, libertarian, and liberal constituencies.

Since it was founded, ALEC has grown into a conservative corporate "bill mill" (Fischer, 2013) that has produced thousands of new bills, with 200 or so becoming state law across the U.S. each year (Mayer, 2016). The fruits of ALEC's activities were seen in Wisconsin's passage of laws limiting the rights of public-sector unions, in Florida's "Stand Your Ground" law, and in Pennsylvania's strict voter ID laws (Anderson & Donchik, 2016). ALEC is a tax-exempt nonprofit, although it operates with a particular political agenda more akin to lobbying (Barkan, 2013; Boldt, 2012; Mayer, 2016). Despite its nonprofit 501(c)(3) status, its activity resembles lobbying more than education or charitable efforts in that it supports specific ideological private-sector interests and is not held accountable by the checks and balances of the U.S. federal government (Kammer, 2013). ALEC is part of a larger network of policy actors, including philanthropists, corporate-funded think tanks, private edubusinesses, lobbyists, and entrepreneurs (Anderson & Donchik, 2016). Through its education task force, ALEC currently spreads a particular brand of free-market and libertarian ideology, as well as what Anderson & Donchik refer to as "the new neoliberal knowledge regime." ALEC is made up of lobbyists and state legislators who promote the advancement of free markets and a reduction in government intervention (Underwood & Mead, 2012).

A State-by-State Strategy

In the scholarly literature related to ALEC and its bill-modeling activities, ALEC's reach has been traced to increasing corporate profit-making in prisons (Green 2015), promoting policies that would eradicate consumer protections (Pridgen, 2015), supporting state laws that have been found to negatively and disproportionately affect African Americans (Cooper, Heldman, Ackerman, & Farrar-Meyers, 2016; Turner, 2014), the privatization of many government services (Dannin, 2012), including the privatization of the police force (Rahall, 2014), various model bills related to the privatization of public schools (Anderson & Donchik, 2016; Attick & Boyles, 2016; Au, 2013; Barkan, 2013; Boston, 2014; Feuerstein, 2015; Fischer, 2013; Graves, 2014; Lahm, 2015; Ujifusa, 2012a, 2012b; Underwood & Mead, 2012) and higher education (Medvetz, 2012; Messer-Davidow, 1993; Neal, 2008; Ness & Gándara, 2014). These varied activities illuminate how ALEC creates coalitions among diverse business actors in order to facilitate corporate involvement in state policymaking (Hertel-Fernandez, 2014).

ALEC has long been associated with and connected to both Jeb Bush's Foundation for Excellence in Education (FEE) and Pearson Education, supporting measures to increase accountability for teacher candidates and teacher preparation programs, as in the case of the development of the Education Teacher Performance Assessment (ETPA). After supporting these measures, Pearson was made an operational partner of ETPA and given access to the teacher education market (Attick & Boyles, 2016). As described by Attick and Boyles, the creation and development of a technology-focused, corporate model of public education has allowed companies like Pearson to see teachers and students as consumers of educational products and to profit from their needs.

Although ALEC ultimately vetoed a resolution supporting the Common Core State Standards (CCSS), disagreements within ALEC led to a failure to reach a consensus on the matter and reflected a larger split of opinion among conservatives, with populist libertarians, states' rights advocates, and Tea Party free-market nationalists from institutes such as the Washington Policy Center, the Pioneer Institute, and the Goldwater Institute rejecting CCSS for its potential to allow more government control over schooling (Au, 2013). These internal disagreements reflect the tenuous nature of ALEC's alliance of various neoliberal, libertarian, liberal, and neoconservative supporters, and call into question how long these alliances can last and in terms of which political issues.

An important key to ALEC's existence is its funding from Big Philanthropy, which influences the kinds of model bills that ALEC develops. Big Philanthropy, as described by Barkan (2013), has long promoted the goal of remaking public education so that it resembles business, believing that this would create competition that would eradicate the achievement gap. The Bill and Melinda Gates, Eli and Edythe Broad, Walton Family, Laura and John Arnold, Anschutz, Annie E. Casey, Michael and Susan Dell, William and Flora Hewlett, and Joyce Foundations have all supported this movement. However, not all Big Philanthropy funders have maintained their funding. For instance, several philanthropic organizations, including the Bill and Melinda Gates Foundation, discontinued their funding of ALEC following negative publicity. This phenomenon is discussed in further detail in subsequent sections in this chapter.

One of the ways in which Big Philanthropy has attempted to remake public education so that it resembles a business is through the act of "astroturfing," which is the creation of fabricated political movements meant to appear as though they were formed at the grassroots level, while actually being funded by Big Philanthropy (Barkan, 2013). ALEC has employed the strategy of introducing "trigger laws," which are laws that are strategically implemented in state legislatures around the United States at the same time. This legislative strategy is another form of astroturfing because of the way it mimics a "ground-up" movement. Trigger laws are based on model bills that are brought up simultaneously at the state level across the United States. In 2013, trigger laws of this sort were disseminated at a rapid pace by ALEC and brought up in at least 25 states in 2013. Many of these trigger laws focused on "school choice" and vouchers for private schools (Boston, 2014).

Ideology, Controversy, and Backlash

ALEC describes itself as a "truly unique organization in the right-of-center policy movement in that it creates an environment for genuine, nonpartisan exchange of policy ideas between elected officials and leaders in commerce" (ALEC, 2016, p. 8). While claiming "nonpartisan" membership, in its 2016 Strategic Plan the organization gave an account of the partisan "attacks" that it has faced in recent years:

> Given its effectiveness, ALEC is closely scrutinized by the Left and has faced especially harsh attacks from those opposed to free-market policy in the past few years. This caused some upheaval in the organization's funding base, as many corporate members and sponsors broke off to avoid controversy. (p. 9)

The "controversy" that ALEC refers to in its strategic plan could refer to the public attention that it received for its involvement in turning Florida's 2005 "Stand Your Ground" law into a model bill that proliferated in state legislatures across the country. ALEC's involvement in the spread of this law was brought to public attention after an unarmed African American teenager named Trayvon Martin was shot and killed by a neighborhood watch volunteer while walking home in his neighborhood in Florida. *The Hill* wrote that the shooter, George Zimmerman, was not initially charged with a crime, and eventually acquitted, because the

"Stand Your Ground" law was interpreted by prosecutors to mean that it was legal to shoot any person who appeared suspicious in "self-defense," even if they were unarmed (Bowden, 2017). According to *The Guardian*, "The Florida law was picked up by ALEC, and, working in partnership with the National Rifle Association (NRA), used as a template for one of its 'model bills,' which was taken up by other states across the country" (Pilkington & Goldenberg, 2013a). ALEC's involvement in the dissemination of the "Stand Your Ground" law as a "model bill" for legislators across the country led to negative publicity for ALEC and resulted in multiple companies such as Coca-Cola, Kraft Foods, the Bill and Melinda Gates Foundation, and Horizon Blue-Cross Blue-Shield announcing that they would discontinue their support for and involvement with ALEC. Based on ALEC's internal documents, *The Guardian* reported an estimated loss of almost 400 state legislators, 60 corporations that formed the core of funding for ALEC (including Amazon, General Electric, McDonald's, and Walmart), and that ALEC was planning to launch a strategy referred to as the "Prodigal Son Project" in order to attract corporate members in 2013. We now turn to the specifics and nature of ALEC's sources of funding.

ALEC's Sources of Funding

ALEC was founded in 1973 by Paul Weyrich, a conservative press aide from Wisconsin who was the co-founder of the Heritage Foundation and the Moral Majority with Jerry Falwell. ALEC received most of its startup funding of the philanthropist Richard Mellon Scaife. From 1973 to 1983, the Scaife and Mellon family trusts gave $500,000 to ALEC (Mayer, 2016). Almost 98% of ALEC's funding comes from sources other than legislative dues, including corporations, trade associations, and corporate foundations. Some of its biggest funders over the years have included ExxonMobil, the Charles G. Koch Foundation, PhRMA, Peter Coors's Castle Rock

Table 5.1. Donations to American Legislative Exchange Council, $100K and Above, 2003–2016.

DONORS	2003	2004	2005	2006	2007	2008	2009	2010	2011	2012	2013	2014	2015	2016	GRAND TOTAL
Searle Freedom Trust		50		100		100	120	125	175	175	135	194	200		1,374,500
The Lynde and Harry Bradley Foundation, Inc.							50	95	75	70	70	200	350		910,000
Charles Koch Foundation							75			71		280.6	449		876,712
ExxonMobil Foundation	290	167	151.5	30	31										669,500
Lumina Foundation						300		295	45						640,000
Gleason Family Foundation								50	50	75	75	75	75		400,000
The UPS Foundation	40	40	40	40	40	40	42.5	32.5	30	40					385,000

Table 5.1 continued on p. 146

Table 5.1 continued from p. 145

DONATIONS TO AMERICAN LEGISLATIVE EXCHANGE COUNCIL, $100K AND ABOVE (INDIVIDUAL YEARS IN THOUSANDS), 2003–2016

DONORS	2003	2004	2005	2006	2007	2008	2009	2010	2011	2012	2013	2014	2015	2016	GRAND TOTAL
Bill & Melinda Gates Foundation									376.6						376,635
Allegheny Foundation			35		50					50	50		50	50	285,000
Jaquelin Hume Foundation	25	25					45	50	50	50					245,000
General Motors Foundation, Inc.	25	95	25												145,000
Vanguard Charitable Endowment Program								60	12		12		11	10	105,500
Silicon Valley Community Foundation												100			100,000

Retrieved January 2018

Foundation, the John M. Olin Foundation, and the Lynde and Harry Bradley Foundation (Graves, 2011). In addition to receiving major funding from the Charles G. Koch Foundation, ALEC has maintained close ties with the Koch-funded organization the State Policy Network (SPN). (For more detailed information on the history of Richard Scaife, the SPN, and its funders, see Chapter Two herein on the history and strategies of philanthropy in the United States.) According to ALEC's 990 IRS tax filings, in 2012 it was one of the top recipients of donations from the conservative Searle Freedom Trust, a foundation that promotes publications on "individual freedom, economic liberties, personal responsibilities, and traditional American values" (https://searlefreedomtrust.org/). Table 5.1 shows which organizations made donations of over $100,000 to ALEC between 2003 and 2017.

Table 5.1 illustrates several patterns in ALEC's funding. The top funder, the Searle Freedom Trust, has made considerable donations on a consistent basis between 2003 and 2016, taking only one year off between funding cycles. However, several other funders stopped funding after 2012. For instance, the Bill and Melinda Gates Foundation made a one-time donation of $376,600 in 2011 but did not contribute to the organization again. Other foundations, including the ExxonMobil Foundation, the Lumina Foundation, the UPS Foundation, the Jaquelin Hume Foundation, and the General Motors Foundation, Inc., stopped funding ALEC between 2005 and 2012. This pullback followed news reports revealing the organization's involvement in Florida's 2005 "Stand Your Ground" law, which led these companies and others to discontinue their financial support of ALEC.

ALEC's second and third top funders, the Lynde and Harry Bradley Foundation, Inc., and the Charles Koch Foundation, did not contribute any funds between 2003 and 2008, but consistently donated considerable sums from 2009 to 2015. Other donors, such as the Gleason Family Foundation, the Allegheny Foundation, and the Vanguard Charitable Endowment, donated more consistently between 2010 and 2015. The Lynde and Harry Bradley Foundation and the Charles Koch Foundation are known for supporting rightwing causes with their philanthropy. (See Chapters Two and Three herein for more detail on these funders.) Similarly, those who have increased their funding since 2010 have ties to conservative causes. For example, the Allegheny Foundation is one of the Scaife foundations focused on civic development and education,[1] and the Gleason Family Foundation has ties to the Center for Education Reform (CER), which promotes charter schools, "school choice," teacher quality, transparency, and online learning,[2] and has received contributions from foundations known to support conservative and neoliberal education policies, including the Anschutz Foundation, the Lynde and Harry Bradley Foundation, and the Walton Family Foundation.[3]

Less is known about the Vanguard Charitable Endowment. According to the endowment's website, The Vanguard Charitable Endowment is "[a]n independent public charity sponsoring donor-advised funds—a low-cost, tax-effective way to consolidate, accrue, and grant assets to charity. Our mission is to increase philanthropy and maximize its charitable impact over time."[4] This endowment may work in a way that is similar to that of Donors Trust, another foundation sponsoring donor-advised funds and potentially serving as an intermediary foundation that does not identify the original donors. This strategy is useful for foundations interested in funding ALEC but not wishing to be identified with the organization because of the negative publicity that such an association might provoke. Despite such negative publicity and the loss of funders, contributions to ALEC remained steady in the years following 2009–2010, with organizations such as the Searle Freedom Trust, the Lynde and Harry Bradley Foundation, the Charles Koch Foundation, the Allegheny Foundation, and the Gleason Family Foundation consistently donating large sums. Tracking future 990s will reveal how ALEC is currently being funded, and by whom.

Donations to ALEC from corporations and corporate foundations go toward subsidizing legislators' trips to ALEC meetings and conventions. This support includes what are called "scholarships" to cover the cost of the trips taken by legislators and their families to resorts where ALEC conventions are held, often covering airfare, hotel costs, and childcare costs. Corporate money is spent on supporting ALEC's various task forces, which serve as forums where legislators and representatives from private industry can discuss model legislation (Graves, 2011). This funding allows for the creation of a unique and unprecedented communication channel between legislators and corporate interests under the umbrella of various ALEC activities. In order to better understand this relationship, we turn next to a description of ALEC's membership structure.

What Is the Membership Structure of ALEC?

Key to understanding how ALEC functions is an understanding of the current leadership and membership structure of the organization. Members of ALEC include the Board of Directors, who are "state legislative leaders from across the country"; the Board of Scholars, who have "distinguished work and dedication to market-based policy innovations"; the Private Enterprise Advisory Council, an "advisory team of private-sector industry leaders"; and ALEC executives, who "guide the day-to-day ALEC staff operations." The current CEO of ALEC is Lisa B. Nelson, formerly of Visa and AOL Time Warner, who worked with Newt Gingrich from 1995 to 1998 when he was U.S. Speaker of the House. Nelson also served as the executive director of GOPAC, a Republican state and local political training organization (categorized as a tax-exempt 527 organization). Figure 5.1 below details the names and affiliations of various members of the ALEC leadership structure.

Members of each of the leadership structure and ALEC staff are members of certain task forces. ALEC's eleven task forces are:

- American City Council Exchange
- Civil Justice, Commerce
- Insurance and Economic Development

Figure 5.1. ALEC's Leadership Structure.

BOARD OF DIRECTORS
- Rep. Jason Saine (R-NC) - National Chair
- Senate President Wayne Niederhauser (R-UT)
- Sen. Andre E. Cushing, III (R-ME)
- Rep. Alan Clemmons (R-SC)
- Sen. Jim Buck (R-IN)
- Sen. Joel C. Anderson (R-CA)
- Del. Kathy Byron (R-VA)
- Sen. Gary Daniels (R-NH)
- Rep. David Frizzell (R-IN)
- Speaker Phillip Gunn (R-MS)
- Rep. Yvette Herrell (R-NM)
- Sen. Brian Kelsey (R-TN)
- Rep. Phil King (R-TX)
- Rep. Dawn Pettengill (R-IA)
- Rep. John Piscopo (R-CT)
- Rep. David Reis (R-IL)
- Rep. Bill Seitz (R-OH)
- Sen. Jim Smith (R-NE)
- Senate Pres Susan Wagle (R-KS)
- Speaker Linda Upmeyer (R-IA)
- Sen. Leah Vukmir (R-WI)

BOARD OF SCHOLARS
- Rob Natelson
- Dr. Richard Vedder
- Dr. Arthur B. Laffer
- Bob Williams—Senior Fellow, Center for State Fiscal Reform
- Victor Schwartz

PRIVATE ENTERPRISE ADVISORY COUNCIL
- Guarantee Trust Life Insurance - Marianne Eterno
- K-12, Inc. - Don Lee
- Peabody Energy - Michael Blank
- Pfizer - Josh Brown
- American Bail Coalition - Bill Carmichael
- NetChoice - Steve DelBianco
- U.S. Chamber of Commerce - Rob Engstrom
- ExxonMobil Corp. - Ken Freeman
- Bright House Networks LLC - Marva Johnson
- PhRMA - Scott LaGanga
- UPS - Mike Kiely
- AT&T - Bill Leahy
- Americans For Prosperity - Frayda Levin
- Heritage Foundation - Stepen Moore
- Koch Companies Public Sector, LLC - Michael Morgan
- Asian American Hotel Owners Association - Chip Rogers
- National Federation of Independent Businesses - Gary Selvy
- Atria Client Services - Daniel Smith
- State Farm Insurance Companies - Roland Spies
- State Budget Solutions - Bob Williams
- Keith Smith

ALEC EXECUTIVES
- Lisa B. Nelson, CEO
- Lisa Bowen, Chief Financial Officer, Executive Vice President of Operations and Administration
- Michael Bowman, Vice President, Policy
- Bartlett Cleland, General Counsel and Chief Strategy and Innovation Officer
- Jeff Lambert, Vice President, Member Relations
- Bill Meierling, Chief Marketing Officer and Executive Vice President, External Relations and Strategic Partnerships
- Jonathan Williams, Chief Economist and Vice President, Center for State Fiscal Reform

- Communications and Technology
- Criminal Justice
- Education and Workforce Development
- Energy, Environment, and Agriculture
- Federalism and International Relations
- Health and Human Services
- Homeland Security
- Tax and Fiscal Policy

Each of these task forces includes one representative from the ALEC staff called an ALEC director, a private chair from industry, and a public chair who is an elected member of a state legislature. As an example of this structure, Figure 5.2 demonstrates the relationship between the larger membership and the ALEC task force on Education and Workforce Development.

Figure 5.2. Task Force on Education and Workforce Development.

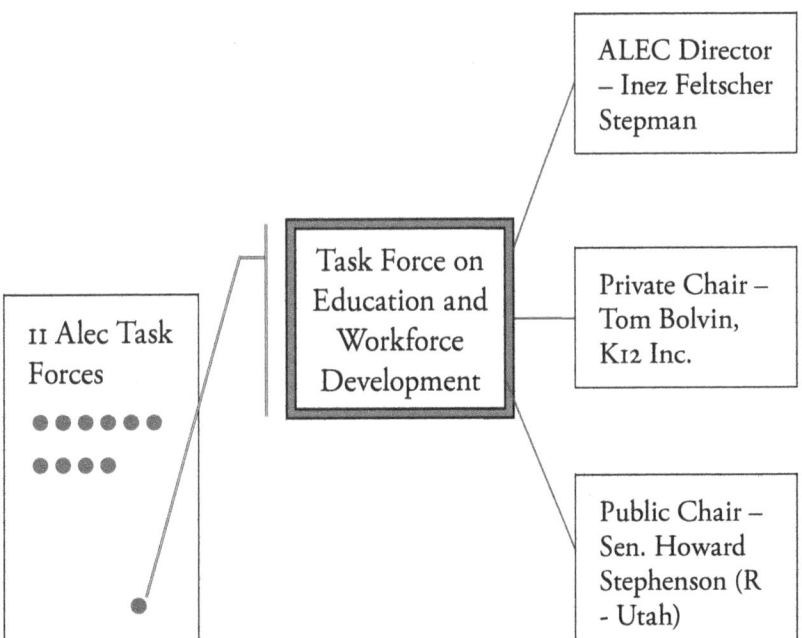

According to ALEC's website, the mission of the Education and Workforce Development Task Force is to:

> Promote excellence in the nation's educational system, to advance reforms through parental choice, to support efficiency, accountability and transparency in all educational institutions, and to ensure America's youth are given the opportunity to succeed. (ALEC, 2016)

Each task force hosts meetings at which model policies are shared and discussed with other members of ALEC from across the United States, including state legislators and representatives of private industry. The identities of other members of ALEC not mentioned in the leadership structure are discussed in the next section.

Who Are Other Non-Leader Members of ALEC?

As ALEC's controversial activities have come to light in recent years, locating records of its membership over time can be difficult. In terms of ALEC's membership, its website reported the following:

> Comprised of nearly one-quarter of the country's state legislators and stakeholders from across the policy spectrum, ALEC members represent more than 60 million Americans and provide jobs to more than 30 million people in the United States. (ALEC, 2016)

ALEC has described its membership and impact in the following way:

> ALEC is the premier free-market organization that provides elected officials the resources they need to make sound policy. It enjoys a broad and growing membership that includes 25 percent of all legislative members and over 200 corporate and nonprofit members. Additionally,

Table 5.2. Non-Leader ALEC Members and Their Roles Reported July 2018.

ALEC MEMBER NAME	ROLE(S) IN ALEC	OCCUPATION AND CITY/STATE (IF KNOWN)
Hon. Billy Hewes	American City County Exchange Task Force	Mayor of Gulfport, MS
Hon. Jon Russell	American City County Exchange Task Force	ALEC staff, Arlington, VA
Ellen Troxclair	American City County Exchange Task Force	District 8 Council Member, Austin, TX
Nick Wachinski	American City County Exchange Task Force	Licensed Attorney in Pennsylvania; Chief Executive Officer for Lexington National Insurance Corporation, Lutherville, MD
Sen. Brian Kelsey	Civil Justice Task Force	Tennessee State Senate, Memphis, TN
Mark Behrens	Civil Justice Task Force	Shook, Hardy & Bacon LLP, Kansas City, MO
Amy Kjose Anderson	Civil Justice Task Force; ALEC Director	ALEC Director, Oklahoma City, OK
Robert Ordway	Commerce, Insurance and Economic Development Task Force	ALEC Task Force Director, Washington DC
Rep. Woody Burton	Commerce, Insurance and Economic Development Task Force	Indiana House of Representatives

Table 5.2 continued on p. 154

Table 5.2 continued from p. 153

ALEC MEMBER NAME	ROLE(S) IN ALEC	OCCUPATION AND CITY/STATE (IF KNOWN)
Frank Morris	Commerce, Insurance and Economic Development Task Force	Vice President Corporate Public Affairs United Parcel Service (UPS), Atlanta, GA
Sen. Michael Hough	Criminal Justice Reform Task Force	Maryland Senate
Bill Carmichael	Criminal Justice Reform Task Force	Chairman of American Bail Coalition Board, Franklinville, NJ
Ronald J. Lampard	Criminal Justice Reform Task Force	ALEC Director, Arlington, VA
Rep. Garry Smith	Communications and Technology Task Force	South Carolina House of Representatives
Rick Cimerman	Communications and Technology Task Force	VP External & State Affairs at NCTA – The Internet and Television Association, Washington DC
Jonathon Hauenschild	Communications and Technology Task Force	ALEC Director
Tom Bolvin	Education and Workforce Development Task Force	K12 Inc., Washington DC (former U.S. Department of Education and Virginia House of Delegates)
Sen. Howard Stephenson	Education and Workforce Development Task Force	Utah State Senate, Salt Lake, UT
Inez Feltscher Stepman	Education and Workforce Development Task Force	ALEC Director

Table 5.2 continued on p. 155

Table 5.2 continued from p. 154

ALEC MEMBER NAME	ROLE(S) IN ALEC	OCCUPATION AND CITY/STATE (IF KNOWN)
Grant Kidwell	Energy, Environment and Agriculture Task Force	ALEC Director, Washington, D.C.
Rep. David B. Reis	Energy, Environment and Agriculture Task Force	Illinois House of Representatives, Olney, IL
Jennifer Jura	Energy, Environment and Agriculture Task Force	Manager, Policy and Political Coalition, National Rural Electric Cooperative Association (NRECA), Alexandria, VA
Rep. Yvette Herrell	Federalism and International Relations Task Force	New Mexico House of Representatives, Alamogordo, NM
Rep. C. Gene Whisnant	Federalism and International Relations Task Force	Oregon State Legislature, Salem, OR
Lorenzo Montanari	Federalism and International Relations Task Force	Director of International Programs & Affairs at Americans for Tax Reform, Executive Director at Property Rights. Washington DC
Karla Jones	Federalism and International Relations Task Force	ALEC Director
Brooklyn Roberts	Health and Human Services Task Force	ALEC Director, Birmingham, AL
Rep. John Nygren	Health and Human Services Task Force	Wisconsin House, Madison, WI

Table 5.2 continued on p. 156

Table 5.2 continued from p. 155		
ALEC MEMBER NAME	ROLE(S) IN ALEC	OCCUPATION AND CITY/ STATE (IF KNOWN)
Joe Arite	Health and Human Services Task Force	Guarantee Trust Life Insurance Company
Sen. Gail Bates	Tax and Fiscal Policy Task Force	Maryland House of Delegates
Jonathan Small	Tax and Fiscal Policy Task Force	Oklahoma Council of Public Affairs
Joel Griffith	Tax and Fiscal Policy Task Force	ALEC Director
Sen. Greg Reed	State Chairs	Alabama
Rep. Terri Collins	State Chairs	Alabama
Rep. John Allen	State Chairs	Arizona
Sen. Debbie Lesko	State Chairs	Arizona
Sen. Missy Irvin	State Chairs	Arkansas
Rep. Jim Dotson	State Chairs	Arkansas
Sen. Joel C. Anderson	State Chairs	California
Sen. Kevin Grantham	State Chairs	Colorado
Rep. Lori Saine	State Chairs	Colorado
Rep. Whit Betts	State Chairs	Connecticut
Sen. Colin Bonini	State Chairs	Delaware
Rep. Mike La Rosa	State Chairs	Florida
Rep. Matt Dollar	State Chairs	Georgia
Sen. Steve Gooch	State Chairs	Georgia
Rep. Gene R. Ward	State Chairs	Hawaii
Sen. Steve Vick	State Chairs	Idaho
Rep. Jeff Thompson	State Chairs	Idaho
Rep. Tom Morrison	State Chairs	Illinois
Rep. David B. Reis	State Chairs	Illinois
Rep. David Frizzell	State Chairs	Indiana
Rep. David A. Wolkins	State Chairs	Indiana

Table 5.2 continued on p. 157

Table 5.2 continued from p. 156		
ALEC MEMBER NAME	ROLE(S) IN ALEC	OCCUPATION AND CITY/STATE (IF KNOWN)
Sen. Charles Schneider	State Chairs	Iowa
Rep. Rob Taylor	State Chairs	Iowa
Sen. Ty Masterson	State Chairs	Kansas
Rep. John Barker	State Chairs	Kansas
Sen. Tom Buford	State Chairs	Kentucky
Rep. Paula Davis	State Chairs	Louisiana
Rep. Ray Garofalo	State Chairs	Louisiana
Rep. Nate Wadsworth	State Chairs	Maine
Sen. Andre E. Cushing, III	State Chairs	Maine
Del. Susan Krebs	State Chairs	Maryland
Sen. Gail Bates	State Chairs	Maryland
Rep. Mike Webber	State Chairs	Michigan
Sen. Michael L. Green	State Chairs	Michigan
Rep. Pat Garofalo	State Chairs	Minnesota
Sen. Mary Kiffmeyer	State Chairs	Minnesota
Rep. Gary Chism	State Chairs	Mississippi
Sen. Josh Harkins	State Chairs	Mississippi
Sen. Wayne Wallingford	State Chairs	Missouri
Rep. Justin Hill	State Chairs	Missouri
Rep. Donna Lichtenegger	State Chairs	Missouri
Sen. Edgar Emery	State Chairs	Missouri
Sen. Roger Webb	State Chairs	Montana
Sen. Lou Ann Linehan	State Chairs	Nebraska
Sen. Jim Smith	State Chairs	Nebraska

Table 5.2 continued on p. 158

Table 5.2 continued from p. 157

ALEC MEMBER NAME	ROLE(S) IN ALEC	OCCUPATION AND CITY/STATE (IF KNOWN)
Sen. James Settelmeyer	State Chairs	Nevada
Rep. Ken Weyler	State Chairs	New Hampshire
Rep. Jordan G. Ulery	State Chairs	New Hampshire
Sen. Gary L. Daniels	State Chairs	New Hampshire
Hon. Jay Webber	State Chairs	New Jersey
Sen. Steve Oroho	State Chairs	New Jersey
Rep. Yvette Herrell	State Chairs	New Mexico
Rep. Dennis Riddell	State Chairs	North Carolina
Rep. Jason Saine	State Chairs	North Carolina
Rep. Karen Rohr	State Chairs	North Dakota
Speaker Cliff Rosenberger	State Chairs	Ohio
Sen. Lou Terhar	State Chairs	Ohio
Rep. Wes Retherford	State Chairs	Ohio
Sen. Bill Coley	State Chairs	Ohio
Sen. AJ Griffin	State Chairs	Oklahoma
Rep. Mark Lepak	State Chairs	Oklahoma
Rep. C. Gene Whisnant	State Chairs	Oregon
Rep. Seth Grove	State Chairs	Pennsylvania
Sen. Rich Alloway	State Chairs	Pennsylvania
Rep. Patricia Morgan	State Chairs	Rhode Island
Rep. Garry Smith	State Chairs	South Carolina
Sen. Tom Alexander	State Chairs	South Carolina
Sen. Jim Stalzer	State Chairs	South Dakota
Rep. Bill Sanderson	State Chairs	Tennessee
Sen. Bill Ketron	State Chairs	Tennessee
Sen. Kelly Hancock	State Chairs	Texas
Rep. Rick Miller	State Chairs	Texas

Table 5.2 continued on p. 159

Table 5.2 continued from p. 158		
ALEC MEMBER NAME	ROLE(S) IN ALEC	OCCUPATION AND CITY/ STATE (IF KNOWN)
Sen. Lincoln Fillmore	State Chairs	Utah
Rep. Kim Coleman	State Chairs	Utah
Rep. Ken Ivory	State Chairs	Utah
Rep. Bob G. Helm	State Chairs	Vermont
Del. Kathy Byron	State Chairs	Virginia
Rep. Matt Shea	State Chairs	Washington
Sen. Jan Angel	State Chairs	Washington
Sen. Patricia Rucker	State Chairs	West Virginia
Rep. Mike Kuglitsch	State Chairs	Wisconsin
Rep. Dan Laursen	State Chairs	Wyoming
*Retrieved from Sourcewatch.org, July 2018		

> ALEC has over 1,800 individual supporters and includes 20 percent of Congress, eight sitting governors and more than 300 local elected officials. (p. 8)

While ALEC does not report a comprehensive list of all of its members, Table 5.2 features the non-leader members whose names have been reported on its website. This list may serve as a resource for readers wanting to investigate how ALEC is influencing laws in their state.

In addition to the current ALEC members, ALEC's website lists its "Alumni." According to the website, "ALEC Alumni advance limited government, free market and federalism priorities at every level of elective office." While it is not clear from the website what the relationship is between ALEC and its alumni, the list includes eight governors, 14 state senators, and 73 state representatives who currently serve. A complete list of ALEC's alumni can be found in Table 5.3 below.

In the next section we turn to a discussion of ALEC's core programs and projects.

Table 5.3. ALEC Alumni List July 2018.

GOVERNORS	U.S. SENATE	U.S. HOUSE OF REPRESENTATIVES		
Jeff Coyler, KS	Michael Enzi (R-WY)	Justin Amash (R-MI)	Tom Graves (R-GA)	Barry Loudermilk (R-GA)
Nathan Deal, GA	Joni Ernst (R-IA)	Jim Banks (R-IN)	Morgan Griffith (R-VA)	Frank Lucas (R-OK)
John Bel Edwards, LA	Cory Gardner (R-CO)	Jaime Herrera Beutler (R-WA)	Glenn Grothman (R-WI)	Blaine Luetkemeyer (R-MO)
Mary Fallin, OK	Lindsey Graham (R-SC)	Andy Biggs (R-AZ)	Sam Graves (R-MO)	Ken Marchant (R-TX)
Kay Ivey, AL	Cindy Hyde-Smith (R-MS)	Diane Black (R-TN)	Brett Guthrie (R-KY)	Tom McClintock (R-CA)
John Kasich, OH	James Inhofe (R-OK)	Marsha Blackburn (R-TN)	Andy Harris (R-MD)	Cathy McMorris-Rodgers (R-WA)
Mike Parson, MO	Joe Manchin (D-WV)	Kevin Brady (R-TX)	Vicky Hartzler (R-MO)	John Moolenaar (R-MI)
Kim Reynolds, IA	Jerry Moran (R-KS)	Tom Cole (R-OK)	Bill Huizenga (R-MI)	Alex Mooney (R-WV)
Scott Walker, WI	Jim Risch (R-ID)	Doug Collins (R-GA)	Lynn Jenkins (R-KS)	Kristi Noem (R-SD)
	Marco Rubio (R-FL)	James Comer (R-KY)	Sam Johnson (R-TX)	Ralph Norman (R-SC)
	Tim Scott (R-SC)	Barbara Comstock (R-VA)	Walter Jones (R-NC)	Tom O'Halleran (D-AZ)
	Thom Tillis (R-NC)	John Culberson (R-TX)	Steve King (R-IA)	Steven Palazzo (R-MS)

Roger Wicker (R-MS)	Jeff Denham (R-CA)	Steve Knight (R-CA)	Erik Paulsen (R-MN)
	Charlie Dent (R-PA)	Raul Labrador (R-ID)	Bill Posey (R-FL)
	Mario Diaz-Balart (R-FL)	Doug Lamborn (R-CO)	Michael D. Rogers (R-AL)
	Jeff Duncan (R-SC)	Al Lawson (D-FL)	Ileana Ros-Lehtinen (R-FL)
	John Faso (R-NY)	Robert Latta (R-OH)	Dennis Ross (R-FL)
	Rodney Frelinghuysen (R-NJ)	Debbie Lesko (R-AZ)	Edward Royce (R-CA)
	Bob Gibbs (R-OH)	Frank LoBiondo (R-NJ)	Steve Scalise (R-LA)
	David Schweikert (R-AZ)	Austin Scott (R-GA)	Michael Simpson (R-ID)
	Adrian Smith (R-NE)	Jason Smith (R-MO)	Lloyd Smucker (R-PA)
	Steve Stivers (R-OH)	Pat Tiberi (R-OH)	Scott Tipton (R-CO)
	Jackie Walorski (R-IN)	Randy Weber (R-TX)	Daniel Webster (R-FL)
	Bruce Westerman (R-AR)	Lynn Westmoreland (R-GA)	Joe Wilson (R-SC)
	Kevin Yoder (R-KS)	Don Young (R-AK)	

ALEC's Core Programs and Projects

ALEC offers a model policy library for legislators as well as various publications. The primary objective of ALEC moving forward, as shaped by the strategic plan, was to significantly expand the reach of ALEC to new audiences and to build up a network of concerned citizens to advance the principles of limited government, free markets, and federalism. Leadership objectives included "strengthening and diversifying" the ALEC Board of Directors and Private Enterprise Advisory Council. Another objective was the creation of a 501(c)(4) board for the ALEC Jeffersonian Project—a sister project of ALEC that engages in political activities—so that it could be developed into a substantial stand-alone project. In order to maintain its tax-exempt status as a 501(c)(3) nonprofit, ALEC's activities are restricted to educational endeavors, and it is not permitted to engage in political lobbying. However, the Jeffersonian Project, categorized as a 501(c)(4), is permitted to engage in political lobbying activities (ALEC, 2016, p. 17). In a memo written by ALEC lawyer Alan Dye that was released by *The Guardian*, the Jeffersonian Project was formed in response to criticism that ALEC was engaging in excessive political lobbying. It was empowered take up any activity that might lead to complaints of violating the 501(c)(3)'s charitable status if engaged in by ALEC (Pilkington & Goldenberg, 2013b).

According to the Center for Media and Democracy's *PRWatch* (Mason, 2014), ALEC established the Jeffersonian Project after a complaint was filed with the IRS that ALEC was violating its status as a 501(c)(3) by sending hundreds of "issue alerts" to legislators across the United States. After the complaint was filed with the IRS in 2012, ALEC stopped sending the issue alerts, but the Jeffersonian Project soon began sending similar "issue alert" lobbying messages to legislators.

On its website, ALEC highlights numerous key policy areas of focus, including education, economic development, international trade, agriculture, tax reform, pension reform, energy, transportation, economic development, regulatory reform, environmental stewardship, business, intellectual property, occupational licensing, lawsuit reform, privacy and security, human services, health, workforce development, cronyism, free speech, insurance, and homeland security. On the topic of education, ALEC describes the K–12 school system as expensive and failing, and promotes neoliberal ideas of school reform such as school choice, vouchers, tax credit scholarships, homeschooling, and education savings accounts. Some of ALEC's promoted "key points" featured on its website state that: (a) "Citizens, legislators, and regulators should separate the concept of public education from the monopolistic delivery system and embrace 21st-century methods of connecting students with learning experiences"; (b) "legislators should improve or pass charter school laws, striking a balance between innovation, autonomy, and accountability"; (c) legislators should create or expand the type(s) of school choice program that best suits their state: vouchers, tax credit scholarships, homeschooling, and education savings accounts"; (d) "legislators and regulatory agencies should be wary of attempts to re-regulate innovative and/or private educational options, which could expose them to the death of the thousand bureaucratic cuts and sacrifice the freedoms that allow them to succeed"; and, (e) "institutions of higher education should be transparent about what outcomes students can expect and how much money they will have to spend or borrow" (ALEC website, 2018, https://www.alec.org/issue/education/). ALEC's website houses multiple model policies organized by issue. In the next section we turn to the model policies ALEC has developed as they relate to education.

ALEC's Model Bills: How ALEC Has Influenced the Lives of Educators

After ALEC drafts its model bills at various gatherings and task force meetings in conjunction with state legislators, representatives in private industry, free-market scholars, and ALEC staff, the resulting model bills are posted directly on ALEC's website, organized according to policy topic. Since 2017, ALEC has posted the following education model bills: the Teacher Quality Assurance Act, Amendments to the Great Schools Tax Credit Program Act (Scholarship Tax Credit), the Amendments to the Next Generation Charter Schools Act, the Student Future's Program Act, the School Turnaround and Leadership Development Act, the Neutrality and Integrity in Software Procurement Act, the Forming Open and Robust University Minds (FORUM) Act, and the Partnerships for Student Success. These model policies relate both to P–12 and higher education. The language used in these model bills follows ALEC's pattern of using neutral-sounding language that masks a conservative agenda. ALEC's model bills promote legislation that has the clear ideological goal of increasing privatization of P–12 and higher education, increasing benefits for charter schools, placing greater burdens and accountability checks on public education and educators, and making schools and universities more business-friendly.

For instance, in a model bill targeted at P–12 education, the Teacher Quality Assurance Act is summarized on ALEC's website as follows:

> This model policy prohibits a school district from utilizing a last-hired, first-fired layoff policy when reducing staff. Additionally, the model policy requires the Education Interim Committee, in consultation with the State Board of Education, to study how the performance of teachers may be evaluated for the purpose of awarding or eliminating teacher career employee status.[5]

While this summary positions the bill as a way to protect newly hired educators from being the "first-fired," a careful reading of the model bill reveals that the policy gives the Education Interim Committee and the State Board of Education more power to evaluate teachers' performance across their careers, for the purpose of "eliminating teacher career employee status." This policy could eliminate certain benefits or special considerations that might be offered to a senior teacher. Another model bill targeted at P–12 education, the School Turnaround and Leadership Development Act, gives power to the State Board of Education to designate low-performing public and charter schools, impose consequences on schools that do not improve by a timeline set by the State Board of Education, funds a program to train school leaders, and requires the State Board of Education to report to the Education Interim Committee (ALEC, 2018, https://www.alec.org/model-policy/school-turnaround-and-leadership-development-act/). Increasing the power of the State Board of Education in deciding matters related to P–12 education gives more power to state governors, since members of state boards of education are typically appointed by the state governor rather than elected by the people.

While many articles have explored the impact of ALEC on shaping the privatization and marketization of P–12 schooling, less attention has been directed toward ALEC's relationship to higher education (with the exception of Medvetz, 2012; Messer-Davidow, 1993; Neal, 2008; and Ness & Gándara, 2014). If ALEC's interest in public education has been to create policy briefs aimed at increasing competition between schools, reducing government intervention, increasing the privatization of schooling through charter and online schools, and expanding standardized testing of teachers and students as a measure of "accountability" (Underwood & Mead, 2012), what is ALEC's vision for and interest in higher education and academia? ALEC's model bills related to higher education reveal similar trends in using neutral-sounding language to promote legislation increasing privatization and marketization. Additionally, ALEC's higher education model bills such as the Forming Open and Robust University Minds (FORUM) Act, which eliminates free-speech zones on college campuses, and the Campus Anti-Harassment Act, which would make "student-on-student speech" on campus protected by the First Amendment, makes it easier for the neoconservative free-speech movement to proliferate on campus.

These model policies help to perpetuate the myth that colleges and universities are exclusively liberal institutions where conservative viewpoints are excluded and open up the possibility for conservative students to sue public universities if they feel that their conservative viewpoints have been dismissed.

More information on ALEC's model bills in education can be found at ALEC's website. ALEC's system of drafting model bills to be adopted across state legislatures in the United States has seen success, and ALEC has reported additional plans to bolster its impact on various policies related to education, as well as other areas. ALEC's intentions regarding project planning and cultivating funding are outlined in in the organization's *2016–2018 Strategic Plan* discussed below.

ALEC's Future Plans

To promote its mission of supporting the creation of particular business-friendly policies supporting free markets and limited government regulations, ALEC creates spaces, materials, and opportunities for individuals representing corporate interests to have direct access and influence over the development of "model policies" that are then brought back by state legislators to their home states. Despite the reported controversy and decrease in funding in 2012–2013, ALEC's *2016–2018 Strategic Plan* presented an optimistic outlook for its future endeavors and influence on American politics and governance. For instance, the organization argued:

> Having withstood vicious attacks from the Left and the media, ALEC is well positioned to capitalize on opportunities to expand its audience, member benefits, programming and funding base. Success in these areas will help ALEC remain the leading organization driving free-market reform at the state level and become the leading organization educating America's elected officials on sound policy that

expends all Americans' economic opportunities and personal liberty. (ALEC, 2016, p. 9)

The leadership of ALEC constructed its current 2016–2018 strategic development plan following a developmental audit with consultants from a consulting firm called American Philanthropic, LLC. ALEC's *Strategic Plan* (2016) described how the organization intends to fulfill its mission through the implementation of core programs and projects that include the creation of multiple policy centers, a model policy library, task forces, publications and studies, and by hosting several major events and meetings. Another key strategy for ALEC's future activities included the creation and use of new ALEC policy centers to manage and promote the organization's policy recommendations. The creation of these policy centers and model bills may be attractive to legislators, as it relieves them of the work involved in creating new policy. It is the nature of this cut-and-paste legislation that has led to the nicknaming of ALEC as a "bill mill."

Fundamental to achieving these goals is ALEC's plan to expand its donor base and bring in new philanthropic investors—particularly foundations—to meet those needs. This effort to expand the organization's donor base echoes a long tradition of philanthropic support for right-wing causes in the United States, such as the powerful philanthropic donor group the Philanthropy Roundtable, which used its money and influence in highly organized and well-funded campaigns to promote various right-wing causes in fighting the "war of ideas" (deMarrais, 2006). In the tradition of the Philanthropy Roundtable's strategies enacted to win that "war of ideas," ALEC places a new spin on these strategies, which it categorizes as "educational activities." While the activities of Big Philanthropy have long operated under the radar, and did so in the early days of ALEC, coverage of ALEC by various media sources has helped alert the American public to ALEC's role in creating model bills that are spread from state to state, and the involvement of corporate interests in funding ALEC's operations. In the concluding section we highlight media and informational resources for educators to become further acquainted with activities of ALEC in order to track how ALEC may be influencing education in its home state.

Conclusion

Since 1973, ALEC has been a formidable organization that has helped connect legislators and members of private industry for the purpose of drafting model bills that support limited government, free markets, and federalism across a spectrum of issues that include tax reform, energy, criminal justice, and education. This chapter has detailed the history of ALEC's activities, namely its state-by-state strategy to serve as a corporate and conservative bill mill. With origins in Big Philanthropy and with start-up funding from Richard Mellon Scaife and continued support from the Charles Koch Foundation, the State Policy Network (SPN), and other key conservative philanthropic backers, ALEC has been successful in turning many of its model bills into state law across the United States.

In some ways, ALEC's success has led to backlash against the organization. For instance, ALEC was instrumental in helping "Stand Your Ground" laws to come to fruition in states including Florida, Alabama, Alaska, Arizona, Georgia, Idaho, Indiana, Iowa, Kansas, Kentucky, Louisiana, Michigan, Missouri, Montana, New Hampshire, North Carolina, Texas, Utah, West Virginia, and Wyoming. However, this success led to increased attention to and scrutiny of ALEC's activities, which had remained mostly out of the public eye until that time. ALEC's goal is to help ghostwrite policy with members of private industry, forming a "legislative exchange" of ideas on policy between elected officials and business. ALEC's bills have impacted, and will continue to impact, the lives of educators at the P–12 level and in higher education. Since ALEC has plans to continue expanding its operations and has made courting new philanthropic investors a top priority, it is important for educators to continue to resist ALEC's efforts to write the policies that impact our school systems without our input and voices being heard. We suggest that educators take the following steps if they are concerned with how ALEC might be impacting their schools and universities:

1. Know the legislators in your state who are connected to ALEC.
2. Know the members of ALEC, including the staff and the scholars who are associated with it.
3. Know the businesses involved.
4. Know the model bills that may be proposed, and learn to recognize the language and strategies for passing particular pieces of legislation.
5. Know who is funding ALEC.
6. Use our list of media and informational resources of educators to "get to know ALEC" (see Chapter Nine) and to help other educators become more informed about how ALEC impacts their schools and universities.

These actions can help educators "get to know ALEC" and to become aware of the impact they have on schools and universities. Getting to know ALEC is the first step toward taking action to make sure that communities, rather than private interest groups, can decide for themselves what educational legislation would be most beneficial for their schools. For more resources, ideas, and information, see Chapter Nine herein.

Notes

1. http://www.scaife.com/alleghen.html
2. https://www.edreform.com/category/press-releases/
3. https://www.edreform.com/about/people/cer-supporters/
4. https://www.guidestar.org/profile/23-2888152
5. https://www.alec.org/model-policy/teacher-quality-assurance-act/

References

American Legislative Exchange Council. (2016). *ALEC 2016–2018 strategic plan*. Arlington, VA: ALEC. Retrieved from https://www.alec.org/app/uploads/2016/06/ALEC-Strat- Plan-Final-051616.pdf

Anderson, G.L., & Donchik, L.M. (2016). Privatizing schooling and policy making: The American Legislative Exchange Council and new political and discursive strategies of education governance. *Educational Policy*, *30*(2), 322–364.

Attick, D., & Boyles, D. (2016). Pearson Learning and the ongoing corporatization of public education. *Journal of Thought*, *50*(1), 5–19.

Au, W. (2013). Coring social studies within corporate education reform: The Common Core State Standards, social justice, and the politics of knowledge in US schools. *Critical Education*, *4*(5).

Barkan, J. (2013). Big philanthropy vs. democracy. *Dissent*, *60*(4), 47–54.

Boldt, A. (2012). Rhetoric vs. reality: ALEC's disguise as a nonprofit despite its extensive lobbying. *Hamline Journal of Public Law & Policy*, *34*(1), 35–71.

Boston, R. (2014). Challenging the "school choice" charade. *Church & State*, *67*(3), 4–5.

Bowden, J. (2017, June 9). Florida governor signs strengthened "stand your ground" bill into law. *The Hill*. Retrieved from http://thehill.com/homenews/news/337215-florida-governor- signs-strengthened-stand-your-ground-bill-into-law

Cooper, R., Heldman, C., Ackerman, A.R., & Farrar-Meyers, V.A. (2016). Hidden corporate profits in the U.S. prison system: The unorthodox policy-making of the American Legislative Exchange Council. *Contemporary Justice Review*, *19*(3), 380–400. doi:10.1080/10282580.2016.1185949

Dannin, E. (2012). Privatizing government services in the era of ALEC and the Great Recession. *University of Toledo Law Review*, *43*, 503.

deMarrais, K. (2006). "The haves and the have mores": Fueling a conservative ideological war on public education (or tracking the money). *Educational Studies*, *39*(3), 201–240.

Feuerstein, A. (2015). Parental trigger laws and the power of framing in educational politics. *Education Policy Analysis Archives*, *23*(79/80), 1–34. doi:10.14507/epaa.v23.1992

Fischer, B. (2013). ALEC's schoolhouse rock. *Progressive, 77*(8), 24–28.
Givan, R.K. (2014). Why teachers unions make such useful scapegoats. *New Labor Forum, 23*(1), 68–75. doi:10.1177/1095796013513010
Graves, B. (2014). Pushing back the ALEC agenda. *School Administrator, 71*(8), 33–37.
Graves, L. (2011, July 13). A CMD special report on ALEC's funding and spending. *The Center for Media and Democracy's PRWatch*. Retrieved from https://www.prwatch.org/news/2011/07/10887/cmd-special-report-alecs-funding-and- spending
Green, D.A. (2015). US penal-reform catalysts, drivers, and prospects. *Punishment and Society: International Journal of Penology, 17*(3), 271–298.
Hertel-Fernandez, A. (2014). Who passes business's "model bills"? Policy capacity and corporate influence in U.S. state politics. *Perspectives on Politics, 12*(3), 582–602. doi:10.1017/S1537592714001601
Kammer, A. (2013). Privatizing the safeguards of federalism. *Journal of Law & Politics, 29*(1), 69–150.
Lahm, S. (2015, May 27). The secret group that wants to take over your school. *Progressive*, 20–23.
Mason, J. (2014, July 31). ALEC's Jeffersonian Project pushes to amend Constitution. *The Center for Media and Democracy's PRWatch*. Retrieved from https://www.prwatch.org/news/2014/07/12554/alecs-jeffersonian-project-pushes-amend- us-constitution
Mayer, J. (2016). *Dark money: The hidden history of the billionaires behind the rise of the Radical Right.* New York: Anchor Books.
Medvetz, T. (2012). "Scholar as sitting duck": The Cronon Affair and the buffer zone in American public debate. *Public Culture, 24*(166), 47–53.
Messer-Davidow, E. (1993). Manufacturing the attack on liberalized higher education. *Social Text, 36*, 40–80.
Neal, A.D. (2008). Seeking higher-ed accountability: Ending federal accreditation. *Change: The Magazine of Higher Learning, 40*(5), 24–31.
Ness, E.C., & Gándara, D. (2014). Ideological think tanks in the states: An inventory of their prevalence, networks, and higher education policy activity. *Educational Policy, 28*(2), 258–280.
Pilkington, E., & Goldenberg, S. (2013a, December 3). ALEC facing funding crisis from donor exodus in wake of Trayvon Martin row.

The Guardian. Retrieved from https://www.theguardian.com/world/2013/dec/03/alec-funding-crisis-big-donors-trayvon- martin

Pilkington, E., & Goldenberg, S. (2013b, December 5). State conservative groups plan US-wide assault on education, health and tax. *The Guardian*. Retrieved from https://www.theguardian.com/world/2013/dec/05/state-conservative-groups-assault- education-health-tax

Pridgen, D. (2015). Wrecking ball disguised as law reform: ALEC's model act on private enforcement of consumer protection statutes. *Review of Law and Social Change, 39*(2), 279.

Rahall, K. (2014). The siren is calling: Economic and ideological trends toward privatization of public police forces. *University of Miami Law Review, 68*(3), 633–675.

Turner, L. (2014). Corporate coup d'état. *Black Scholar, 44*(1), 29–46. doi:10.5816/blackscholar.44.1.0030

Ujifusa, A. (2012a). Policy shop casts long K–12 shadow. *Education Week, 31*(29), 1–31.

Ujifusa, A. (2012b). Conservative group kills anti-common-core proposal. *Education Week, 32*(13), 26.

Underwood, J., & Mead, J.F. (2012). A smart ALEC threatens public education. *Phi Delta Kappan, 93*(6), 51–55.

Chapter Six

PHILANTHROPY GOES TO COLLEGE:
TRACKING THE MONEY

In 1971, corporate lawyer and future federal Supreme Court justice Lewis Powell wrote a detailed memo designed to enlist powerful individuals in a concerted effort to win "the war of ideas" in academia. This confidential memo, dated August 23, 1971, and addressed to Eugene B. Sydnor, Jr., Chair of the Education Committee, U.S. Chamber of Commerce, described an "assault" on the American enterprise system from a variety of sources, but primarily from extremists on the left, whom Powell described as "far more numerous, better financed, and increasingly... more welcomed and encouraged by other elements of society, than ever before in our history." Relevant portions of his memo are worth quoting at length:

> The most disquieting voices joining the chorus of criticism come from perfectly respectable elements of society: from the college campus, the pulpit, the media, the intellectual and literary journals, the arts and sciences, and from politicians. In most of these groups the movement against the system is participated in only by minorities. Yet, these often are the most articulate, the most vocal, the most prolific in their writing and speaking.
>
> Moreover, much of the media—for varying motives and in varying degrees—either voluntarily accords unique publicity to these "attackers," or at least allows them to

> exploit the media for their purposes. This is especially true of television, which now plays such a predominant role in shaping the thinking, attitudes and emotions of our people. One of the bewildering paradoxes of our time is the extent to which the enterprise system tolerates, if not participates in, its own destruction.
>
> The campuses from which much of the criticism emanates are supported by (i) tax funds generated largely from American business, and (ii) contributions from capital funds controlled or generated by American business. The boards of trustees of our universities overwhelmingly are composed of men and women who are leaders in the system. (Powell Memo, 1971)

Further, Powell attributed the assault on enterprise, the capitalist system, and individual freedom to social science faculty in political science, economics, sociology, and historians who "tend to be leftist or liberal, resulting in the absence of balanced views on campuses. He called on the U.S. Chamber of Commerce to establish a staff of social science scholars who believe in the free enterprise system (thereby providing more "balance" on campuses), a speaker's bureau, evaluation of textbooks for balance, and equal time on campuses to present views supporting the American system of government and business, to develop relationships with schools of business, to monitor media outlets, scholarly journals, and other print media with the goal of supporting and contributing to more pro-free enterprise views, and to take a "vigorous role in the political arena."[1] Following this memo, free-market philanthropists came together to establish the Philanthropy Roundtable, whose purpose was to implement Powell's call to action. These efforts are detailed in Chapter Two above, which is reprinted from deMarrais (2006). Over the course of the last five decades, influential philanthropic donors have turned their attention to addressing Powell's concerns about what he believed to be the leftist, liberal, and collectivist ideologies promoted by social science faculties on university campuses. By using philanthropic organizations to influence academia and create university-associated institutes, a few ultra-wealthy donors have attempted to leverage control over the kinds of research that is produced, who produces the research, and what faculty are hired at particular institutions, with the aim of promoting an individualist, free-market agenda.

This chapter focuses on the Charles Koch Foundation (CKF), a top donor in the effort to create a strategic approach to promoting a free-market ideology within colleges and universities across the United States. An afternoon session of the Freedom Partners Donors Summit, a Koch-sponsored meeting on June 15, 2014, featured a panel entitled "Leverage Science and the Universities," comprised of scholars trained and supported by Koch's network of scholars, institutes, and funding programs. At the panel, Kevin Gentry, a vice present of the Charles G. Koch Charitable Foundation and aide to Charles and David H. Koch, introduced Ryan Stowers, Vice President of the Koch Foundation, with these words:

> Ryan leads the effort and has worked with a number of you all in this room to identify market-friendly scholars at your alma maters, and universities, and states that are worthy of traditional investment maybe with fellowships, or development of research centers, or what have you. And this is key if we're going to help people understand not only the threats associated with collectivism, but also the advantages of a free society.

In his comments to the audience during that meeting, Stowers detailed the strategic efforts of Koch and like-minded free-market philanthropists to promote their views on college and university campuses:

> Now, let's take a look at this network and how it's grown in recent years. Between 2004 when the seminar started and 2008, we saw solid growth in the network of scholars,

and those are represented by the small dots on the map. Out of the growing network of scholars, we built university centers starting with the Mercatus Center at George Mason University. That center is critical to a lot of [inaudible] policy. It's played a major role in many of the [inaudible] efforts. We've also developed university programs for undergraduate students. Professors educate thousands of students in the ideas of a free society, in courses and outside the classroom [inaudible] and group settings, and then help those students see the message to fight for freedom.

Now these programs also act as a talent pipeline. Professors refer the most passionate students from these programs and graduate programs, so they're training the next generation of the freedom movement. So this cycle constantly repeats itself, and you can see the multiplier effect it's had on our network since 2008. Today we work with a network of nearly 5,000 scholars. Now, this network is the backbone of our higher ed investment [inaudible] what we need to do about this, this network. We work with 24 university-based research centers. The number of university-based research centers has almost doubled in the last two to three years due primarily to the partnership of this group here and the leadership [inaudible] Charles is continuing to [inaudible] in over 400 on-campus undergraduate programs.

Now, consider that on average a professor leaves a year with 6,000 students, and this is their career, over a network of 5,000 scholars. That's 80 million students [in a 30-week?] period.... We've made significant progress, there's no question, but this capability pales in comparison to the opposition. Our network is still greatly outnumbered by professors and faculty who hold a collectivist worldview. (Leverage Science and the Universities transcript, pp. 5–7)[2, 3]

Clearly, the efforts initiated by Lewis Powell in 1971 have reached fruition in the sentiment of Stower's statement, where individual and corporate interests, deregulation, and similar initiatives take precedence over the common, community good. In contrast to the remarks of the Koch Foundation above, with its mission to build a network of scholars, policy advocates, and citizen activists trained to pursue a conservative, free-market agenda, the stated public purposes of the CKF are much more tempered in their language, as described by the Foundation on its webpage:

> The Charles Koch Foundation supports students and faculty members at more than 300 colleges and universities across the country. Our grants fund a variety of undergraduate programs, graduate fellowships, academic research, and university centers, with one important goal: To encourage scholarship that addresses challenges preventing all people from living successful and fulfilling lives.[4]

The Foundation lists three major issues on which it focuses support for scholars, including (a) Criminal Justice and Policing Reform ("We believe that a criminal justice system focused on human dignity is the best way to keep our communities safe"); (b) Toleration and Free Speech ("We support research, educational programs, and dialogue focused on enabling a more tolerant society through modeling civil discourse and protecting press freedom"); and (c) Foreign Policy ("We support new voices and sound scholarship that speak to America's enduring interests and policies that will make our country safer"). While the issues addressed and the support described may be open to scholars across a range of ideological positions, the funding tends to be focused on projects and research that reflect conservative or neoconservative ideologies.

To reach these goals at its consistent ideological network of colleges, universities, and scholars, the CKF has contributed significant funding. According to *PolluterWatch*, a project of Greenpeace, between 2005 and 2015 the CKF contributed $144,714,489 to universities in the United States.[5] This organization provides a searchable database for all Koch contributions to universities. Drawn from this database, Table 6.1 below highlights universities funded in amounts over $1 million.

Table 6.1 highlights 14 universities known to have received over $1 million in funding from the Koch Family Foundations between 2005 and 2016. The largest contributions went to George Mason University and its associated centers and institutes, for a total of around $114.65 million. Other universities received smaller sums but share the characteristic of being located in the American south and southwest, with the exception of Suffolk University in Boston, Massachusetts, and the Catholic University of America in Washington, D.C. The cases of George Mason University (GMU) and Florida State University (FSU), the top recipients of Koch funding, are discussed in greater detail in the remainder of this chapter. The chapter also includes the case of Western Carolina University (WCU), not shown in Table 1 because of the recent nature of its funding, to illustrate Koch's ability to impact smaller universities with less funding.

More recent data accessed in January 2018 show that between 2003 and 2016, the latest year in which complete funding data are available, the CKF contributed $170,878,886 to U.S. colleges and universities (Foundation Directory Online, 2018). In the case of wealth built through their private corporation, the Koch brothers are keenly aware of their Return on Investment (ROI). The investments of the CKF are no different, carrying an expectation that significant investment will produce scholars, institutes, and students who will create and work toward policies and political parties that reflect the ideals of the conservative, free-market right. To illustrate how the CKF has worked on the ground at colleges and universities, we present three case studies. The first, GMU, represents the initial and most highly funded of the Koch efforts and has served to create a pipeline of scholars to other institutions.

Table 6.1. Contributions over $1 Million to U.S. Universities from Charles Koch Foundation 2005–2016.

SCHOOL	CITY	STATE	TOTAL CONTRIBUTIONS*
George Mason University*+	Fairfax	VA	2005–2015: $58,827,554 2016: $13,399,270 Total: $72,226,824
George Mason University–Institute for Humane Studies (IHS)*	Arlington	VA	2005–2015: $28,077,092 2016: $5,691,250 Total: $33,768,342
George Mason University – Mercatus Center	Arlington	VA	$8,658,500
Florida State University*+	Tallahassee	FL	$2,391,687
Texas Tech University*	Lubbock	TX	2005–2015: $2,159,500 2016: $3,364,000 Total: $5,523,500
Utah State University	Logan	UT	$2,048,500
West Virginia University Foundation	Morgantown	WV	$1,596,150
Clemson University	Clemson	SC	$1,527,456
Utah State University–Strata Policy, Inc.*	Logan	UT	2005–2015: $1,481,600 2016: $1,677,500 Total: $3,159,100
University of Texas, Austin	Austin	TX	$1,387,608
Southern Methodist University	Dallas	TX	$1,221,800
Arizona State University Foundation	Tempe	AZ	$1,172,927

Table 6.1 continued on p. 180

Table 6.1 continued from p. 179			
SCHOOL	**CITY**	**STATE**	**TOTAL CONTRIBUTIONS***
University of Arizona Foundation	Tucson	AZ	$1,155,565
Troy University Foundation	Troy	AL	$1,110,960
Catholic University of America*	Washington	DC	2005–2015: $1,045,500 2016: $2,172,500 Total: $3,218,000
Suffolk University	Boston	MA	$1,005,328

* 2005–2015 data were retrieved from polluterwatch.org. 2016; updated data were retrieved from Foundation Directory Online.
+ Includes University Foundation Funds.

The other two cases, FSU and WCU, illustrate the ways in which funding comes into universities, along with the resulting resistance from faculty at those institutions. Table 6.2 details the funding to GMU, FSU, and WCU from the Charles Koch Foundation from 2003 to 2016.

As shown in Table 6.2, the CKF contributed $113,850,611 between 2003 and 2016 to these three institutions. This table highlights how Koch funding is delivered to universities through different foundations, centers, and institutes associated with particular universities.

While the CKF is not the only foundation to provide significant funding to colleges and universities, these cases narrate how a family of billionaires has used a consistent focus, strategy, and ideology to fund programs that train faculty and students who possess a particular ideological frame, then support the placement of those faculty within the institutions through faculty lines, distinguished professorships, and institutes in a way that serves to further the Kochs' conservative beliefs. The cases detail faculty and institutional resistance to these efforts to infringe on the academic freedom that for so long has characterized higher education. Following a presentation of the cases, we turn to a brief summary of overall Koch Foundation strategies and a listing of institutions that have accepted Koch funding. We conclude the chapter by suggesting strategies by which administrators, faculty, and students can resist these funding efforts and decline these "gifts." Data for this study were generated from multiple sources, including many websites, books, and articles focused on the CKF, and data from tax filings using sources such as the Foundation Center Online, a database of philanthropic funding, and organizations dedicated to transparency in philanthropic funding.

Table 6.2. Total Funding to GMU, FSU, and WCU from Charles Koch Foundation, 2003–2016.

RECIPIENTS	TOTAL
George Mason University Foundation	$56,767,454 2016: $13,399,270 **Total: $70,166,724**
George Mason University	**$2,924,572**
Institute for Humane Studies, George Mason University	$23,402,030 2016: $5,836,462 **Total: $29,238,492**
Mercatus Center, George Mason University	**$7,670,500**
Florida State University	$2,099,687 2016: $185,000 **Total: $2,284,687**
Florida State University Foundation	$292,000 2016: $819,136 **Total: $1,111,136**
Western Carolina University	**$454,500**
Total	**$113,850,611**

The Case of George Mason University

With a student population of around 33,729, GMU is the largest public research university in Virginia. Originally established as a branch of the University of Virginia in 1949, GMU became independent in 1972. The University is a 4-year and doctoral university with its main campus in Fairfax, Virginia, and other Virginia campuses in Arlington, Front Royal, and Prince William, and an international campus in Songdo, South Korea (George Mason University Office of Institutional Research and Effectiveness, 2017). According to the Carnegie classification of institutions of higher education, GMU is a doctoral research institution with the highest research activity.[6] IRS tax filings show that between 2003 and 2016 Koch Foundation support of GMU (including donations to the George Mason University Foundation) amounted to $59,692,026, not including substantial donations to its affiliated units, the Institute for Humane Studies and the Mercatus Center. Table 6.3 illustrates the annual and total funding for GMU and its affiliated units, the Mercatus Center and the Institute for Humane Studies from the Koch family foundations between 2003 and 2016.

Table 6.3 shows the complex pattern of Koch funding received by GMU and its associated Foundation, Center, and Institute over a period of 11 years. Conducting a search for the amount donated to GMU would only reveal $2,924,572, but expanding the search to include the GMU Foundation, the Institute for Humane Studies, and the Mercatus Center yields total donations of $109,948,716. The multiple avenues by which funding can enter into a university system should be considered by anyone interested in exploring how much funding a university is actually receiving from a single donor, and how this might be impacting the institution, if at all.

As Ryan Stowers indicated in his remarks at the Koch gathering described above, GMU is critical to building the Koch network and is recognized as welcoming libertarian-leaning law scholars

Table 6.3. Annual and Total Funding for George Mason University from Koch, 2003–2016.

YEAR	GEORGE MASON UNIVERSITY	GEORGE MASON UNIVERSITY FOUNDATION	INSTITUTE FOR HUMANE STUDIES	MERCATUS CENTER	TOTAL
2003		1.9M	15K	27K	1.9M
2006		350K	1.1M	3.9M	5.3M
2007		408K	885K	2.7M	3.9M
2008	2.9M		1.2M	1.1M	5.1M
2009		4.9M	2.5M		7.5M
2010		3.7M	2.2M		5.8M
2011		4.4M	3.7M		8.1M
2012	51.6K	5.5M	3M	11K	8.4M
2013		10.4M	4.1M	14.5M	
2014		11.8M	4.9M		16.8M
2015		13.3M			13.3M
2016		13.3M	5.8 M		19.1M
Total	$2,924,572	$70,166,724	$29,238,492	$7,670,500	$109,948,716

to its Law and Economics Center in the University's Law School and housing many free-market-supporting academics producing scholarship reflecting these positions. For instance, in 2018, GMU economics professor Bryan Caplan published *The Case Against Education: Why the Education System Is a Waste of Time*, which argued against public funds being used to support education (2018). The book was published by Princeton University Press and received positive reviews from the *National Review Online* and endorsements by members of the Independent Institute and the American Enterprise Institute.[7]

Professors and students at GMU, as well as others in the surrounding community, have raised questions about possible restrictions and stipulations on curriculum in university departments with substantial Koch funding (DeSmogBlog, 2014). Over time, GMU faculty and students began to question whether Koch's philanthropic giving was perpetuating a Radical Right ideology in GMU's academic scholarship in the fields of law and economics and breaking traditional norms of academic integrity observed in philanthropic donations to higher education institutions. Due in part to the raised profile of Charles Koch's strategy of ideologically fueled philanthropy provided in Jane Mayer's book *Dark Money* (2016), students and faculty raised questions and demanded transparency in the regulations concerning giving to GMU by foundations, particularly those associated with the wide-reaching and financially robust Koch philanthropy network (DeSmogBlog, 2014).

History of Koch's involvement with George Mason University.

GMU's connection to libertarian billionaire Charles G. Koch has a long and involved history that was recently explored by Nancy MacLean, a professor of history and public policy at Duke University, in her 2017 book *Democracy in Chains: The Deep History of the Radical Right's Stealth Plan for America*. MacLean draws primarily from GMU's archival resources, including the personal papers of James McGill Buchanan. MacLean identifies Buchanan—a political economist, GMU professor, and Nobel Prize winner—as a key architect in the Radical Right's plan to increase the free flow of power and capital to America's ultra-wealthy. MacLean argues that it was Buchanan, upset by racial desegregation of schools as a result of *Brown v. Board of Education*, who developed a plan to wage a counterattack on increasing democratic participation in America during and after the Civil Rights Movement. Buchanan theorized a divide in the

United States between "makers" and "takers," an idea that took hold in ultra-conservative political and philanthropic circles. Many corporations and right-wing organizations were drawn to Buchanan's strategy, but it was Charles G. Koch who provided enough money to enable that strategy to come to life. The John Birch Society, of which Charles Koch was a member and his father, Fred Koch, was a co-founder, shared an anti-civil rights and anti-desegregation stance, citing the Civil Rights Movement as a plot to spread communism in the United States. This membership and history demonstrate the kinship between Charles Koch's political beliefs and the ideology of Buchanan's strategy.[8] Buchanan's ideas, bolstered by Koch's financial support, allowed the libertarian right to gain prominence in the Republican Party and to execute a plan to pass legislation to undermine unions, privatize education, privatize healthcare and Social Security, and make it more difficult for Americans to vote and participate in democratic processes (MacLean, 2017).

In 1978, newly hired GMU President George W. Johnson began fostering an entrepreneur-friendly campus at GMU by actively cultivating relationships between GMU and local CEOs in Fairfax, Virginia. In 1981, GMU's Economics Department recruited Buchanan, then a professor at Virginia Tech. According to MacLean,

> Karen Vaughn, of the George Mason University Economics Department, was stunned that Buchanan would even consider the underfunded and, as she later put it, "spectacularly undistinguished" school. Knowing what a difference a hire like this could make to her department and the university administration, Vaughn discussed it with an ally and then "jumped on the chance." She assured Buchanan that with no "entrenched interest groups to oppose the public choice agenda... they could pretty much run the place." (p. 172)

At GMU, Buchanan's presence and fundraising abilities reportedly brought millions of dollars to the university in the 1980s, including funds from one of Buchanan's long-time funders, the Scaife Family Charitable Trust. The consequences of increased funds to GMU from right-wing philanthropic organizations and the private sector were discussed by MacLean, who wrote:

> Over time, especially with Buchanan's talent for fund-raising with businessmen, the institution found a purpose that it never announced publicly, but which enabled its ambitious administrators to realize their dreams of expansion in a tight-fisted state. The campus—or rather, members of its economics department and law school—created the research and design center of a right-wing political movement determined to undo the modern democratic state. (p. 169)

One example of Buchanan's ideology as a vehicle to undermine modern democratic processes was represented in his attitude toward the passage of the National Voter Registration Act of 1993, espoused later in his life. The legislation, also known as the Motor Voter Act, allowed U.S. citizens to register to vote by mail, when visiting a government agency for public assistance, or when getting a driver's license at their Department of Motor Vehicles. According to MacLean:

> To believers in voting rights, it was a huge achievement. To those who scorned the idea of a broad and inclusive electorate, it was cause for mourning. "We are increasingly enfranchising the illiterate," grumbled Jim Buchanan, "moving rapidly toward electoral reform that will not expect voters to be able to read or follow instructions." (p. 197)

Buchanan's fears of enfranchising the illiterate to participate in the democratic process aligned with many of the espoused ideologies of right-wing philanthropists that he courted.

Once James M. Buchanan came to GMU, Charles Koch called on him to help create what would become the Koch-funded Cato

Institute. Koch also invested millions of dollars in Buchanan's Center of Study for Public Choice, which Buchanan founded at the University of Virginia in 1956, later relocating it to GMU. Buchanan's center envisioned training intellectuals who would fight against federal policies that enforced racial desegregation after *Brown v. Board of Education*. The purpose of the center was to train intellectuals who would populate the intricate network of Koch-funded institutions, supported by a network of additional wealthy donors. These institutions included the Cato Institute, the Heritage Foundation, Citizens for a Sound Economy, Americans for Prosperity, Freedom Works, the Club for Growth, the State Policy Network, the Competitive Enterprise Institute, and many others (MacLean, 2017). These centers would provide the intellectual prowess to change ideas and interpretations of laws and policies and to advise primarily Republican politicians. For instance, many economists who trained at George Mason under Buchanan went on to serve important roles in the Reagan administration, including James C. Miller III, Paul Craig Roberts, and Robert D. Tollison. Other GMU master's degree students obtained jobs at think tanks such as the Koch-funded Cato Institute, the Scaife- and Coors-funded Heritage Foundation, and the American Enterprise Institute. The influence of these centers remains to this day. For instance, the current U.S. Vice President, Mike Pence, is an example of a Republican politician who worked closely with many of these organizations, including the American Legislative Exchange Council (ALEC), an organization committed to the goals and values of these conservative/neoconservative organizations and described in depth in Chapter Five herein. Social scientists Skocpol and Hertel-Fernandez (2016) referred to the Koch network as operating on the scale of a national, yet hidden, political party seeking to overwhelm normal political processes with the intent of disrupting and replacing them.

Another key player in Koch's connection to GMU is Richard Fink, who taught at GMU from 1980 to 1986. Fink graduated from the Austrian economics program at New York University before going to GMU to work with Karen Vaughn and her Austrian Economics forum. While in graduate school, Fink reached out to Koch to fund a small training program that he brought to GMU when he became an assistant professor there (MacLean, 2017). According to MacLean (2017), Fink was a militant advocate for the promotion of Austrian economic principles:

> "We're gonna be like Malcolm X," Fink goaded them. Except where Malcolm X promoted Black Power and pride, the GMU alumni would be "Austrian and proud." He urged that they be "in your face with Austrian economics." (p. 173)

Since then, Fink has served as president of the CKF and the Claude R. Lambe Foundation. He has served on the board of directors of the Mercatus Center and the Institute for Humane Studies, and is the former executive vice president for Koch Industries, Inc. He has served as a board member for the Center for the Study of Public Choice, the Board of Visitors, and the Student Affairs Committee at GMU. Richard Fink and Charles Koch founded the Mercatus Center, an important center that continues to connect Koch to GMU.

The Mercatus Center.

The Mercatus Center was founded by Richard Fink in the late 1970s, originally as the Center for Market Processes at Rutgers University. In the 1980s, the center moved to GMU, where it received millions of dollars in Koch funding, support that continues to this day. In 1999, the name of the think tank was changed to the Mercatus Center, a reference to the Latin word "mercatus," meaning market. According to the Mercatus Center's website, board members include Charles G. Koch; Richard Fink, senior fellow at the F.A. Hayek Program for Advanced Study in Philosophy, Politics, and Economics; Donald J. Boudreaux, president and CEO of the

Institute for Humane Studies; Emily Chamlee-Wright, Holbert L. Harris chair of Economics at GMU and general director of the Mercatus Center; Tyler Cowen, the 75th attorney general of the United States and counselor and policy advisor to President Ronald Reagan; Edwin Meese; and Vernon Smith, Professor Emeritus at GMU and Nobel Prize winner in economics, among others (Mercatus Center, 2018, https://www.mercatus.org/).

Along with its influential and prestigious board members with strong ties to GMU, the Mercatus website purports to be the largest supporter of graduate students at GMU. One way in which the Mercatus Center supports graduate students is through its F.A. Hayek Program for Advanced Study in Politics, Philosophy, and Economics. Four fellowships are offered: a PhD fellowship, an MA fellowship, the Adam Smith Fellowship, and the Bastiat Fellowship. Mercatus offers the Joseph Schumpeter Fellowship for undergraduate students at GMU who are "interested in learning more about political economy." According to GMU professor Peter Boettke,

> The best students in our program find our "economics with attitude" contagious and many have gone on to stellar careers in research and teaching. The one defining characteristic of our program is the open invitation to inquiry that we offer to all who are serious about using economics to study human beings in all walks of life.

Boettke's reference to "economics with attitude" harkens back to Fink's original promotion of an "in your face attitude" about Austrian economics. The words "to all who are serious" in Boettke's quote are a red flag that contradicts the depiction of the program as an "open invitation to inquiry." The catchphrase "economics with attitude" adorns the Mercatus website, along with quotes by F.A. Hayek and research publications on the subjects of Federal Fiscal Policy, Healthcare, Regulation, Technology Policy, Financial Markets, State and Local Policy, Monetary Policy, the Study of American Capitalism, and Trade and Immigration. While the subject lines seem neutral, closer inspection reveals a Radical Right agenda in line with the political ideologies supported by Koch and other conservative donors. For instance, the summary of Federal Fiscal Policy research reads:

> The U.S. budget is on an unsustainable path. Improving the nation's federal and economic outlook will require fundamental reforms to spending—particularly in the largest entitlement programs, the tax system, and the budget process itself. Mercatus fiscal policy research focuses on how the right reforms, applied to these key areas of the federal budget, can put the United States on the path to sustainable growth and increased economic opportunity.

This summary reflects a perspective in line with traditional free-market, capitalist ideas of de-regulating government, rather than promoting research.

The titles of the "research" publications on the Mercatus website provide clues to the organization's focus and what Boettke might have meant when he referred to "using economics to study human beings in all walks of life"—that is, economics that focuses on benefiting the ultra-wealthy. For instance, publication titles include "How Much Federal Spending Can the Rich Buy Us?" by Veronique de Rugy and Justin Levinthal (2018), "What Defines 'the Rich'?" (de Rugy, 2018a), and "Is Tax Reform Already Working?" (de Rugy, 2018b). For instance, de Rugy and Levinthal (2018) argue that taxing the top income earners, or the one percent, would not yield enough revenue to pay for the federal government's spending, and they encourage cuts to government spending as opposed to increased taxes (with no mention of taxing corporations and businesses). The scholars at Mercatus engage in expanding their particular message through the publication of op-ed pieces, blogs, radio, and television appearances. Recent news on the Mercatus Center website promoted the release of the book *Exploring the*

Political Economy and Social Philosophy of James M. Buchanan (Alijica et al., 2018), demonstrating the center's lingering connection to Buchanan's economic philosophy. Mercatus's sister organization, the Institute for Humane Studies (IHS), promotes a similar political philosophy and serves a talent-development pipeline for young libertarians as early as high school, with the support of similar donors with radical ideological leanings. We turn now to a description of IHS's history and activities.

The Institute for Humane Studies.

The Institute for Humane Studies (IHS) was founded in 1961 by F.A. Harper and has been associated with GMU since 1985 (DeSmogBlog, 2014). It has received substantial funding over the years from the Koch Family Foundations and other conservative foundations such as the Carthage Foundation, the Sarah Scaife Foundation, and the Lynde and Harry Bradley Foundation (SourceWatch, 2017), and Charles Koch has played an influential role in directing the organization since the 1960s. The institute's mission is:

> To support the achievement of a free society by discovering and facilitating the development of talented, productive students, scholars and other intellectuals who share a commitment to liberty and who demonstrate the potential to change significantly the current climate of opinion to one more congenial to the principles and practices of freedom.[9]

Like the statements and mission of the Mercatus Center, The IHS mission statement signals its free-market philosophy by using the words "free society," "liberty," and "freedom." However, these terms refer to the freedom of markets without consideration of the potential of unregulated capitalism to allow those with the most capital to gain unrestricted profit without any guaranteed protections of the rights of people with less capital. The IHS's mission fulfills

Buchanan and Koch's strategies for developing future scholars, academics, and policymakers who will go on to promote free-market ideals. The development of this talent pipeline is accomplished through substantial funding in the form of scholarships, seminars, and career assistance to undergraduate and graduate students. According to the *Huffington Post* (Wilkie & Resmovits, 2014), leaked Google documents from the CKF indicated that IHS staff had been involved in offering training and course content for high school teachers under the program "Youth Entrepreneurs" (YE), founded by Charles and Elizabeth Koch in 1991. The YE program used teaching videos identified as misrepresenting facts to align with Koch's political agenda.

The IHS program "Learn Liberty" has produced multiple education videos on libertarian and conservative topics,[10] some of which defend price-gouging and argue that the gender pay gap is a myth, the cost of living is not rising, and the gap between rich and poor is not widening. The YE program is an example of how Charles Koch has attempted to influence young adults to carry on his own espoused ideologies, regardless of historical and scientific facts (Wilkie & Resmovits, 2014). With increased scrutiny placed on the activities of Koch-funded and Koch-organized institutions associated with GMU, concerns about threats to academic freedom at the university have grown in recent years, and resistance from students and faculty has been noted (Strauss, 2014) at various universities, as well as at GMU (Fandos, 2016).

Controversy in naming.

One example of resistance to Koch and other donor influences at GMU surrounded the naming of George Mason's law school. In 2016, GMU announced it would name its law school for the late Supreme Court justice and frequent champion of conservative causes, Antonin Scalia. The name change was initiated and tied to a $10 million gift from the CKF and another $20 million gift from an anonymous conservative donor. The choice to name the Law School for Scalia led to intense criticism directed at the administration and trustees at George Mason, and questions were raised by students, faculty, and politicians who were concerned about whether Koch and other conservative donors were shaping GMU, Virginia's largest public university, to promote their particular brand of radical conservatism (Fandos, 2016).

Significant pressure was exerted on GMU to hold off on accepting the donations and naming the Law School after Scalia, including a Faculty Senate request for more time to review the agreement behind the naming. A letter signed by 140 GMU faculty and staff expressed disapproval of the name change. Comments from the Faculty Senate expressed concern that the agreement required the university to make complicated organizational changes that were unclear, involved the creation of two new centers to be affiliated with the Law School, and committed taxpayer monies to hiring several tenured and senior-level professors, along with an unspecified number of support staff. Faculty argued that redirecting funds like this would impact resources for other important academic programs at George Mason. Resistance to the movement of resources to the Koch-funded centers highlighted GMU's limited, publicly funded financial resources and the low and declining enrollment numbers at the Law School (Flaherty, 2016). Although the stipulation to use taxpayer monies to fund a portion of the law school's program could be seen as a coercive measure to keep limited resources focused on the Law School at George Mason, university president Angel Cabrera argued that naming the law school after Scalia did not signal an endorsement of the former Supreme Court justice's views.

The American Association of University Professors (AAUP) released a statement expressing its strong concern about the renaming of GMU's law school and the terms of the agreement, which would exclude faculty from involvement in decisions related to the college's objectives, the appointment of faculty, and the structure of academic programs (AAUP, 2016). Citing the AAUP's statement regarding donor agreements, a heated debate in the Faculty Senate ensued when faculty demanded that the donor agreements be subjected to a process of further review. Faculty cited a provision in the agreement stipulating that donors be notified if the Law School's dean, Henry N. Butler, were to be replaced, arguing that this could give donors undue leverage regarding faculty hiring practices and thus threaten academic integrity at the institution (Schmidt, 2016). A 1,300-signature petition opposed the name change, arguing that the change and acceptance of donations would harm the University's academic reputation. Despite this resistance, the State Council for Higher Education in Virginia decided that GMU was free to rename the Law School after Scalia, and that the state board had no oversight on the matter (Barakat, 2016a). Although the name was officially changed, and today the school is known as the Antonin Scalia Law School,[11] resistance continues. On April 30, 2018, UnKoch My Campus released hundreds of documents and emails that illuminated ties between the Law School and the conservative and libertarian-leaning Federalist Society for Law and Public Policy Studies[12] (Woolsey, 2018).

Students sue for open public records.

Student resistance grew at GMU in light of the questionable donations and possible strings attached to the renaming of the law school. In 2017, GMU students filed a lawsuit against the University to obtain records related to Koch Foundation donations. The lawsuit was filed after student requests to obtain donor agreement records under the Virginia Freedom of Information Act (FOIA) were denied by the University. The administration argued that the information was not obtainable by Virginia's FOIA because it was the property of the George Mason University Foundation, a private foundation not under government jurisdiction. Such creation of private foundations at various universities has made it harder for students and faculty to monitor private influence over public institutions. Disturbed by this trend, students at GMU formed an advocacy group called Transparent GMU to advocate for transparency in university donor agreements, and other students from GMU joined forces with a national group called UnKoch My Campus, which shares the same goals of transparency surrounding donor agreements involving the Koch Family Foundations (Woolsey, 2018). On November 29, 2017, the Fairfax Circuit Court in Virginia threw out several claims from the students, and an order by Judge John M. Tran declared that the University was entitled to the protected status of Sovereign Immunity.[13] The legal case went to trial in the Fairfax County Circuit Court on April 24, 2018, and, as the judge has not yet made a ruling, is still ongoing.[14] In the next section, we turn to FSU, where the Koch Foundation used similar strategies to further its ideological interests.

The Case of Florida State University

FSU is a large doctoral research university located in Tallahassee, Florida. The case of Koch involvement at FSU began between 2008 and 2009, when the Florida State University Foundation (FSUF) signed a Memorandum of Understanding (MOU) with the CKF wherein the Koch Foundation agreed to bestow $1.5 million on the University over a period of six years. As a part of this agreement, the FSUF agreed that the money would be used to establish two programs: a program for the study of political economy and free enterprise and a program for excellence in economic education. Additionally, FSUF agreed to use the money to create two faculty positions in the Economics Department (Levinthal, 2014). Table 6.4 shows the funding received by FSU and the FSUF from the Koch Family Foundations between 2003 and 2016, according to the CKF's 990 tax filings (Foundation Directory Online, 2018).

As shown in Table 6.4, the donations to FSU and FSUF from the CKF, according to the organizations' tax filings, illustrate that the agreement was upheld and the CKF donated a total of $3,395,823 to FSU between 2007 and 2016.

Table 6.4. Total Funding to FSU from Charles Koch Foundation, 2003–2016.

YEAR	FLORIDA STATE UNIVERSITY	FLORIDA STATE UNIVERSITY FOUNDATION	TOTAL
2003			-
2006			-
2007	50,000		50,000
2008			-
2009	289,150		289,150
2010	350,544		350,544
2011	123,765	250,000	373,765
2012	297,341		297,341
2013	358,140		358,140
2014	626,247		626,247
2015	4,500	42,000	46,500
2016	185,000	819,136	1,004,136
Total	$2,284,687	$1,111,272	$ 3,395,823

On the surface, nothing about the donor agreements between FSU and the CKF appeared to be out of step with standard philanthropic giving to a university. However, in the years following the agreement, after observing what was happening in the Economics Department and learning more about the profile of the Koch brothers' ideologically guided philanthropic giving, faculty at FSU began to ask questions about possible strings attached that afforded the Kochs' excess influence on curriculum and hiring. Through this process of questioning, speaking out, and investigative journalism, the details about the strings attached to the CKF's giving to FSU were brought to the attention of the public, revealing that the agreement was not as typical or innocent as once believed (Levinthal, 2014; Strauss, 2014).

Seeking a return on investment through strings attached.

In 2012, Professors Kent S. Miller and Ray Bellamy wrote an op-ed piece for the *Tallahassee Democrat* (Miller & Bellamy, 2012) that detailed investigative journalist Jane Mayer's 2010 profile on the ideologically guided philanthropy of the Koch brothers, David and Charles, for *The New Yorker*. The article played a significant part in raising awareness about the Kochs and exploring the motivations behind their philanthropic giving to universities (Mayer, 2010). The two professors were the first to speak out about the CKF's gifts to the Economics Department at FSU, and soon the story was picked up by the *Tampa Bay Times*. Further reports revealed the details of the possible strings attached written into the language of the MOU between the FSUF and the CKF, showing how the CKF attempted to replicate the business world's idea of gaining "a return on investment" in the sphere of higher education.

Close inspection of the MOU revealed that the CKF attempted to forge agreements that would allow it to exert undue control on faculty hiring, evaluation, and curriculum development in the period 2008–2009 (Chandler, 2011). As Dan Berret argued in a piece for *Inside Higher Education* (2011), the Kochs' attempts to exert influence over personnel matters exceeded the norms of typical donor involvement, which tend not to go beyond designating an area of study or suggesting a name for a chair or program. In terms of faculty hiring, the Memorandum of Understanding (MOU) for the Koch donations at FSU allowed the Foundation to have unprecedented say and input into the process of hiring faculty. Specifically, the agreement stated that the hiring process of the two professors using Koch money would be conducted by a three-person advisory board, with two FSU representatives—not necessarily faculty members—and one CKF foundation representative. According to the

MOU, the three-person advisory board would have to unanimously agree on hiring suggestions. In addition to one-third representation on the advisory board, this gave the Koch representative veto power over any potential candidate. Another provision allowed Koch representatives to participate in the evaluation of the professors' job performance, which was against FSU policy and was allegedly never put into practice, according to a report released by FSU faculty (Chandler, 2011).

Another section of the MOU stipulated that the Koch donations be used to support the creation of a new economics course called "Morals and Ethics," which listed libertarian novelist Ayn Rand's *Atlas Shrugged*, as well as Murray Rothbard's *The Ethics of Liberty*, as required textbooks (FSU Progress Coalition–UnKoch My Campus, 2017). According to an official 2011 FSU faculty report (as cited in Chandler, 2011), the course was changed to "Market Ethics," and Rand's materials were moved to a supplementary readings list on the syllabus (Chandler, 2011). The "Market Ethics" course was originally created through the BB&T Program of Free Enterprise, and two "Professor of Free Enterprise" positions were created to promote the free enterprise curriculum, a new speaker series, and the new economics course. The Department of Finance hired Dr. William Christiansen, and the Department of Economics hired Dr. Bruce Benson to serve in these positions. Bruce Benson would go on to become a key player in the CKF donor agreement (FSU Progress Coalition–UnKoch My Campus, 2017), as detailed below.

Bruce Benson, a free-market libertarian, was the chair of FSU's Economics Department at the time of the 2008–2009 CKF donor agreement (Pilkington, 2014). Internal memos and documents from Benson dating back to 2007 were leaked in 2014 by Dave Levinthal of the Center for Public Integrity and revealed Benson to be deeply involved in, and knowledgeable about, the Koch donation and the constraints that came with the foundation's philanthropic giving. For instance, in a memo dated November 2007, Benson wrote that the CKF would not "give us money to hire anyone we want and fund any graduate student that we choose. There are constraints." And later in the memo, he wrote: "Koch cannot tell a university who to hire, but they are going to try and make sure, through contractual terms and monitoring, that people hired are [to] be consistent with 'donor intent.'" In another email of November 2007, Benson asked CKF officials to review his correspondence with FSU associates about the potential for Koch funding (Levinthal, 2014). Additional documents, memos, and records released in 2017 showed that the MOU with the CKF was drafted jointly by a CKF employee and Matt Brown, Bruce Benson's doctoral student. The original Faculty Senate investigation report found that Brown helped negotiate $105,000 for Benson to stay on as the department chair of Economics, which the original Faculty Senate report, before it was rewritten and released to the public, called "egregious." In a 2007 memo, Benson wrote about how the $105,000 was payment to incentivize him to remain in the department chair position:

> I also told the Koch representatives that I did not intend to stay on as chair after the current three-year term. However, Koch has indicated that they would not be willing to commit the proposed level of funding if I do not continue to serve as chair until the proposal is implemented. They are willing to help induce me to do so and this line item reflects that effort. (FSU Progress Coalition–UnKoch My Campus, 2017, p. 162)

Although the payment was taken off the negotiation table and Benson continued as department chair despite this fact (Levinthal, 2014), Benson was eventually forced to step down as chair, with FSU President Eric Barron calling the incident a "clear conflict of interest" (FSU Progress Coalition–UnKoch My Campus, 2017, p. 163). According to the FSU Progress Coalition–UnKoch My Campus report (2017), Benson continued to receive Koch Foundation funding as of April 4, 2016. Further, Dr. Bruce Benson and Dr. Matt Brown have continued their professional relationship, serving as co-panelists at a meeting of the Association of Private Enterprise Education in Las Vegas, Nevada.

These internal memos from Benson illustrate how the Koch-funded talent pipeline influenced the development of the Koch MOU with FSU. These documents and revelations were carefully hidden and may never have come to light if not for resistance put up by students, faculty, and alumni at FSU, and the careful research and activism that they engaged in to push back against threats to academic integrity in Florida.

Resistance.

In 2011, a liberal advocacy group called Progress Florida helped gather 9,000 petition signatures against the FSU agreement with the CKF, and 1,000 of the signatures were individuals with ties to FSU (Chandler, 2011). This pressure culminated in a university-led investigation by FSU faculty at the request of FSU's then-president Eric Barron, who asked that the group review the CK foundation arrangements for any impropriety. The FSU faculty report, released in 2011, claimed that FSU had done nothing wrong in allowing the Koch Foundation's input into the hiring of the two professors. The report concluded that the faculty selected candidates they wanted to work with, but the report did acknowledge that the language of the agreement raised the possibility that Koch and other private donors could exert more influence on hiring and course development than intended. Ultimately, the faculty review suggested that the course on "Market Ethics," with Ayn Rand in the supplemental readings, be suspended and re-submitted for curricular approval at a later date. However, according to the 2017 report by FSU Progress Coalition–UnKoch My Campus, private donors such as Koch and BB&T have created certificate/minor programs with a particular free-market curriculum at FSU, including the Charles Koch-funded Certificate in Markets and Institutions, the BB&T-funded minor in Free Enterprise and Ethics, and the DeVoe L. Moore Center's

Specialized Study in Political Economy (FSU Progress Coalition–UnKoch My Campus, 2017).

According to the FSU Progress Coalition–UnKoch My Campus report (2017), although no majors were created in the Koch/BB&T donor agreements, Koch and BB&T set up graduate fellowships. In the BB&T Program of Free Enterprise Graduate Fellowship, the fellows were required to lead a discussion series on Rand's *Atlas Shrugged*, assist in teaching undergraduate courses in Financial Institutions and Investments, and serve as teaching assistants for the Morals and Ethics in Economics Systems class. The Koch agreement founded an "Economics Club" providing $200 scholarships to host a book club using a book list developed by the Koch-funded program. An "Undergraduate Program" receiving $30,000 per year from the DeVoe L. Moore Center was supported in the agreement and offered $200 scholarships to students for participation in the program. Notably, the faculty advisor of the Economics Club in 2009, Lora Holcombe, was previously employed by the James Madison Institute. A spinoff of the Economics Club called "Students for Healthcare Reform" was also formed. According to its website (as of 2009), the Students for Healthcare Reform "began as a group of free market students" whose "long term goals...are to help write legislation to keep health care in the free market in Florida," despite the fact that legislative initiatives were specifically prohibited by the terms of the Koch MOU (p. 134).

Several reading groups and clubs were sponsored by the DeVoe L. Moore Center, Koch, BB&T, and the Walton Family Foundation, illustrating how foundations, banks, and think tanks could work together to support these programs. A paid reading group called the Freedom Reader's Scholarship Group was funded by the DeVoe L. Moore Center and was hosted by the Economics Club. BB&T sponsored the Students in Free Enterprise Club, now known as Enactus, which has received at least $1,950,000 from the Walton Family Foundation and at least $40,000 from the Koch Family Foundations since 2003. On its website, The Koch-funded Economics Club actively recruits students for graduate programs at GMU, as well as internships for the Koch Foundation and the Institute for Humane Studies. Past Economics Club presidents have ties to the DeVoe L. Moore Center, the Mercatus Center, the FSU College Libertarians, the Charles Koch Institute, the James Madison Institute, and the Institute for Humane Studies, illuminating the "talent pipeline" these Koch-funded clubs aim to develop. During the 2015–2016 school year, the Economics Club hosted Sal Nuzzo of the James Madison Institute, a think tank located in Tallahassee, Florida, and member of the State Policy Network (SPN), further demonstrating how think tanks and individuals associated with the SPN gain campus access through donor-sponsored clubs and spaces (p. 134).

According to a publication by the American Association of University Professors (AAUP), Kent S. Miller and Ray Bellamy reported that they first took their concerns about the Koch Foundation's agreement with FSU to FSU President Eric Barron and to Dean David W. Rasmussen of the College of Social Sciences and Public Policy before writing their op-ed about the Koch involvement at FSU for the *Tallahassee Democrat* in May 2011 (as cited in American Association of University Professors (AAUP), 2016, May 10). According to Miller and Bellamy, their concerns were not taken seriously by Barron and Rasmussen, who saw no problem with the agreement laid out between FSUF and the CKF. Rasmussen reportedly told Miller and Bellamy, and later the *Tampa Bay Times* (May 9, 2011, as cited in American Association of University Professors (AAUP), 2016, May 10), that not taking the money would have been financially irresponsible, regardless of its perceived threat to academic freedom (Miller & Bellamy, 2012). They argued that in 2007, before the agreement was made with the CKF, FSU was struggling for money, as the Florida state budget had reduced its support for higher education institutions to increase support of prisons. Miller and Bellamy argued that the media had misplaced its emphasis on the Kochs' influence on hiring faculty, and instead feared that the most damage would come from the their ability to impact the curriculum at higher education institutions.

Further developments.

In 2013, FSU President Eric Barron and Interim President Garnett Stokes authorized and amended the agreement between FSUF and the Koch Foundation. Then, in 2014, HB115, known by its detractors as the "Koch Cover-Up Bill," was passed by the state legislature. This bill allowed private donors to keep all contracts with universities out of public view by blocking access to meetings between private donors and public university foundations. Under this law, universities were not required to disclose donor funding, and in the future it would be up to whistleblowers to draw attention to any wrongdoing, and only after corrupt contracts have been signed. The bill was championed by both the American Legislative Exchange Council (ALEC), an organization discussed in depth in Chapter Six, and the Koch-funded Americans for Prosperity, and its passage marked a new age of dark money coming to FSU and other higher education institutions in the state of Florida (Wilson, Lakey, Joseph, & Schultz, 2014).

Although they were unsuccessful in stopping the Florida Senate from passing into law the "Koch Cover-Up Bill," significant numbers of students and faculty organized protests and other resistance efforts aimed at preventing this erosion of donor transparency in public universities (Kotch, 2016; Wilson et al., 2014). In 2014, representatives from student organizations such as the FSU Progress Coalition, UFF-FSU Graduate Assistants United, the Tallahassee Dream Defenders, and the Tallahassee Students for a Democratic Society demanded that the selection of FSU's next president be independent of corporate influence and called for a restructuring of the Presidential Search Advisory Committee (PSAC) to include one-third student representation. The PSAC was chaired by Allan Bense, an appointee of Florida Governor Rick Scott. Bense was also a member of the board of directors of the Koch-funded, SPN-affiliated James Madison Institute, which had been instrumental in implementing the 2008 contract between CKF and FSUF. Bense's PSAC was comprised of 26% faculty-student representation and 64% corporate and political interests.

Many of the members of Bense's PSAC had direct ties to the ALEC and Koch-funded institutes (Wilson et al., 2014). Along with 14 other non-academic members, Bense voted to accept businessman and Republican State Senator John Thrasher as the sole candidate for consideration, a former businessman who violated ethics laws twice while senator and who voted to cut funding to higher education in Florida (Kotch, 2016). Thrasher, who voted for the "Koch Cover-Up Bill," was also the chair of Governor Rick Scott's re-election campaign, which received donations from Koch foundations (Kotch, 2016; Wilson et al., 2014). Thrasher's personal political campaigns received $3,000 from Koch Industries over three election cycles, and he was named Legislator of the Year by the Koch-supported ALEC in 1998 (Kotch, 2016). The connections between individuals, institutions, and organizations reveal an entrenched network funded by the Koch Foundation in the selection of FSU's president. Despite protests by student and faculty organizations and the presence of three other candidates whom many viewed as more qualified to serve as the University's president, John Thrasher became president of FSU on November 10, 2014. (As of June 2018, he continued to hold that position.)

In the spring of 2017 a joint report, *A Case Study in Academic Crime: The Charles Koch Foundation at Florida State University*, was released by the FSU Progress Coalition and UnKoch My Campus. This report revealed further details about how the CKF bought academic influence at Florida State. The findings of the report are based on the work of students, faculty, and alumni of FSU and include evidence drawn from the University's public records and the colleges and departments involved, as well as hundreds of pages of documents and correspondence generated by student record requests between 2014 and 2016. The report provides evidence that, contrary to statements made by FSU officials, the Koch Foundation and partner donors were granted undue influence in an agreement violating academic freedom, faculty governance, the faculty's collective bargaining agreement, and departmental and university donor policies. Further, the report revealed that although some wrongdoing was revealed in the 2011 Faculty Senate investigation, many key findings and recommendations were omitted from the public report, including descriptions of "threats," "an atmosphere of intimidation," and conflicts of interest surrounding the agreement between CKF and FSU, and concerns about Koch and BB&T graduate fellowships that allowed a Koch-appointed advisory board to screen the dissertation topics of fellows. *A Case Study in Academic Crime* (FSU Progress Coalition–UnKoch My Campus, 2017) found that a second Faculty Senate report produced in 2014 lacked rigor, lacked sources and findings, and was essentially a one-paragraph press statement. Finally, this study argued that the influence of Koch at FSU has expanded to include an increase in donations to undergraduate programs and the creation of two centers, the L. Charles Hinton Center and the Project on Accountable Justice, both with ties to the Koch-funded conservative State Policy Network (SPN), both of which were not subjected to faculty review or approval. These Koch Foundation activities at FSU provide an example of how Koch and its donor partners have attempted to buy legitimacy for their ideologies by associating themselves with the academic credibility and power that come from a research university and ultimately influence public policy in ways that further their ideological interests (FSU Progress Coalition–UnKoch My Campus, 2017).

Since Thrasher became president of FSU, the University has removed a previous requirement guaranteeing that gifts of over $25,000 to the University include a formal, written gift agreement (Kotch, 2016; Zeballos, 2015). In removing this safeguard, it has become increasingly difficult, if not impossible, to identify violations and threats to academic integrity such as those brought to light in the case of the $1.5 million agreement between CKF and FSUF in 2008–2009. Despite significant activism on the part of students, faculty, and concerned citizens that challenged potential threats to academic integrity in the process of philanthropic giving at FSU, holding the University accountable will require persistent vigilance on the part of those groups. Given FSU's history, Thrasher's choice to eliminate formal, written agreements regarding gifts to the University in excess of $25,000 begs the question: Why hide the terms of agreements and MOUs around philanthropic giving at a university if no wrongdoing or shameful action is occurring? This pattern of hiding the terms under which money is given to higher education institutions and making it more difficult to identify donors and their influence fits into a larger strategy that has been enacted by conservative and Koch-related foundations for decades. According to the nonprofit UnKoch My Campus, the case at FSU is not unique (2017). We turn next to a recent example of the Kochs' influence in higher education in the case of WCU.

The Case of Western Carolina University

The story of the Koch Foundation's involvement at WCU begins with Professor Ed Lopez, WCU's BB&T Distinguished Professor of Capitalism and Research Fellow at the Independent Institute, a free-market think tank. He earned his Ph.D. in economics in 1997 at GMU, where he was a Mercatus Center Ph.D. Fellow. In 2012, Lopez was hired through a BB&T Foundation grant of $1 million with the stipulation that he teach Ayn Rand's *Atlas Shrugged*, considered the Bible of libertarian economic philosophy (Vegan Body Project, 2016). Initially, *Atlas Shrugged* was to be required reading in College of Business courses, and the grant required a copy of the book to be given to all business majors in their junior year. This incursion into the academic program was met with faculty pushback and resulted in the creation of *Policy 104*, which states:

> If a proposed gift has curricular implications, that is, if it contains any restrictions, conditions, implications, and/or makes suggestions with regard to academic content, the Chancellor, or his/her designee, will immediately be

informed and will inform Legal Counsel. The Chancellor, or his/her designee, will then appoint an ad hoc committee of five faculty members to review the curricular implications of the gift and to make specific recommendations regarding the acceptability of such implications.

The policy further stipulates that the committee be composed of a faculty member from the affected department, a member of the affected college's curriculum committee, and two from curriculum committees in other academic units. Additionally, the committee is to be led by the chair of the Faculty Senate or his/her designee as a voting member of the committee. The ad hoc committee then makes recommendations to the chancellor of the University regarding any implications the gift poses to the curriculum, as well as the need for further review or modification of the proposed funding agreement (Vegan Body Project, 2016).

Lopez has been affiliated with other Koch-funded organizations, including the Bastiat Society, the Public Choice Society, the Association for Private Enterprise Education, and the John Locke Foundation. SourceWatch reported that his "2012 speaking engagements were hosted by Koch supported university departments and think tanks" (2016).

Table 6.5 shows the total funding that WCU received from the CKF between 2003 and 2015, according to the most recent CKF tax filings. While Table 6.5 reveals small donations that increase incrementally, records do not yet show the results of more recent donor agreements between WCU and the CKF. However, records indicate that $378,000 was given in 2016, the beginning of an incremental $2 million agreement struck in 2015 that will unfold over the next five years to establish a Center for the Study of Free Enterprise.

When the proposed gift from CKF of $2 million to establish a Center for the Study of Free Enterprise was announced in October 2015, faculty at WCU immediately raised questions about the need for the center, the political ideology of the donor, and the process

Table 6.5. Funding to WCU from Charles Koch Foundation, 2009–2016.

YEAR	WESTERN CAROLINA UNIVERSITY
2009	$12,000
2010	–
2011	$12,000
2012	$14,000
2013	$12,000
2014	$26,500
2015	–
2016	$378,000
Total	$454,500

around the decision to create the center. On October 28, 2015, the Faculty Senate debated a draft Position Statement on the Proposed Center for the Study of Free Enterprise (Economics). Concerns expressed included (a) the need for the Center, especially since there was no economics major at WCU; (b) the absence of peer review; (c) constraints on academic freedom; (d) the long-term cost of the Center to the University; and (e) the reputational costs to the University. In reference to the cost to the University, it was argued that the match would come from two existing faculty lines in the business school that would then be named to the Center, so it would not be new money. However, in another article using email exchanges between Lopez and the Koch Foundations as sources, it was stated that two additional professors would be hired for the center and that Lopez had already allowed the CKF to review the position announcements before they were posted.

The faculty were not convinced. Professor David McCord, chair of the Faculty Senate, reported faculty concerns that the center would cost WCU $1.4 million and stated, "We aren't convinced there is no extra cost burden on the university" (Johnson, 2016). The Faculty Senate Position Statement argued:

> The Charles Koch Foundation has previously set forth explicit expectations in line with their political views in exchange for monetary gifts to universities, thereby constraining academic freedom by influencing and interfering with the development of new knowledge [long statement between here].... Furthermore, any research conclusions consistent with the Foundation's ideological perspective may be considered fruit from the poisoned tree, and therefore dismissed by reputable scientific communities.

The vote on this position statement within the Faculty Senate was 24 endorsing the statement and 2 not endorsing. On the proposal to establish the Center for the Study of Free Enterprise, the vote was 21 opposing, 3 in favor, and 4 neither supporting nor opposing. Professor Bruce Henderson, a WCU psychology professor, commented on the implications of the Koch donations to the larger university community:

> Here, a tiny, unrepresentative portion of the university faculty has decided on a strategic direction that has major consequences for the university, not in discussion with the rest of the faculty, but with an outside group with a decidedly biased perspective. To my amazement, the administration bought it. That, in my experience, is extraordinary. The university faculty has been left out of the discussions and the Koch Foundation and Dr. Lopez are clearly the beneficiaries of the decisions that have been made. The process was off the rails. (Johnson, 2016)

From Ed Lopez's perspective, "The mission of the center as proposed is to conduct sound research. Engaging in abstract research, it plays a role of guiding the subsequent discussion among the intellectual class and ultimately among the political debate. It can provide important input."

On November 20, 2015, despite the Faculty Senate's Position Statement, Provost Alison Morrison-Shetlar recommended that WCU move forward with the Center for the Study of Free Enterprise. In response to the faculty resolution, Provost Morrison-Shetlar stated: "Their resolution was based on alleged academic freedom restrictions and curricular control." She, WCU Chancellor David Belcher, and Lopez pledged that that wouldn't be the case. In early December 2015, the University's Board of Trustees unanimously endorsed the creation of the center. One trustee, Bryant Kinney, stated: "Free enterprise is how we do business in this country. It is what makes our county great" (Johnson, 2016).

This approval by the trustees is particularly interesting given the context at the system level where, in 2015, the UNC Board of Governors reviewed all centers across the system and voted to close three other centers: a privately funded Center on Poverty, Work and Opportunity at UNC Chapel Hill, the Institute for Civic Engagement and Social Change at North Carolina Central University, and the Center for Biodiversity at East Carolina University. All three were criticized for having liberal agendas (Johnson, 2016).

In response to faculty resistance to the proposal, Jay Schalin of the John William Pope Center for Higher Education Policy in North Carolina (now called the James G. Martin Center for Academic Renewal), who also has ties to the CKF, submitted an open records request for emails of professors critical of the center. (These events were related in an online article by WCU Professor Laura Wright, a target of the request.) Schalin is the author of an article, "Faculty Hiring Needs Proper Checks and Balances," (Johnson, 2016).

On December 16, 2015, due to overwhelming faculty resistance to the proposed center, WCU Chancellor David Belcher announced that he would use Policy 104 to trigger a review of the center and its implications for the academic curriculum. He stated:

"In this case, because there are many concerns that the gift might result in an infringement of academic freedom, I am going to go ahead and involve an ad hoc committee just to assure and reassure people. Because there is so much concern about this I will appoint an ad hoc review committee and let them be involved." Subsequently, a "blue ribbon" committee was selected and began its work in February 2016.

Interestingly, throughout this process there was no formal, written gift agreement from the Koch Foundation. The proposed center was a creation of Lopez communicating informally with the CKF, as well as through a visit from two CKF representatives in the fall of 2015. According to newspaper accounts, Lopez benefited from the establishment of the Center as director and would receive an additional $45,000 (funded with Koch money) over his base salary of $136,000 to move his 10-month position to a 12-month position. In addition, the Center would receive $128,000 a year in operational funds from Koch monies to support student and faculty research and travel to conferences, and an additional $550,000 a year in salaries and staff support ($250,000 from existing WCU faculty positions and $300,000 in salaries and staffing from Koch money). According to *Smoky Mountain News* (SMN), Lopez had previously received annual funding of $15,000 in Koch funds to support a Free Enterprise student club to take students to conferences and to bring in speakers, for which students earned extra credit for attendance. Lopez used these activities to establish WCU as fertile ground for further Koch funding.

A January 20, 2016, a *Smoky Mountain News* article based on a public records request of strategy documents between Lopez and the Koch Foundation reported that Lopez aimed to fill the faculty positions with professors who supported conservative economic theory with the goal of making "WCU a hub for the promotion of the free enterprise school of thought, a socio-economic philosophy rooted in conservative principles" (Johnson, 2016). The article described the idea of "clusters" or "groupings of universities in a geographic region that also have Koch-funded free enterprise activities," where "professors could serve as 'thought leaders' for the advancement of free enterprise ideals." This list of deliverables sent to the CKF by Lopez highlighted the cultivation of students in the free enterprise discipline, including developing a "pipeline of students" exposed to free enterprise teachings and cultivating students' long-term interest and participation in the larger community of free enterprise scholars, implementers, activists and related professions. After summarizing the backgrounds of the WCU economics faculty in a July 27, 2015, memo to Andrew Gillin of the CKF, Lopez described a strategy for free enterprise faculty hires, establishing an economics major at the institution, and expanding economics course offerings to achieve the following:

> Establish WCU as a respected authority in producing sound research and policy analysis for North Carolina, the region, and nationally. Establish WCU as a hub of free enterprise idea entrepreneurs, with productive links to individual scholars and program builders at UNC-Charlotte, Johnson & Wales, Wake Forest, Winston-Salem State, College of Charleston, Coastal Carolina, UNC-Wilmington, Fayetteville State, Berry College, and others to form a regional cluster. (Strategy Document from Dr. Ed Lopez to the Koch Foundation [Johnson, 2016])

As of March 31, 2016, no grant agreement had been made public; SourceWatch then reported that the WCU general counsel was drafting an agreement with the CKF (2016).

On September 18, 2016, the ad hoc committee presented its findings to Chancellor Belcher with a recommendation to oversee structure and process for establishing a permanent advisory board (with assurances that such board reflect interdisciplinary membership with faculty members from other colleges). The board was to be appointed by the Faculty Senate, which would consist of the chair of Institutional Review Board (IRB), an administrator from the Office of Research Administration, a member of the Library faculty, an administrator from the Office of the Provost, and two faculty members and the dean of the College of Business (Source-Watch, 2016).

Lopez was authorized to revise his proposal based on recommendations and to request $2 million in seed money for a five-year period to support the center. On September 22, 2016, WCU received a Koch gift of $1.8 million to launch the Center for the Study of Free Enterprise. An article detailing more information about the center's Speaker's Series provided the following descriptions:

> In the Center's information on the Speaker's Series, a speaker from the Cato Institute, Robert A. Levy (chair) "will contrast discrimination by private parties and discrimination by governments, and emphasize the argument of why private parties should not be required to perform expressive acts that violate their beliefs," Lopez said. "In addition, WCU's Todd Collins, Steed Distinguished Professor in Public Policy and director of the university's Public Policy Institute, will emphasize arguments for the appropriate role of governments in assuring equal access and treatment," Lopez said.[15]

While the Koch Foundation's overall funding to WCU (see Table 6.5) has been more recent and less than that of either GMU or FSU, it illustrates Koch's continued efforts, particularly in southeastern institutions, to advance a network of conservative, free-market ideologues. One consistent thread throughout the case studies described above is their connection to BB&T's assistance to regional programs that support professorships, centers, and other programs focused on the study of capitalism. Table 6.6 illustrates the ways in which the BB&T Foundation worked in conjunction with Koch and other corporate funders to further the same ideological influences on the curriculum at institutions in North Carolina, the corporation's home state, and across the southeast, primarily public and private institutions facing decreased state and endowment funding.

Table 6.6. Examples of BB&T Program of Free Enterprise.

NAME	INSTITUTION	UNIT/DIRECTOR	PROGRAMS	ABOUT
The BB&T Center for Free Enterprise	Florida State University	Colleges of Business and Social Sciences (joint), Dr. Bill Christiansen, Director	Support for professorship to develop and promote free enterprise curriculum, minor program in Free Enterprise and Ethics, 4 doctoral fellowships	
The BB&T Center for Free Enterprise Education (Est. 2009)	Barton College, Wilson, NC		Lecture series; workshops for teachers; course called "Capitalism: Implications and Applications"	Featuring lectures from key figures in business, the BB&T Center for Free Enterprise Education gives our students the opportunity to meet and learn from prominent leaders in free enterprise.
The BB&T Scholar Program	Wingate University, Hendersonville, NC	Dr. Peter M. Frank	Student scholarships of $2,000, renewed annually for full-time students who minor in economics.	The purpose of the BB&T Scholar Program is to assist students in the intellectual pursuit of understanding the foundations of free enterprise. BB&T Scholars are economics minors who study the market process and the American capitalist system

BB&T Program on the Moral Foundations of Free Enterprise	Jesse Helms Center, Wingate University	Dr. Peter M. Franks	Lecture series on capitalism and other economics-based topics; Jesse Helms Fellowships (est. 2010).	The Jesse Helms Center exists to promote our nation's founding principles that Senator Jesse Helms advanced throughout his career: to become one of our nation's leading advocates of free enterprise and traditional American values through education, public policy promotion, and historical preservation.
BB&T Program for the Study of Capitalism (est. 2003)	University of Kentucky, Lexington, Kentucky	John H. Schnatter Institute for the Study of Free Enterprise (est. 2015 with $8 million gift from John H. Schnatter Family Foundation of Papa John's Pizza and $4 million from the CKF) in the Gatton College of Business & Economics; John Garen, BB&T Director and Professor for the Study of Capitalism	Supports faculty research funding, open discussions with undergraduate and graduate students, and public events.	The John H. Schnatter Institute for the Study of Free Enterprise is dedicated to understanding the role that markets play in the economy and in society. The Institute's mission is to generate intellectually rigorous research and an open dialogue to discover and understand how free enterprise affects peoples' lives and the well-being of society.

In his article in the *Journal of Academic Ethics*, "BB&T, *Atlas Shrugged*, and the Ethics of Corporation Influence on College Curricula," Beets (2015) details how BB&T funded grants averaging $1.2 million to more than 60 colleges and universities in the United States. The grant agreements stipulated "the creation of faculty positions, library reading rooms, designated capitalism centers, speaker series, scholarships, and the distribution of free student copies of *Atlas Shrugged*" (p. 311). According to Beets, the BB&T Moral Foundations Programs overlapped Koch funding at 42 institutions, and both BB&T and Koch were supporters of the Ayn Rand Institute. Under the leadership of John Allison, then president and CEO, The BB&T Foundation donated several million dollars for a Moral Foundations of Capitalism (MFOC) Program. Allison viewed colleges and universities as controlled by the left, with "many defenders of communism on university campuses" (2013, p. 233), and believed that these institutions needed to be recaptured (Allison, 2013; Beets, 2015). From 2002 to 2012, donations to 60 colleges and universities varied, with amounts ranging from $150,000 (Shenandoah University) to $4.9 million (Clemson University). Grants averaging over $1.2 million per school required the establishment of a Moral Foundations of Capitalism program that included readings consistent with Allison's free-market ideology and included Ayn Rand's *Atlas Shrugged*, a novel given to bank employees (Beets, 2015).

To illustrate the requirements of BB&T donor funding, Beets included two letters of agreement in his article's appendix, one between BB&T and the University of North Carolina at Charlotte, and the other with FSU. After retiring from BB&T in 2008, Allison served as president and CEO of the Cato Institute, a think tank "dedicated to the principles of individual liberty, limited government, free markets and peace" (www.cato.org), from 2012 to 2015. In recent years, BB&T discontinued its funding of the Moral Foundations of Capitalism program and established BB&T Financial Foundations, an online program designed to promote financial knowledge by way of short tutorials for high school students and adults.[16]

In response to increased media attention to and public awareness of BB&T's Moral Foundations of Capitalism, faculty and student resistance has grown. For example, in response to the BB&T programs, Meredith College in Raleigh, North Carolina, rejected a $420,000 Moral Foundations of Capitalism (MFOC) grant in 2006 by a faculty vote of 54–34 (*Inside Higher Ed*, October 16, 2015). In addition, at Auburn University in Alabama in 2009, a university curriculum committee turned down $1.5 million in BB&T funding (Flaherty, 2015). The grounds on which faculty protested BB&T contracts with universities was summarized by Beets (2015):

> While the concerns expressed by faculty and students were many and varied, several of the concerns can be synthesized to five: (1) that a non-faculty entity could influence the curriculum and thereby threaten academic freedom, (2) that the influencing party was offering payments of hundreds of thousands or millions of dollars in quid pro quo arrangements thereby clouding the judgment of some administrators and faculty, (3) that the author whose work is promoted in the quid pro quo arrangement would probably not be included in the curriculum without the funding, (4) that the purpose of the arrangement was to promote a specific corporation-sponsored ideology, and (5) that there was an intentional absence of transparency between those university officials who agreed to the MFOC contracts and the remainder of the university community. (p. 329)

We now turn to a summary of the specific strategies used by the CKF to influence the curricula on college and university campuses, the ways in which these efforts have been successfully resisted, and suggestions for faculty, students, and other

Table 6.7. Koch-Funded Universities and Colleges with Total Funding over $1 Million, 2003–2016.

RECIPIENTS	2003	2006	2007	2008	2009	2010	2011	2012	2013	2014	2015	2016	GRAND TOTAL	TOTAL FOR INST.
George Mason University*	$1.9M	$350K	$408K	$2.8M	$4.9M	$3.7M	$4.4M	$5.5M	$10.4M	$11.8M	$13.2M	$13.3M	$73M	
George Mason Environmental Law Clinic										$13K	$2.9K		$16K	
Institute for Humane Studies	$15K	$1M	$885K	$1.1M	$2.5M	$2.15M	$3.7M	$2.9M	$4M	$4.9M		$5.8M	$28.8M	
Mercatus Center	$27K	$3.9M	$2.7M	$1M				$11K					$7.7M	
TOTAL GMU														$109.5M
Florida State University*			$50K	$89K	$289K	$350K	$373K	$297K	$358K	$626K	$46.5K	$1M	$3.4M	$3.4M
Utah State University*			$32.5K		$172K	$170K	$205K	$170K	$145K	$65K	$1M	$288K	$2.3M	$2.3M

West Virginia University*	$15K	$155K		$200K	$272K	$283K	$1183K		$239K	$258K	$462K	$1.9M	$1.9M
University of Texas				$22K	$11K	$17K		$12K	$9K	$1.3M	$114K	$1.5M	$1.5 M
Lindenwood University					$5K		$6K	$13.5K	$10K	$2M	$565K	$2.5M	$2.5M
University of Arizona Foundation				$13.5K	$512K	$200K	$249K	$40K	$23.5K	$117K	$800K	$2.0M	$2.0M
Troy University Foundation					$240K	$240K	$275K	$50K	$298K			$1.1M	$1.1M
Catholic University of America							$8K	$215K	$610K	$212K	$2.1M	$3.1M	$3.1M
Suffolk University		$375K	$97K	$137K	$209K	$110K	$45K	$17K	$5K	$9K		1.01M	1.01M
Clemson University		$52K	$130K	$250K	$250K	$250K	$165K	$140K	$55K	$235K	$420K	1.9M	1.9M
GRAND TOTAL	$1.9M	$5.3M	$4.6M	$5.4M	$8.5M	$7.8M	$9.9M	$9.9M	$15.8M	$19.2M	$22M	$24M	$130.2M	$130.2M

*Includes money to University Foundations

interested individuals should Koch offer to support its programs in your institutions.

Koch Strategies and Resistance Efforts

As demonstrated in this chapter, the CKF, with the support of a network of other wealthy philanthropists, has made a concerted attempt to introduce a conservative, free-market ideology into targeted colleges and universities through efforts to influence the curriculum, hiring practices, and creation of right-leaning centers and institutes. The scope of these efforts is growing as the result of increased funding to 404 U.S. colleges and universities in almost all of the 50 states, including the District of Columbia but excluding Wyoming. Additionally, Koch has funded colleges and universities outside of the United States, including the University of Manchester and King's College London in the UK, Ludwig-Maximillians University in Munich, Germany, and McGill University and the Fraser Institute in Canada. See Table 6.7 for a list of Koch-funded institutions with total funding over $1 million from 2003 to 2016 and Table 6.8 for institutions with Koch funding in amounts ranging from $100,000 to $999,999 during this same time period. The number of such institutions has grown since 2014, when it was reported that 163 colleges and universities in 41 states and the District of Columbia received Koch funding (Levinthal, 2014). In addition to those amounts, another 316 institutions received a total of $7,872,184 in donations under $100,000.

The Koch Foundation and corporate and private foundations collaborating with it use similar strategies to promote their ideological beliefs at both private and public colleges and universities in the United States. As a reminder, these private foundations are approved 501(c)(3) organizations with educational, charitable, and similar purposes, so they qualify for tax exemptions, as we described in Chapter Four. Therefore they can establish foundations with gifts from a family or corporation, then use the foundations

Table 6.8. Koch-Funded Universities and Colleges with Total Funding over $100K but under $1 Million, 2003–2016.

RECIPIENTS	2003	2006	2007	2008	2009	2010	2011	2012	2013	2014	2015	2016	GRAND TOTAL
Brown University				$136K	$147K	$117K	$37.5K	$13K			$378K		$828K
George Washington University						$15K	$91K	$116K	$62K	$60K	$421K	$322K	$1.08M
University of Louisville						$31K		$14K	$20.5K	$18.5K	$621K		$705K
Indiana University*					$10K			$34K	$15K	$292	$231K	$262K	$844K
Georgetown University							$14K				$657K	$545K	$1.2M
University of North Carolina						$5K	$108K	$117K	$12K	$139K		$263K	$643K

Table 6.8 continued on p. 222

Table 6.8 continued from p. 221

RECIPIENTS	2003	2006	2007	2008	2009	2010	2011	2012	2013	2014	2015	2016	GRAND TOTAL
Purdue Research Foundation											$624K	$559K	$1.1M
Florida Southern College									$400K	$200K		$200K	$800K
Creighton University										$300K	$294K		$594K
University of Chicago										$5K	$455K	$156K	$616K
Northwestern University					$200K	$250K			$8.8K			$73K	$532K
Baylor University						$6K			$172K	$12.5K	$254K	$398K	$443.5K
Massachusetts Institute of Technology			$250K			$45.5K	$25K	$25K		$50K	$11K	$104K	$510.5K

Table 6.8 continued on p. 223

Table 6.8 continued from p. 222

RECIPIENTS	2003	2006	2007	2008	2009	2010	2011	2012	2013	2014	2015	2016	GRAND TOTAL
Ohio State University*		$20K	$28.7K	$46.6K	$37.3K	$32.2K		$11K	$130K	$132K		$405.6K	$779.6K
Grove City College							$38.1K	$33K	$34K	$36.5K	$48K	$56.6K	$410.6K
New York University					$9K	$10K	$35.5K	$35.5K	$35.5K	$35.5K	$95K	$580K	$924K
Texas A & M University*							$9K	$16.7K	$253K	$84K	$35.5K		$398.2K
University of Wisconsin*				$19.7K	$32.2K	$13.9K	$7K	$11K	$23.5K	$99K	$173K	$692.3K	$1M
College of Charleston*						$30K	$36.7K	$40K	$52K	$40K	$8K	$84.5K	$343K
Oklahoma State University Foundation*							$36.4K		$69K		$137K	$68.5K	$310.9K

Table 6.8 continued on p. 224

Table 6.8 continued from p. 223

RECIPIENTS	2003	2006	2007	2008	2009	2010	2011	2012	2013	2014	2015	2016	GRAND TOTAL
Auburn University				$300K									$300K
McGill University						$6K	$8K	$10K	$10K	$93K	$126.4K	$107.6K	$360.7K
Hillsdale College				$33K	$28K	$26K	$23.4K	$34K	$32K	$35K	$39K	$70.2K	$321.2K
Brooklyn Law School									$100K	$150K		$150K	$400K
Mississippi State University								$10K	$20K	$22K	$177.3K		$229K
Ohio University*				$75K		$19K	$14K	$41.9K	$50K	$52.2K	$60K		$237.1K
Loyola University*						$20K	$25K	$42K	$42K	$23K		$48K	$275K
Hampden-Sydney College		$25K	$25K	$18.5K	$14K	$16K	$35K	$30.6K	$14K	$21K			$199K

Table 6.8 continued on p. 225

Table 6.8 continued from p. 224

RECIPIENTS	2003	2006	2007	2008	2009	2010	2011	2012	2013	2014	2015	2016	GRAND TOTAL
Beloit College			$40K	$31K	$32K	$32K	$32K	$6K	$4.5K	$7K	$7K	$7K	$198.5K
University of Missouri				$17.5K	$14K	$14K	$34.5K	$27K	$33K	$36K	$11.1K	$10K	$197K
Florida Gulf Coast University*				$16K		$36.2K	$26K	$37.5K	$36K	$42K	$28K		$221.6K
University of Kentucky*						$2K							
Johnson and Wales University								$8K	$33K	$1119.5K	$28K	$473K	$655.5K
Harvard University								$75K	$40K		$170K		$178K
Saint John's University						$22K	$29.5K	$32K	$29.5K	$46.5K	$115K	$772.5K	$935K
											$59.6K		$219.1K

Table 6.8 continued on p. 226

Table 6.8 continued from p. 225

RECIPIENTS	2003	2006	2007	2008	2009	2010	2011	2012	2013	2014	2015	2016	GRAND TOTAL
Claremont McKenna College					$22K	$14K	$14K	$29.4K	$14K	$27K	$27K		$147.4K
Claremont Graduate University										$70K	$75K		$145K
Chapman University					$25K	$40K	$24K	$18K	$15K	$10K		$225K	$357K
University of Georgia Foundation								$3.8K		$9K	$118.3K	$30K	$161.1K
Purdue University										$84K	$46K	$530K	$660K
Michigan State University				$15.4K		$10.6K	$15K	$20K	$22.5K	$20K	$24K		$127.5K

Table 6.8 continued on p. 227

PHILANTHROPY GOES TO COLLEGE

Table 6.8 continued from p. 226

RECIPIENTS	2003	2006	2007	2008	2009	2010	2011	2012	2013	2014	2015	2016	GRAND TOTAL
Duquesne University of the Holy Spirit				$18K	$20K	$17K	$25K	$22K	$23.5K				$125.5K
Berry College			$32K	$10.8K	$12.1K	$9.6K	$15K	$11.9K	$10.8K	$6.8K	$8.6K	$12K	$129.6K
Wake Forest University						$6.8K		$8K	$5K	$87K	$10K	$316.6K	$433.4K
Stanford University										$40K	$75K	$259.7K	$374.7K
The Tower Foundation of San Jose State University				$15K	$19.5K		$25K	$25K		$30K			$114.5K
Trinity College				$20K	$30K	$11.1K	$11.2K	$10K	$7.5K	$13K	$10K	$15K	$127.7K
Azusa Pacific University						$22K	$23.5K	$15K	$15K	$18K	$18K	$25K	$135.5K

Table 6.8 continued on p. 228

Table 6.8 continued from p. 227

RECIPIENTS	2003	2006	2007	2008	2009	2010	2011	2012	2013	2014	2015	2016	GRAND TOTAL
Regent University						$7.5K	$10K	$23K		$45.5K	$25K	$74.6K	$185.6K
Saint Lawrence University			$12K		$10K	$10K	$14K	$15.2K	$15K	$15.3K	$16K		$107.5K
Duke University						$111.5K	$16.3K		$37K	$40K		$185.7K	$290.5K
Mercer University				$16K	$16K	$10.5K		$21.3K	$15.2K	$20.5K	$3K	$19.4K	$121.9K
Metropolitan State University of Denver*				$17K	$12K	$15.4K	$15.5K	$18K	$15K	$15K	$20K		$127.8K
San Jose State University*		$25K	$11.9K			$16.5K					$54K		$107.4K
TOTAL FOR ALL COLLEGES AND UNIVERSITIES	$0	$70K	$399.6K	$1.03M	$828K	$863K	$880.8K	$1.1M	$2.06M	$2.7M	$5.8M	$8.1M	$23.7M

*Includes money to University Foundations

to further causes of their choice, as long as these programs fulfill the IRS requirements for 501(c)(3) status. In the cases described above, the foundations are engaged in giving to specific educational causes. However, in those cases, the agreements made with the institutions were viewed by faculty, students, and administrators as having undue influence in hiring faculty with specific ideological qualifications and through veto power in the search process, as well as undue influence on the curriculum, with specific requirements for readings and lectures that were in keeping with libertarian economic ideologies espoused by Koch (Levinthal, 2014). UnKoch My Campus's report, *Oversteps of Academic Freedom, Faculty Governance, and Academic Integrity*, details six major strategies used by Koch to exert undue influence over academic and administrative decisions, including: (a) contractual control with conditions for donor withdrawal and annual disbursements awarded after compliance with donor's objectives, (b) influence over hiring early in the process, as well as through veto power, (c) influence over programing through curriculum, certificates, majors, minors, and introductory courses, (d) influence over student programming through graduate fellowships and donor-created groups such as reading groups, (e) bypassing transparency and dissent through secret agreements and without faculty knowledge or approval, (f) influence through political activity with academic programming as part of a strategy for policy change and through working with other donors with consistent political agendas.[17]

In this chapter we have described resistance efforts in the three cases highlighted, but there are numerous other institutions where Koch funding was refused, including Suffolk University, the University of Dayton, and Brooklyn College. As we have seen, through faculty governance structures, faculty resisted Koch donations at FSU and WCU. The faculties at other institutions—including Syracuse University and Wake Forest University—have pushed back against undue Koch influence on academics.

Resisting the Gift

Given the reduced state funding of institutions across the United States, it is difficult to turn away significant gifts at the level offered by the Kochs and other wealthy philanthropists. Based on the cases we have detailed here, as well as other resources, the following steps are offered as suggested resistance activities in the event that Koch comes calling at your institution:

1. Become aware of the funding streams into your college or university. Who are the major donors? This information is publicly available through your development office and can be easily accessed through a search of Foundation Center Online, a subscription-based database often available at university libraries and used to identify grantors, grantees, and types of grants. It can be searched for specific grantors, grantees, years, geographic areas, fund amounts, etc.
2. Know the Freedom of Information Act's (FOIA) open records law, or what is commonly referred to as the "sunshine law" in your state, which enables access to public records. For example, in Georgia, the Open Records Law (O.C.G.A. 50-18017) "is meant to provide interested individuals with the public records they are looking for. These documents are open to 'any citizen of this state' and to everybody who is an employee of a nonresident corporation." Use these open records laws to request access to documents such as the Memorandum of Understanding or written agreement entered into by the university with the donor.
3. Become informed about the influence of philanthropy in higher education through online resources and work with groups such as UnKoch My Campus (http://www.unkochmycampus.org/). See the resources noted in Chapter Ten.
4. Use your faculty governance structure, such as the college or university Faculty Senate, to review and organize regarding undue influence over the academic curriculum.

Work with faculty and administrators to establish policies that prohibit any ideological criteria in donor funding agreements.
5. Contact faculty at other institutions who have experienced similar issues with ideological philanthropy.
6. Contact your local and state journalists who cover educational issues, and keep them informed as to the faculty's perspectives and activities.
7. Use social media to support and promote transparency in donor-university agreements and their purposes when undue influence is evident.
8. Use petitions to demonstrate resistance levels to the university administration.

As demonstrated throughout this chapter in the cases of GMU, FSU, and WCU, it was only through the vigilance and collective resistance of faculty, students, alumni, and concerned community members that the nature of Koch agreements with colleges and universities was brought to light. These cases demonstrate how crucial it is to "track the money" and examine the accompanying conditions of donations in order to maintain transparency around philanthropic giving to colleges and universities. The history of neoliberal ideology at work in higher education has led to fewer public resources going into public universities. With fewer funding resources, colleges and universities are more reliant on Big Philanthropy to support their institutions. The work of community members is essential to ensure that college and university communities are aware of and have input into the conditions surrounding funding. For more information and resources on what you can do to track the money at your institution, see Chapter Ten for an extensive list of resources for change and collective resistance. With these resources, we hope that educators and concerned individuals will become knowledgeable about the histories and conditions that may be informing philanthropic giving in education and thus be enabled to make the best choices about when to accept or resist the gift.

Notes

1. http://reclaimdemocracy.org/powell_memo_lewis/
2. https://archive.org/stream/FreedomPartnersLeveragingScienceAndUniversities/Freedom%20Partners%20Leveraging%20Science%20and%20Universities_djvu.txt
3. This recording and transcript of Koch aides discussing education funding strategy with potential donors was provided to the Center for Public Integrity by The Undercurrent, an online program produced by liberal political activists and available at: https://www.publicintegrity.org/2015/10/30/18715/kochs-higher-education-funding-strategy
4. https://www.charleskochfoundation.org/our-giving-and-support/higher-education/
5. http://polluterwatch.org/charles-koch-university-funding-database
6. http://carnegieclassifications.iu.edu/lookup/view_institution.php?unit_id=232186&start_page=lookup.php
7. https://press.princeton.edu/titles/11225.html
8. https://www.prwatch.org/news/2016/01/13017/how-charles-koch-backed-john-birch-society-height-its-attacks-martin-luther-king
9. Institute of Humane Studies, 2018, https://theihs.org/
10. https://theihs.org/learnliberty16/
11. https://law.gmu.edu/
12. http://www.fairfaxtimes.com/articles/gmu-law-school-under-scrutiny-for-possible-federalist-society-ties/article_0e6a6570-5531-11e8-a3a5-9b2db33b86c9.html
13. http://www.splc.org/article/2017/02/students-file-complaint-against-george-mason-university-for-records-on-koch-donations
14. https://www.washingtonpost.com/local/education/george-mason-gets-koch-money-now-this-group-wants-to-know-more/2018/04/24/dfc7ccda-4766-11e8-827e-190efaf1f1ee_story.html?noredirect=on&utm_term=.539e3e048080
15. https://www.jamesgmartin.center/2017/10/faculty-hiring-needs-proper-checks-balances/
16. https://www.bbt.com/education-center/video/financial-foundations-program.page
17. http://www.unkochmycampus.org/introduction/

References

Alijica, P.D., Coyne, C.J., & Haeffele, S. (Eds.). (2018). *Exploring the political economy and social philosophy of James M. Buchanan*. Lanham, MD: Rowman & Littlefield.

Allison, J.A. (2013). *The financial crisis and the free market cure*. New York: McGraw-Hill.

American Association of University Professors (AAUP). (2016, May 10). *AAUP expresses strong concern over renaming GMU law school and issues of shared governance*. Retrieved from https://www.aaup.org/news/aaup-expresses-strong-concern-over-renaming-gmu-law-school-and-issues-shared-governance#.W1tNx9VKiM8

Barakat, M. (2016a, April 1). *George Mason University becomes a favorite of Charles Koch*. Fairfax, VA: Associated Press. Retrieved from http://www.bostonherald.com/news/national/2016/04/george_mason_university_becomes_a_favorite_of_charles_koch

Beets, S.D. (2015). BB&T, *Atlas Shrugged*, and the ethics of corporation influence on college curricula. *Journal of Academic Ethics, 13*(3), 311–344.

Berret, D. (2011, June 28). Not just Florida State. *Inside Higher Education*. Retrieved from https://www.insidehighered.com/news/2011/06/28/not-just-florida-state

Caplan, B.D. (2018). *The case against education: Why the education system is a waste of time and money*. Princeton, NJ: Princeton University Press.

Chandler, J. (2011, July 18). *[Update] FSU faculty approves Koch deal, with caveats*. Tallahassee, FL: Associate Press. Retrieved from http://www.wctv.tv/home/headlines/UPDATE_FSU_Faculty_Senate_Releases_Review_of_Koch_Deal.html

deMarrais, K. (2006). "The haves and the have mores": Fueling a conservative ideological war on public education (or tracking the money). *Educational Studies, 39*(3), 201–240.

de Rugy, V. (2018a, January 19). What defines "the Rich"? *Mercatus Center: George Mason University*. Retrieved from https://www.mercatus.org/publications/what-defines-rich

de Rugy, V. (2018b, January 19). Is tax reform already working? *Mercatus Center: George Mason University*. Retrieved from https://www.mercatus.org/commentary/tax-reform-already-working

de Rugy, V., & Levinthal, J. (2018, January 26). How much federal spending can the rich buy us? *Mercatus Center: George Mason University*. Retrieved from https://www.mercatus.org/publications/how-much-federal-spending-can-rich-buy-us

DeSmogBlog. (2014). *Koch and George Mason University*. [web log]. Retrieved from https://www.desmogblog.com/koch-and-george-mason-university

Fandos, N. (2016, April 28). University in turmoil over Scalia tribute and Koch role. *The New York Times*. Retrieved from https://www.nytimes.com/2016/04/29/us/koch-brothers-antonin-scalia-george-mason-law-school.html

Flaherty, C. (2015, October 16). Banking on curriculum. *Inside Higher Ed*. Retrieved from https://www.insidehighered.com/news/2015/10/16/new-paper-details-extent-bbt-banks-ayn-rand-inspired-grant-program

Flaherty, C. (2016, May 5). George Mason faculty senate asks university to hold off on Koch-funded law school renaming. *Inside Higher Ed*. Retrieved from https://www.insidehighered.com/news/2016/05/05/george-mason-faculty-senate-asks-university-hold-koch-funded-law-school-renaming

Foundation Directory Online. (2018). Retrieved from https://foundationcenter.org

FSU Progress Coalition–UnKoch My Campus. (2017, Spring). A case study in academic crime: The Charles Koch Foundation at Florida State University (a joint report by FSU Progress Coalition and UnKoch My Campus). Retrieved from http://www.unkochmycampus.org/progress-coalition-2017/

George Mason University Office of Institutional Research and Effectiveness. (2017). Factbook. Retrieved from https://irr2.gmu.edu/Factbooks

Johnson, B. (2016, January 20). Koch money at WCU remains under scrutiny. *Smoky Mountain News*. Retrieved from https://www.smokymountainnews.com/archives/item/17027-koch-money-at-wcu-remains-under-scrutiny

Kotch, A. (2016, January 14). Koch influence on Southern schools remains in the spotlight. *Facing South: A Voice for a Changing South*. Retrieved from https://www.facingsouth.org/2016/01/koch-influence-on-southern-schools-remains-in-the-.html

Levinthal, D. (2014, March 27). Inside the Koch brothers' campus crusade: The billionaire industrialists aren't just investing in politicians, but also young hearts and minds. *Center for Public Integrity*. Retrieved from https://www.publicintegrity.org/2014/03/27/14497/inside-koch-brothers-campus-crusade

MacLean, N. (2017). *Democracy in chains: The deep history of the Radical Right's stealth plan for America*. London: Scribe Publications.

Mayer, J. (2010, August 30). Covert operations: The billionaire brothers who are waging a war against Obama. *The New Yorker*. Retrieved from https://www.newyorker.com/magazine/2010/08/30/covert-operations

Mayer, J. (2016). *Dark money: The hidden history of the billionaires behind the rise of the Radical Right*. New York: Anchor Books.

Miller, K. S., & Bellamy, R. (2012, May–June). Fine print, restrictive grants, and academic freedom: The limits to "free" in free-market foundation donations at Florida State University. *American Association of University Professors (AAUP)*. Retrieved from https://www.aaup.org/article/fine-print-restrictive-grants-and-academic-freedom#.W1oN7tVKiM-

Pilkington, E. (2014, September 12). Koch brothers sought say in academic hiring in return for university donation. *The Guardian*. Retrieved from https://www.theguardian.com/world/2014/sep/12/koch-brothers-sought-say-academic-hiring-university-donation

Powell memo (also known as the *Powell manifesto*). (1971.) Retrieved from http://reclaimdemocracy.org/corporate_accountability/powell_memo_lewis.html

Schmidt, P. (2016, May 13). George Mason faculty demands review of agreements with donors. *Chronicle of Higher Education*. Retrieved from https://www.chronicle.com/article/George-Mason-Faculty-Demands/236365

Skocpol, T., & Hertel-Fernandez, A. (2016). *The Koch effect: The impact of a cadre-led network on American politics*. Paper presented at the Inequality Mini-Conference, Southern Political Science Association, San Juan, Puerto Rico, January 8, 2016. Retrieved from https://www.scholarsstrategynetwork.org/sites/default/files/the_koch_effect_for_spsa_w_apps_skocpol_and_hertel-fernandez-corrected_1-4-16_1.pdf

SourceWatch. (2016). Koch and Western Carolina University. Retrieved from https://www.sourcewatch.org/index.php/Koch_and_Western_Carolina_Univers ity
SourceWatch. (2017, August 3). Institute for Humane Studies. *Center for Media and Democracy.* Retrieved from https://www.sourcewatch.org/index.php/Institute_for_Humane_Studies
Strauss, V. (2014, November 7). Charles Koch Foundation's unique definition of "academic freedom." *Washington Post.* Retrieved from https://www.washingtonpost.com/news/answer-sheet/wp/2014/11/07/charles-koch-foundations-unique-definition-of-academic-freedom/?utm_term=.659c0c5d970b
The Vegan Body Project. (2016, February 21). *The Charles Koch Foundation, the Pope Center, Western Carolina University, and my email* [web log]. Retrieved from http://veganbodyproject.blogspot.com/2016/02/the-charles-koch-foundation-pope-center.html
Wilkie, C., & Resmovits, J. (2014, July 21). Koch high: How the Koch brothers are buying their way into the minds of public school students. *Huffington Post.* Retrieved from https://www.huffingtonpost.com/2014/07/16/koch-brothers-education_n_5587577.html
Wilson, R., Lakey, Joseph, R., & Schultz, Z. (2014, August 27). My view: Free FSU search from corporate influence. *Tallahassee Democrat.* Retrieved from https://www.tallahassee.com/story/opinion/columnists/2014/08/27/view-free-fsu-search-corporate-influence/14709875/
Woolsey, A. (2018, May 11). GMU law school under scrutiny for possible Federalist Society ties. *Fairfax County Times.* Retrieved from http://www.fairfaxtimes.com/articles/gmu-law-school-under-scrutiny-for-possible-federalist-society-ties/article_0e6a6570-5531-11e8-a3a5-9b2db33b86c9.html
Zeballos, J. (2015, June 4). Progress Coalition report uncovers alleged violation of university donor policy. *FSU News.* Retrieved from https://www.fsunews.com/story/news/2015/06/04/progress-coalition-report-uncovers-alleged-violation-university-donor-policy/28490341/

Chapter Seven

IDEOLOGICAL AND PHILANTHROPIC BEDFELLOWS: ELEVATING THE INDIVIDUAL OVER THE COLLECTIVE GOOD IN EDUCATION

A myriad of education reforms explicitly reimagine schooling as an individual activity producing individualized commodities rather than a collective effort benefiting the common good. Those reforms include school vouchers, charter schools, homeschooling, alternative teacher certification, and hyper-accountability through standardization. Embedded in each iteration of these school reforms, particularly those centered around notions of school "choice," is the assumption that public schools in the United States have failed our nation's students for decades. The belief in the failure of schools and the subsequent need to reform them has ideological roots in the work of Milton Friedman (1955, 1997, 2002) and anecdotal roots in the launch of Sputnik.

Friedmanism and Sputnik were launched in the 1950s. This belief of public schools as failed social institutions has been prevalent in the national discourse and psyche since that time. The launch of Sputnik signaled new economic and security challenges as well as a national conversation, largely guided by fear, about the need to reform schools in what was then a new post-WWII globalized world. With the Soviets beating the United States in the initial space race, schools became a target for reforms that would, according to the reactionary logic, prepare the current and future generations to compete with the communists economically, scientifically, and militarily. The fact that the United States "won" the space race in the years that followed the launch of Sputnik by being the first to land on the moon played no role in suppressing the myth of failed schools and the purported benefit of reforms. Contrary to mainstream discourse, there was not enough time for the reforms that were put into place as reactionary policy to Sputnik to have played any role in providing the academic and educational insights that fostered the Gemini and Apollo programs. The brilliant engineers, mathematicians, physicians, and astronauts who triumphed in what had become a proxy war of science education were not the result of new reforms and a hyper-focus on science (a precursor to the modern hyper-focus on STEM education). Rather, these remarkable individuals were the result of the era of schooling that reformers claimed had failed.

The mania over reforming education converged with anecdotal "evidence" of school failure and the ideology of Friedmanism in the Reagan administration's release of *A Nation at Risk* (The National Commision on Excellence in Education, 1983). Once again, drawing assumptions about the state of education in the United States through the lens of global warfare and conflict, the policy position document refreshed discursive commitments about the myth of the failed school and the need to inject more accountability. Modern school reforms such as vouchers, charters, homeschooling, alternative teacher certification, and standardized testing are ideologically grounded in Reagan's push to decrease social spending and deregulate governmental control over public sectors, instead turning them over to fundamental free-market idealism. This phenomenon is known colloquially as Reaganomics. President Reagan's Reaganomics "reshaped the contours of public discourse by replacing regulation and assistance with deregulation, free markets, and the interests of the individual, especially the individual as entrepreneur" (Fischer, 2003, p. 25) and, as a result, ushered neoliberal ideology to the forefront of U.S. policy and discourse in the 1980s, while Thatcherism (a neoliberal ideology pushed by the United Kingdom's Margaret Thatcher, and predating Reaganomics) pushed for similar privatization and individualization in Europe. Surprisingly, policies informed by this ideology of reducing governmental influence in public institutions and shifting financial and oversight responsibility onto the individual have been supported not only by Republicans, but also by Democrats. The spread of neoliberal ideology supporting the ideas of meritocracy and individualism has allowed these policies to find support across party lines within the United States.

Meritocracy and Individualism

At its core, neoliberal ideology within education in the United States has sought to replicate social inequity, implement social control, limit the distribution of social and cultural capital, restrict democratic engagement, reduce teaching to a technocratic process, and reduce curriculum to atomized standards that can be assessed for profit with standardized testing (Brewer & Myers, 2015). The employment of this meritocratic ideology specifically relies on dehumanization and stratification that reinforces racial and socioeconomic injustice. The idea of meritocracy within a capitalist economy imagines schools and schooling as a level playing field where a variety of outcomes and the stratification of economic and social rewards are seen as the direct result of the individual work ethic. Further, this conception fails to recognize how schools and schooling are artifacts of systemic economic and racial inequality. Such myopic thinking reinforces and reproduces a population of "haves and have nots" that falls along racial and economic lines and allows reformers from the political left and right to ignore systemic injustice.

While the "mainstream political left" has lent surface-level rhetorical attention to systemic socioeconomic and racial inequality, some notable individuals and organizations who identify with the political left vehemently deny that reforms must start with the foundational causes of inequality and injustice. Rather than addressing the root cause of inequality—such as systemic and targeted poverty and racism—the vast majority of reformers on the political left approach school reform primarily through the lens of individualized meritocracy and "hard work" or "big goals."

The convergence of a shared ideological conception of the purpose of schooling from all points across the political spectrum begins to make sense as we consider the pervasiveness of the myth of the failed school and conceptions of meritocracy and individualization. Our use of the term individualization should not be understood as an individualized or tailored education, but rather as an "everyone for themselves" mantra. The new imaginary of individualization has further reinforced schooling as both a means and end to credentialing (Labaree, 1988, 1997a), which stands in stark contrast to what we might consider an education (Dewey, 1963, 1997). While "rugged individualism" finds its roots firmly within the conservative political ideology, there has been a convergence of support for such reforms by the political right and left. On the face of it, Democrats and neoliberals have fully embraced the myth of meritocracy and the individualization and competition that such a myth necessitates, despite the fact that these political ideologies are historically associated with conservative thought. Similarly, the political right has fully embraced the language and rhetoric of civil rights that has historically been associated with the political left. While both sides of the political spectrum push for identical reforms, both have utilized phrases such as "equity" and "equality" in the process. Democrats—for example, Secretary of Education Arne Duncan, appointed by President Obama—have referred to education as the "civil rights issue of our time" (Gordy, 2010), as have Republicans such as President Donald Trump (Powell, 2017). While each side of the political spectrum has adopted and co-opted ideology and language from the other side, this has not resulted in balancing how these ideologies and language manifest in schools. In short, the adoption of conservative ideology by the left represents a greater overall shift in how we conceptualize and *do* schooling to the political right.

Education Reforms

Education reforms centered on school organization, elevating the individual and "choices," and promoting competition can be seen in homeschooling, charter schools, and school vouchers. Homeschooling has become the *pièce de résistance* in the quiver of those who favor education privatization for the sake of elevating the individual student over the collective good. However, given the relatively small number of homeschooled children in the United States, the practice does not offer much competition to traditional public schools (Ray, 2015). Despite this fact, homeschooling represents the epitome of conceptualizing education as an individualistic good (Brewer & Lubienski, 2017a, 2017b; Lubienski, 2000; Lubienski & Brewer, 2014). In this form of school organization, the individual student is elevated above all other students as the curriculum, teacher focus (often a parent), and support systems center around ensuring the success of one student with little to no regard for the success of other students. In this form of school organization, students and their parents are the ultimate consumers on the free market, with a wide berth of choice among curricula and pedagogical approaches. In this view, curricula can be tailored to individualistic choices, much like shopping at a grocery store. However, this conception of schooling as an individualistic good and a commodity raises significant questions about the types of curriculum taught and not taught at home. Students who are homeschooled may not necessarily learn a curriculum to provide them with a common vocabulary and a common understanding necessary to engage in a collective society.

Homeschooling and school vouchers.

While homeschooling, with its intense focus on the individual, is the epitome of privatized education, school vouchers also reimagine education as an individualistic good and represent the literal transfer of public dollars into private coffers. The logic of school vouchers argues that parents who are dissatisfied with the local public school, for religious or any other reasons, can "vote with their feet" and transfer their child from a public school to a private one. While parents have long held the right to have their children educated in private schools if they have the financial means, vouchers redirect federal and state money that is allocated per student to offset the private costs associated with private schools. In this practice, what is earmarked for the individual within the public sphere is redirected to benefit the individual within the private sphere. The push for school vouchers has firm roots in Friedmanism and has found a staunch cheerleader in Trump's secretary of education, Betsy DeVos, who has pushed school vouchers for numerous decades in keeping with her alignment with Friedmanism (Barkan, 2017) and as a way to "advance God's kingdom" (Wermund, 2016). Unlike homeschooling, vouchers seek to shift public funds from the local public school to the private school of a parent's choice. When public money is transferred into the hands of religious organizations who oversee private schools, such as the Catholic Church, it violates the Constitution's Establishment Clause, which restricts the government from establishing religion—not to mention that it removes the public's ability to engage in oversight of how its tax dollars are being used. This transfer of public money into private hands becomes problematic because private schools are not required to adhere to federal laws such as the Individuals with Disabilities Act (IDEA) (Strauss, 2017) and anti-discrimination laws. During Secretary DeVos's confirmation hearings, she was repeatedly asked if private schools would, as the result of receiving federal funds, be obligated to follow the guidelines set forth in IDEA. DeVos wavered in her response and suggested that it would be up to the individual states to decide this issue for themselves, thus demonstrating that from her perspective states should have the ability to override federal law despite the ethical implications—or simply showcasing her ineptitude in understanding educational and federal law.

In some cases, school vouchers do not fully offset the cost of private school tuition. As such, parents must pay the balance, which often limits this form of school choice to affluent individuals. The fact that vouchers do not always cover the full costs of private school tuition highlights how deceptive the rhetoric about the freedom of free markets and the marketing of school "choice" is, since it is not free and is limited to those who are relatively wealthy. Within the competitive environment of school vouchers, private schools purport to offer a better education for the individual. Additionally, public schools are said to be incentivized to improve student outcomes and customer service (parental satisfaction) to avoid losing students and funding. Yet research has shown that when socioeconomic status is controlled for, private schools do not actually outperform public schools (Lubienski & Lubienski, 2014). Ignoring the less-than-stellar history of private school performance, it is troubling that the political right has sought to use school vouchers as a justifiable means to segregate along racial lines (Persson, 2015).

Charter schools.

Charter schools represent another iteration of school organization reform that has individualization, privatization, and marketization at its core. Similar to the competitive threat represented by school vouchers, proponents of charter schools argue that the competitive environment created by charter schools incentivizes public schools to improve. Beyond considerations of first-order effects (benefits to those who participate in school choice) and second-order effects (collateral benefits to public school students who do not actively participate in school choice) (Linick & Lubienski, 2013), vouchers and charters are often promoted because they represent an ideological commitment to free-market ideals (DeBray-Pelot, Lubienski, & Scott, 2007). Given that research suggests charters often do no better than traditional public schools, proponents on the political right have, like ALEC's justification of vouchers for the purpose of White segregation (Persson, 2015), suggested charter schools as a justifiable mechanism for parents to self-segregate along racial lines (Brewer & Lubienski, 2017c). While the political right has relied on the myth of the failed school to promote school organization reforms such as homeschooling, vouchers, and charters, when confronted with research suggesting the failure of those reforms, the political right often admits a sinister rationale for the reforms: racial segregation.

Teacher preparation.

Additionally, implications of market-oriented ideology have not been limited to school organization. While the promotion of market ideology rests on the myth of the failed school, that myth hinges on the assumption of the "bad" teacher (Goldstein, 2014; Kumashiro, 2012; Olsen, 2015; Rothstein, 2010). As such, neoliberal reforms have targeted teacher preparation in an attempt to privatize and otherwise inject competition into the process of training educators.

Teach for America (TFA) is likely the most discussed organization providing alternative teacher certification for would-be teachers. TFA, along with many other alternative certification programs, represents an attempt at privatizing teacher education that has enjoyed some success (Lahann & Reagan, 2011). This form of competition within teacher education serves multiple purposes. One purpose is to break up the so-called "monopoly" that colleges of education have on teacher preparation and certification. Additionally, the rise of privatized teacher preparation, particularly fast-entry teacher preparation programs like TFA, seeks to de-professionalize and delegitimize teaching as a profession while pursuing the neoliberal agenda of reducing spending on public goods (Brewer, Kretchmar, Sondel, Ishmael, & Manfra, 2016). Given neoliberalism's attempt to de-professionalize teaching by way of de-skilling (Weiner, 2011), alternative teacher certification programs that employ fast-entry training explicitly view teaching as nonprofessional work (Brewer & deMarrais, 2015). Specifically, the aim of neoliberal efforts is to "deprofessionalize the role of teachers so that they are seen as interchangeable cogs whose craft can, according to neoliberal philosophy, be quantified into student test outcomes and comparatively measured" (Brewer & Cody, 2014, p. 80) within the scope of commodification and monetary competition. Given the nature of fast-entry teacher preparation programs, many rely on test-prep pedagogy, since a 5-week "crash course" in training doesn't lend itself to learning a broad range of pedagogical approaches. As a result, alternative teacher certification has been largely connected to the growth of charter schools (Crawford-Garrett, 2013; Horn, 2011, 2016; Kretchmar, Sondel, & Ferrare, 2014; Labaree, 2010; Lack, 2011).

In this era of education reforms that elevate individualism and competition, teachers are commodified, and students are increasingly reduced to their test scores. A focus on teaching to the test aligns with the viewpoint that the purpose of schools is to increase and compare quantifiable student outcomes. Since the era of normal schools, professors in colleges of education across the country have been responsible for educating and assessing pre-service teachers and their readiness to enter the profession of teaching. Yet the rise in distrust of professors at public institutions and the desire to commodify teacher education for profit ushered in Pearson's edTPA (Teacher Performance Assessment). The pre-service assessment mechanism of edTPA not only seeks to standardize teacher preparation training; it also takes the assessment and evaluation of teacher candidates away from the universities and places them in private corporate hands that will profit from the practice.

Accountability.

Testing and test-prep pedagogy are situated firmly within Friedmanism's push for more governmental accountability. While the ideology simultaneously pushes for a reduction in governmental activity in public spheres, it demands an increased level of scrutiny of the government and its actors by way of increased accountability measures. Following the publication of *A Nation at Risk*, the United States ushered in policy after policy seeking to address the perceived failures of schools by increasing accountability measures. Within the conservative right and neoliberal ideology also embraced by the political left, government and its agents are perceived as naturally inefficient. The perpetuation of the myth of the failed school and the scapegoat of the "bad" teacher present an opportunity to increase accountability measures. With the rise of conceptualizing education as a process of credentialing (Labaree, 1988, 1997a, 1997b; Maier, 2012) and individualistic competition by way of test scores, accountability measures have sought to tie both students' and teachers' worth to their performance on such measures. Recent policy trends have called for a significant portion of a teacher's annual evaluation to consider student test scores and tie those test scores to merit-pay structures for teachers, despite evidence that competitive incentives are not a silver bullet (Springer et al., 2010). Given the hyper-focus on increasing test scores, it should come as no surprise that many teachers focus their instruction on test preparation, and that there have been cases of cheating on state standardized tests (Brumback, 2013; Flock, 2011). In fact, test-prep pedagogy has been explicitly adopted by organizations like TFA as a necessary component in their work to reform education along the lines of competition and meritocracy.

In recent years, even the USDOE has pushed for colleges of education to be held accountable regarding the ability of their graduates to raise student test scores (Kumashiro, 2015). In essence, because marketization and competition are presented as a taken-for-granted ideology and disposition, school organization, teacher preparation, and pedagogy have become weaponized in an attempt to advance narrow-minded political agendas. Unfortunately, as the Democratic and Republican parties have aligned their interests in education and assumed that public school education is broken and must be reinvigorated with markets, the future state of education will likely include more competition and individualization.

These reforms have not occurred in a vacuum, and none have succeeded without help from other reforms. The political landscape is fertile for reforms that elevate the individual and meritocracy over the collective good and quality education. These silver-bullet reforms rely on the myth of the failed school and the bad teacher, working together to reimagine schooling. Alternative certification programs like TFA partner with and support the growth of the charter school sector while also promoting accountability by way of standardized tests in their "backwards planning" pedagogy. Homeschooling, vouchers, and charters all benefit equally from the ideology that the introduction of competition into a public sphere will benefit all parties involved. Because these reforms rely on a general understanding and shared ideology, individuals and organizations across the political spectrum have become bedfellows within the education reform network.

The Education Reform Network

We want to pause here to share a few caveats: (1) our critique of education reform is not to be understood as a wholesale endorsement for the status quo of education in the United States; and (2) our critique of market-oriented reforms and individualization is to be understood in juxtaposition to collective governance and the common good. To the former point, when controlling for socioeconomic status, schools with a low percentage of students living in poverty consistently score among the highest in the world when we compare PISA results (Berliner, 2013). That said, this highlights two realities: (1) that we don't have a schooling problem per se in the United States; rather, we have an income inequality problem; and (2) the design of schooling in the United States, when understood within the country's historical and contemporary context, explains how schools and curricula were designed to reproduce socioeconomic inequality and, on that measure alone, schools have fully achieved their aim (Anyon, 1980; Bowles & Gintis, 1976; Brewer & Myers, 2015; Coleman et al., 1966; Jencks et al., 1972; Rothstein, 2004; Sacks, 2007; Willis, 1977). Income inequality in the United States, the world's wealthiest country, has become so rampant that a United Nations report of extreme poverty in the United States raised questions about whether Americans in poverty could even experience fundamental human rights (Pilkington, 2017).

So, while schools in the United States are functioning exactly as they were designed—to reproduce haves and have nots along classed and racial lines—theorizing a better approach to schooling policies is needed. While there is room to reform schooling policies in an effort to stymie inequalities, it makes more sense to focus more on reforms that address inequality at its core. However, this is the opposite goal of the education reform network.

With those caveats in place, it becomes clear(er) why silver-bullet reforms that center on privatization and individualistic competition will only reinforce systemic inequalities and the reproduction of class and racial inequity in the United States. However, each education reform mentioned above has found ardent support from Republicans and Democrats alike. The vast majority of those who are in policymaking positions have bought into the myth of the failed school, the bad teacher, meritocracy, and individualization, and these reforms represent promising silver bullets. It takes little political capital to join the bandwagon of education reform, given the rampant nature of the myth that schools need to be reformed.

In what follows, we illustrate the growing network of organizations and individuals funded by venture philanthropists who have the primary goal of privatizing education, elevating the individual over the collective good, ignoring decades of research, and profiting from the education marketplace. While we have mentioned that, broadly, Republicans and Democrats have converged around education reform, in this section we name those individuals. We have suggested that the majority of policymakers, regardless of their political affiliation, have not only bought into the myth that schools have failed, but they share a common support for the same types of reforms. It may seem odd that far-right organizations like the American Legislative Exchange Council (ALEC) and the Koch brothers would be bedfellows with purportedly left-leaning organizations like Students for Education Reform (SFER), TFA, and the Clinton Foundation. Day-to-day activities and policies supported by the Koch brothers are fully at odds with an organization like the Clinton Foundation. However, these individuals and organizations are supportive of market-oriented educational reforms and are connected within the reform network. Because they support similar reforms, we can assume that on some level they share similar values, since "...alliances over policy can be primarily about sharing values" (Fischer, 2003, p. 32). Considering the alignment of values and policy ideas about silver-bullet reforms, we suggest that the education reform network has developed an advocacy coalition. Accordingly:

> An advocacy coalition is conceived of as an alliance of political groups in a policy subsystem sharing the same interests and ideas that come together to argue against other policy coalitions concerned with the same policy issues. Involving more participants than the traditional policy sector decision-makers—administrators, congressional committee members, and relevant industry lobbyists—advocacy coalitions, like policy communities more generally, include journalists [media], interested politicians, public interest groups, policy analysts and researchers, state and local officials, among others. All play a role in the dissemination of policy ideas. In contrast to policy-network theory, advocacy coalition members bargain and form alliances within a policy subsystem. (p. 95)

This advocacy coalition of right- and left-wing politicians, varied ideological organizations, philanthropic donors, and the media (a topic we take up in Chapter Eight) is not only a growing network but, increasingly, a network that continues to grow more incestuous. We provide a visual representation of this network online (http://ow.ly/xydk3oilRza) in order to show those individuals and organizations that are the most centrally connected, and those that have multiple points of connection within the reform network.

In the Education Reform Network, so-called bastions of liberalism and champions of equality such as Democrats for Education Reform (DFER), TFA, and Education Reform Now (ERN) are not only directly connected to pro-market and pro-privatization organizations like NewSchools Venture Fund (NSVF), 50CAN, the Walton Foundation, the Gates Foundation, the Broad Foundation, the Robertson Foundation, and the Laura and John Arnold Foundation. Rather, by extension, they are also connected to far-right donors and organizations like the Koch brothers and ALEC. Of additional interest are the growing connections that the reform network has with the United States Department of Education (USDOE). As suggested above, market-oriented education reforms have centered on accountability through testing as a mainstay of pedagogy, so it is not surprising that Pearson is also well connected within this network.

Over the past few years, the National Council for Teacher Quality (NCTQ) has rated teacher preparation programs (traditional and alternative certification) across the country (National Council for Teacher Quality, 2014). And while many have pointed out the methodological flaws in NCTQ's reports (Darling-Hammond, 2013; Eduventures, 2010; Fuller, 2013; Kumashiro, 2015), understanding their direct and close organizational and funding connections to groups that are connected to TFA and the Relay Graduate School shed light on why those connected organizations receive such high praise from NCTQ. NCTQ has promoted the myth that traditional colleges of education are complicit in the production of "bad teachers," all the while promoting market-oriented reforms like those through their connections to StudentsFirst/50CAN (a charter advocacy organization that also works to fight teacher tenure and teacher unions), Educators4Excellence, TFA, SFER, DFER, and Education Reform Now. In fact, TFA has become a central point of connection within the reform network, suggesting that the myth of the "bad teacher" is firmly at the center of the blame levied on schools (see Figure 7.1 at: bit.ly/Figure7-1). In addition to its central role in placing the blame for failed schools on teachers, TFA has played a key role in producing alumni who are often elevated to positions of political power that they can use to reinforce neoliberal conceptions of the individual versus the collective good and schooling as a competitive, individualistic practice. In fact, three of the top five contenders for promotion to New York City Schools Chancellor are TFA alumni (*New York Times*, 2018), and the top education advisor at the White House is a TFA alum who worked at the TFA-founded KIPP charter network (Bowie & Marbella, 2017).

These instances are not isolated. A major goal of the reform network is to increase its control over the political and policymaking processes. All three finalists for Commissioner of Massachusetts are TFA alums (Larkin, 2018); Mark Johnson, the newly elected North Carolina State Superintendent, is a TFA alum (Teach for America, n.d.-b); TFA alum Michael Johnston is running for governor of Colorado (Teach for America, n.d.-c); John White, a TFA alum and former TFA staffer, is the Louisiana State Superintendent of Education (Louisiana Department of Education, n.d.); Tennessee, a hotbed of charter school reform, was recently led by Kevin Huffman, who, along with Ryan Wise, the Iowa Director of Education appointed by Republican Governor Terry Branstad, was heavily involved in TFA. DeRay McKesson, notable for his role in the Black Lives Matter movement, ran an unsuccessful bid for mayor of Baltimore despite heavy support from TFA and LEE (Teach for America, n.d.-a) after advocating for education reform by combining the language of the myth of meritocracy with the language of Civil Rights.

Intermediary organizations within the reform network, like TFA, are heavily funded by venture philanthropic organizations such as the Gates Foundation, the Broad Foundation, the Walton Foundation, the Laura and John Arnold Foundation, the Robertson Foundation, the Doris and Donald Fisher Fund, the Carnegie Corporation, the Bezos Foundation, the Michael and Susan Dell Foundation, Arthur Rock, and the Koch Family Foundations. These multi-millionaire and multi-billionaire donors have financed a network of reformers that continue to drive silver-bullet reforms such as homeschooling, vouchers, charters, alternative teacher certification, and standardization and testing while influencing policy decisions. For example, with the help of philanthropic money from the Broad Foundation, Michelle Rhee (a TFA alumna herself and the founder of the New Teacher Project) and StudentsFirst/50CAN have promoted parent "trigger laws" (Vasquez Heilig, 2013). These laws include language crafted by ALEC and allow parents to "pull the trigger" and force a public school to convert to a charter school. ALEC, a far-right organization, successfully promoted legislative language concerning the conversion of public schools into charter schools and garnered support for those laws by purportedly left-leaning individuals and organizations.

The financial support from venture philanthropic organizations is a vital component of the education reform network, and among the largest donors to the network has been the Gates Foundation (see Figure 7.2 at: bit.ly/Figure7-2). While the Gates Foundation and other venture philanthropists have funneled money into organizations like TFA, the Charter School Growth Fund, and the Relay Graduate School, it has been Students for Education Reform (SFER) that has seen a significant amount of support and partnership from both individuals and organizations that are historically right- and left-leaning (see Figure 7.3 at: bit.ly/Figure7-3). SFER, founded by two TFA alums, and now with chapters on more than 100 college campuses since its founding in 2009, recruits college students by drawing them into the myths of the failed public school, the "bad teacher," and the need to reform education. SFER approaches education reform by supporting lawsuits that challenge teacher tenure (a leading target of right-leaning ideology), thus seeking to open the door for districts to fire more veteran teachers in an effort save money by hiring novice, alternatively certified teachers like TFA corps members. Additionally, SFER has received $1.6 million from Education Reform Now, whose PAC, Democrats for Education Reform (DFER), shelled out $1 million to attack the Chicago Teachers Union and partnered with the Koch brothers and ALEC to promote the passage of Proposition 32 which, if passed, would have prevented teacher unions from using automatic payroll deductions for "political purposes."

As we have discussed in previous chapters, college campuses, in their attempt to impose their free-market ideology on the next generation, have been a primary target of the political right for decades, which explains the Koch brothers' and ALEC's support for SFER. In aligning themselves with the broader education reform movement, the Koch brothers and ALEC seek to influence educational reform by preying on the liberal optimism of naïve students and recent college graduates who have little to no training or expertise in educational policy to parrot and reinforce the policies that they desire.

The appointment of Secretary of Education Betsy DeVos (a Republican) by Donald Trump continues the practice of filling the USDOE position with a staunch supporter of the reform network and the reforms that they champion. Like Arne Duncan (a Democrat) and his predecessors, the Secretaries of Education—despite their own political affiliation or the political affiliation of the president who chose them—have facilitated the growing flow of venture philanthropic money into the reform network while bolstering the USDOE's support for market-oriented reforms. During DeVos's confirmation hearing, ideas were discussed instead of evidence. Myths were allowed to become the foundation for discussion in a Senate committee hearing. The same familiar myths of failure, bad teachers, the purity of marketization, and privatization were promoted by DeVos, who has no formal experience in the field of education, but whose family tree of radically conservative and predatory philanthropists may have influenced her views on education reform. DeVos and her agenda are decidedly anti-public schools, as she pushes for the expansion of for-profit charters (putting money into investors' portfolios), expansion of vouchers (putting money into church coffers), and expanding alternative certification to further de-skill teaching and pay teachers less money (Mead, 2016; Rizga, 2017).

As we detailed in a previous chapter, ALEC has been at the center of many ideological reforms over the past few decades. Like the rest of the reform network, ALEC's leaders have relied heavily on perpetuating the myth of failed schools and bad teachers and have sought to promote market-oriented reforms through their political affiliations. Notably, ALEC has worked over the years to establish a broad network of state- and federal-level policymakers who, as a part of their Education Taskforce (see Figure 7.4 at: bit.

ly/Figure7-4), promote reforms that elevate rugged individualism over the collective good and policies that seek to reduce the role of government.

As illustrated in Figure 7.4, the majority of those elected officials who are on ALEC's Education Taskforce are Republicans, although there are also a handful of Democrats. Political affiliation aside, the primary focus of ALEC's education reforms have targeted state-level efforts to promote school vouchers, charters, homeschooling, and other market-oriented reforms. This state-level focus includes both the state legislature and the governor's office. As a by-product of ALEC's focus on governors, there are two state-level superintendents/secretaries of education who have been directly appointed by governors connected to ALEC, and Governor Chris Christie, who, as a member of Trump's transition team, is a regular, vocal supporter of Trump. ALEC's focus on state-level reforms is best understood through the organization's annual *Report Card on Education*. ALEC does not hide the fact that its grading scheme is primarily ideological (Lubienski & Brewer, 2013)—that is, a state's grades are based entirely on how friendly (or unfriendly) the state is to the types of reforms discussed above.

Both the political right and left have become strange bedfellows when it comes to education reforms. While it is clear that the political right and left are incredibly divided on almost every issue, especially in the era of Trump, it remains an anomaly that they are so committed to the same types of education reform. Specifically, it is clear that the decades-long myth of the failed school and the bad teacher who is to blame is not a partisan myth; rather, it is a myth that is so ingrained in our national discourse and psyche that it costs little political capital to jump on the bandwagon of reform. Consequently, the support for reforms that seek to reinvest in public education would not be politically savvy. The political right has co-opted educational reform and has benefited from individuals on the left who have been all too willing to become foot soldiers for the conservative and neoliberal ideologies. In effect, the convergence of support for educational reforms that are historically favored by the ideological right in the United States represents ideological laundering. Conservatives have been successful in their use of dark money to fund a growing network of education reform organizations that are primarily led by left-leaning individuals who are doing the right's bidding, passing off the ideology as not only their own, but an ideology whitewashed in the co-opted narratives of the Civil Rights Movement.

References

Anyon, J. (1980). Social class and the hidden curriculum of work. *Journal of Education, 162*(1), 67–92.

Barkan, J. (2017). *Milton Friedman, Betsy DeVos, and the privatization of public education*. Retrieved from https://www.dissentmagazine.org/online_articles/betsy-devos-milton-friedman-public-education-privatization

Berliner, D.C. (2013). Effects of inequality and poverty vs. teachers and schooling on America's youth. *Teachers College Record, 115*, 1–26.

Bowie, L., & Marbella, J. (2017). *Jason Botel, KIPP School founder and education advocate, said to become White House adviser*. Retrieved from http://www.baltimoresun.com/news/maryland/politics/bs-md-botel-named-white-house-advisor-20170125-story.html

Bowles, S., & Gintis, H. (1976). *Schooling in capitalist America*. New York: HarperCollins.

Brewer, T.J., & Cody, A. (2014). Teach for America: The neoliberal alternative to teacher professionalism. In J.A. Gorlewski, B. Porfilio, D.A. Gorlewski, & J. Hopkins (Eds.), *Effective or wise? Teaching and the meaning of professional dispositions in education* (pp. 77–94). New York: Peter Lang.

Brewer, T.J., & deMarrais, K. (Eds.). (2015). *Teach for America counternarratives: Alumni speak up and speak out*. New York: Peter Lang.

Brewer, T.J., Kretchmar, K., Sondel, B., Ishmael, S., & Manfra, M. (2016). Teach for America's preferential treatment: School district contracts, hiring decisions, and employment practices. *Educational Evaluation and Policy Analysis, 24*(15), 1–38.

Brewer, T.J., & Lubienski, C. (2017a). *Does homeschooling improve educational opportunities?* Retrieved from http://www.scholarsstrategynetwork.org/brief/does-homeschooling-improve-educational-opportunities

Brewer, T.J., & Lubienski, C. (2017b). Homeschooling in the United States: Examining the rationales for individualizing education. *Pro-Posições, 28*(2), 21–38.

Brewer, T.J., & Lubienski, C. (2017c). *NEPC review: Differences by design? Student composition in charter schools with different academic models.* Retrieved from http://nepc.colorado.edu/thinktank/review-charters

Brewer, T.J., & Myers, P.S. (2015). How neoliberalism subverts equality and perpetuates poverty in our nation's schools. In S.N. Haymes, M.V. de Haymes, & R. Miller (Eds.), *The Routledge handbook of poverty in the United States* (pp. 190–198). New York: Routledge.

Brumback, K. (2013). *Former Atlanta schools chief indicted in cheating scandal.* Retrieved from http://www.huffingtonpost.com/2013/03/29/former-atlanta-schools-chief-indicted_n_2982272.html

Coleman, J., Campbell, E.Q., Hobson, C.J., McPartland, J., Mood, A.M., Weinfeld, F.D., & York, R.L. (1966). *Equality of educational opportunity.* Washington, DC: U.S. Department of Health, Education & Welfare. Office of Education (OE-38001 and supp.)

Crawford-Garrett, K. (2013). *Teach for America and the struggle for urban school reform.* New York: Peter Lang.

Darling-Hammond, L. (2013). *Why the NCTQ teacher prep ratings are nonsense.* Retrieved from https://www.washingtonpost.com/news/answer-sheet/wp/2013/06/18/why-the-nctq-teacher-prep-ratings-are-nonsense/?utm_term=.c9718fcc6142

DeBray-Pelot, E.H., Lubienski, C., & Scott, J.T. (2007). The institutional landscape of interest group politics and school choice. *Peabody Journal of Education, 82*(2–3), 204–230.

Dewey, J. (1963). *Experience & education.* New York: Macmillan.

Dewey, J. (1997). *Democracy and education: An introduction to the philosophy of education.* New York: Free Press.

Eduventures. (2010, February). *Review & critique of the national council on teacher quality (NCTQ) methodology to rate schools of education.* Retrieved from Eduventures.com

Fischer, F. (2003). *Reframing public policy: Discursive politics and deliberative practices.* Oxford: Oxford University Press.

Flock, E. (2011). *APS [Atlanta Public Schools] embroiled in cheating scandal.* Retrieved from http://www.washingtonpost.com/blogs/blogpost/post/aps-atlanta-public-schools-embroiled-in-cheating-scandal/2011/07/11/gIQAJl9m8H_blog.html

Friedman, M. (1955). *The role of government in education.* Retrieved from http://www.schoolchoices.org/roo/fried1.htm

Friedman, M. (1997). *Public schools: Make them private.* Retrieved from http://www.cato.org/pubs/briefs/bp-023.html

Friedman, M. (2002). *Capitalism and freedom.* Chicago: University of Chicago Press.

Fuller, E.J. (2013). *NCTQ ranking of teacher prep programs gets an F.* Retrieved from http://nepc.colorado.edu/blog/nctq-ranking-teacher-prep-programs-gets-f

Goldstein, D. (2014). *The teacher wars: A history of America's most embattled profession.* New York: Doubleday.

Gordy, C. (2010). *Education is the civil rights issue of our time.* Retrieved from https://www.essence.com/2010/03/01/arne-duncan-education-reform

Horn, J. (2011). Corporatism, KIPP, and cultural eugenics. In P.E. Kovacs (Ed.), *The Gates Foundation and the future of U.S. "public" schools* (pp. 80–103). New York: Routledge.

Horn, J. (2016). *Work hard, be hard: Journeys through "no excuses" teaching.* Lanham, MD: Rowman & Littlefield.

Jencks, C., Smith, M., Acland, H., Bane, M.J., Cohen, D., Gintis, H.... Michelson, S. (1972). *Inequality: A reassessment of the effect of family and schooling in America.* New York: Basic Books.

Kretchmar, K., Sondel, B., & Ferrare, J. (2014). Mapping the terrain: Teach for America, charter school reform, and corporate sponsorship. *Journal of Education Policy, 29*(6), 742–759.

Kumashiro, K. (2012). *Bad teacher! How blaming teachers distorts the bigger picture.* New York: Teachers College Press.

Kumashiro, K. (2015). *Review of proposed 2015 federal teacher preparation regulations.* Retrieved from http://nepc.colorado.edu/thinktank/review-proposed-teacher-preparation

Labaree, D. (1988). *The making of an American high school: The credentials market & the central high school of Philadelphia, 1838–1939.* New Haven, CT: Yale University Press.

Labaree, D. (1997a). *How to succeed in school without really learning: The credentials race in American education*. New Haven, CT: Yale University Press.

Labaree, D. (1997b). Public goods, private goods: The American struggle over educational goals. *American Educational Research Journal, 34*(1), 39–81.

Labaree, D. (2010). Teach for America and teacher ed: Heads they win, tails we lose. *Journal of Teacher Education, 61*(1–2), 48–55.

Lack, B. (2011). Anti-democratic militaristic education: An overview and critical analysis of KIPP schools. In R. Ahlquist, P.C. Gorski, & T. Montano (Eds.), *Assault on kids: How hyper-accountability, corporatization, deficit ideologies, and Ruby Payne are destroying our schools* (pp. 65–90). New York: Peter Lang.

Lahann, R., & Reagan, E.M. (2011). Teach for America and the politics of progressive neoliberalism. *Teacher Education Quarterly, 38*(1), 7–27.

Larkin, M. (2018). *Finalists for Mass.' next Ed Commissioner are in: 1 state receiver, and 2 female outsiders*. Retrieved from http://www.wbur.org/edify/2018/01/16/next-education-commissioner

Linick, M., & Lubienski, C.A. (2013). How charter schools do, and don't inspire change in traditional public school districts. *Childhood Education, 89*(2), 99–104.

Louisiana Department of Education. (n.d.). *Meet John White*. Retrieved from http://www.louisianabelieves.com/resources/about-us/meet-john-white

Lubienski, C. (2000). Whither the common good? A critique of home schooling. *Peabody Journal of Education, 75*(1/2), 207–232.

Lubienski, C., & Brewer, T.J. (2013). *Review of report card on American education*. Retrieved from http://nepc.colorado.edu/thinktank/review-report-card-ALEC-2013

Lubienski, C., & Brewer, T.J. (2014). Does home education "work"? Challenging the assumptions behind the home education movement. In P. Rothermel (Ed.), *International perspectives on home education: Do we still need schools?* (pp. 136–147). London: Palgrave.

Lubienski, C., & Lubienski, S. (2014). *The public school advantage: Why public schools outperform private schools*. Chicago: University of Chicago Press.

Maier, A. (2012). Doing good and doing well: Credentialism and Teach for America. *Journal of Teacher Education, 63*(1), 10–22.

Mead, R. (2016). *Betsy DeVos and the plan to break public schools.* Retrieved from https://www.newyorker.com/news/daily-comment/betsy-devos-and-the-plan-to-break-public-schools

The National Commission on Excellence in Education (April, 1983). A nation at risk: The imperative for educational reform. Washington, DC: United States Department of Education. Retrieved from https://www2.ed.gov/pubs/NatAtRisk/risk.html

National Council for Teacher Quality. (2014). *2014 teacher prep review: A review of the nation's teacher preparation programs.* Retrieved from http://www.nctq.org/dmsView/Teacher_Prep_Review_2014_Report

New York Times. (2018). *Some bright hopes for New York's schools.* Retrieved from https://www.nytimes.com/2018/01/14/opinion/some-bright-hopes-for-new-yorks-schools.html

Olsen, R. (2015). *The toxic myth of good and bad teachers.* Retrieved from https://www.richardolsen.me/b/2015/05/the-toxic-myth-of-good-and-bad-teachers/

Persson, J. (2015). *ALEC admits school vouchers are for kids in suburbia.* Retrieved from http://www.prwatch.org/news/2015/07/12869/alec-school-vouchers-are-kids-suburbia

Pilkington, E. (2017, December 1). *Why the UN is investigating extreme poverty... in America, the world's richest nation.* Retrieved from https://www.theguardian.com/world/2017/dec/01/un-extreme-poverty-america-special-rapporteur

Powell, D. (2017). *No, education isn't the civil rights issue of our time: We shouldn't buy school choice rhetoric masquerading as civil rights.* Retrieved from https://www.edweek.org/ew/articles/2017/05/17/no-education-isnt-the-civil-rights-issue.html

Ray, B.D. (2015). *Research facts on homeschooling.* Retrieved from http://www.nheri.org/ResearchFacts.pdf

Rizga, K. (2017). *Betsy DeVos wants to use America's schools to build "God's kingdom.".* Retrieved from https://www.motherjones.com/politics/2017/01/betsy-devos-christian-schools-vouchers-charter-education-secretary/

Rothstein, R. (2004). *Class and schools: Using social, economic, and educational reform to close the Black-White achievement gap.* Washington DC: Economic Policy Institute.

Rothstein, R. (2010). Rothstein: Why teacher quality can't be only centerpiece of reform. Retrieved from http://voices.washingtonpost.com/answer-sheet/school-turnaroundsreform/rothstein-on-the-manifestos-ma.html

Sacks, P. (2007). *Tearing down the gates: Confronting the class divide in American education.* Los Angeles, CA: University of California Press.

Springer, M. G., Ballou, D., Hamilton, L., Le, V.-N., Lockwood, J. R., McCaffrey, D. F., . . .Stecher, B. M. (2010). *Teacher pay performance: Experimental evidence from the project on incentives in teaching.* Retrieved from Nashville, TN: http://www.rand.org/content/dam/rand/pubs/reprints/2010/RAND_RP1416.pdf

Strauss, V. (2017). Betsy devos apparently 'confused' about federal law protecting students with disabilities. Retrieved from https://www.washingtonpost.com/news/answer-sheet/wp/2017/01/17/betsy-devos-confused-about-federal-law-protecting-students-with-disabilities/?utm_term=.3bb63793a142

Teach For America. (n.d.-a). Deray mckesson. Retrieved from https://www.teachforamerica.org/person/deray-mckesson

Teach For America. (n.d.-b). Mark johnson. Retrieved from https://www.teachforamerica.org/person/mark-johnson

Teach For America. (n.d.-c). Michael johnston. Retrieved from https://www.teachforamerica.org/person/michael-johnston

Vasquez Heilig, J. (2013). *The teat: Where does parent trigger movement get their $?* Retrieved from https://cloakinginequity.com/2013/04/12/the-teat-where-does-parent-trigger-get-their/

Weiner, L. (2011). Neoliberalism's global reconstruction of schooling, teachers' work, and teacher education. In S. Tozer, B.P. Gallegos, A.M. Henry, M.B. Greiner, & P.G. Price (Eds.), *Handbook of research in the social foundations of education* (pp. 308–318). New York: Routledge.

Wermund, B. (2016). *Trump's education pick says reform can "advance God's kingdom."* Retrieved from http://www.politico.com/story/2016/12/betsy-devos-education-trump-religion-232150

Willis, P. (1977). Learning to labor: How working class kids get working class jobs. New York: Columbia University Press.

Chapter Eight

THE MEGAPHONE BEHIND THE MYTH:
THE MEDIA'S ROLE IN SHAPING PUBLIC DISCOURSE ABOUT EDUCATION REFORM

This chapter examines the role that traditional and non-traditional media have played in shaping and influencing public discourse related to school reforms. Following a comprehensive discussion of how the media reinforce commonsense language about the need to reform "failing" schools, the chapter provides a social network analysis of ownership and connections across various media platforms (e.g., television, local news, national news, social media platforms, etc.) in order to show how right-wing philanthropic groups have worked to synthesize the media narrative while simultaneously working to concentrate ownership of and power over media outlets.

The media, in their various iterations, are leveraged by individuals and organizations pushing neoliberal agendas of education reform (Wubbena, Ford, & Porfilio, 2016). These intertwined agendas reimagine and understand schools as the primary determinant of merit that informs capital accumulation. Accordingly, the "neoliberal agenda for education is an extension of the neoliberal political project that seeks to re-establish the conditions for capital accumulation and to restore the power of economic elites through processes of dispossession and restructuration of the market, state, and citizenship" (García, 2015, p. 4). Capital accumulation is seen as the natural outcome of successful efforts that begin in schooling by the individual. If an individual is wealthy, then she must be smart and is a hard worker. Poverty, comparatively, is an artifact of a poor work ethic and poor choices—often stemming from poor performance in school.

The assumption that schools offer a level playing field for all students regardless of their predispositions of poverty or relative wealth reinforces the ideology that schools offer equal opportunities to all and that variance among individual success is attributable to bad schools and poor individual choices. While there is much to be said about the conservative and neoliberal belief that individual choices inform socioeconomic outcomes, it is the foundational assertion that schools are largely responsible for the persistence of achievement gaps and economic inequality in our society. The belief in level playing fields becomes harder to sustain in the face of data showing that there is a racial divide in academic and economic outcomes, lest the believer admit to overt deficit ideologies and notions of White supremacy. Confronting that reality requires tough discussions on systemic racism that most individuals in power are not eager to have. The latter presumption—that inequality is a function of bad schools and bad teachers—creates the façade that policy is a viable remedy to a perceived problem while simultaneously and conveniently ignoring systemic racism. Nonetheless, it is the latter argument of failed schools that drives the discourse of education reformers, and this discourse is magnified by all forms of media, particularly those controlled or otherwise connected to education reformers and venture philanthropists.

Drawing from the same venture philanthropic donors who seek to promote a right-wing, market-oriented approach to educational reform, this chapter provides a social network analysis and discussion of the shared connections across myriad educational documentaries that, while packaged under the guise of liberal commitments to equality and equity, have in fact promoted the same discourse of school failure and silver-bullet reforms such as charter schools, school vouchers, and homeschooling. In the era of "fake news," conversations about how the media influence public perception of schools and the resulting reforms that are promoted are essential. The consolidation of media control into smaller, mostly conservative hands has bolstered the right wing's ability to promote market-oriented reforms like those advocated by the Koch brothers and organizations such as the American Legislative Exchange Council (ALEC).

Without a doubt, the general national consensus on the state of schooling in the United States is a negative one: failed schools, caused by bad teachers (Kumashiro, 2012). But how did we get here? How did the nation develop what is seemingly a general consensus about the failure of schools, and how is that consensus maintained? Without a doubt, the media are part of that answer. During every election cycle, politicians running for a wide range of offices—from the local, small-town mayoral office to state legislative offices, gubernatorial offices, and the presidency—will, with few exceptions, include education as part of their platforms. In fact, the larger the race, the more likely it seems that education is included in the platform. Without fail, the national Democratic and Republican platforms include educational reforms as part of their official national platforms (Spring, 2010, 2011).

Politicians talk about reforming education because they are wont to propose solutions to perceived problems in a bid to get elected. What is interesting here is that the general consensus that schools have failed is a national perspective, but it is not necessarily a local one. Gallup and Phi Delta Kappa (PDK) have, since 1985, conducted polls on how the general public views the state of education (Lopez, 2010). Consistent across the years is the finding that respondents are highly likely to rate the local school that their children attend with an "A" or a "B." Most respondents (both parents and non-parents) graded other local schools (the ones their children did not attend, if the respondent was a parent) as "average or above," giving those schools a grade of "C." However, when asked about the state of schooling in the broader context of the nation, respondents were far more likely to grade them as "C" or lower.

What is often excluded from conversations surrounding the Gallup/PDK poll is how such a disparity in perception is possible. What is clear is that parents with students in local schools are, overall, incredibly satisfied with the quality of education their child is receiving. In most cases, this is informed by concrete information—that is, the parents are directly connected to the school, and their children are able to accurately evaluate the quality of education. Being disconnected personally from other local schools, parents and residents without student-age children must rely on secondhand knowledge about the quality of those schools, either by word of mouth or local news media reporting. But how can an individual provide an evaluation of the state of education broadly throughout the United States? Again, the media are likely to play a considerable role in shaping that assessment.

What is often excluded from conversations surrounding the poll is this question: how it is that if almost all individuals grade their local schools as good, how can there be any bad ones? That is, if individuals using firsthand knowledge of their local schools suggest that the grass is, in fact, greener on *their* side of the fence at the same rate that other individuals rate their local schools similarly (or the grass on *the other* side of the fence, to continue the metaphor), then the perception of failing schools *over there* is wholly unwarranted. In a seminal work, Berliner and Biddle (1995) explain how education reformers have outright manufactured the crisis of failing schools. This "manufactured crisis" is advertised through our media outlets. The news media have exacerbated "the sense of crisis through the production of spectacle, fear, and manufactured crisis" (Ford, Porfilio, & Goldstein, 2015, p. 5). Parents see these advertisements of crisis (and hear of the need to reform) and conclude that this crisis must be *over there*, that it must be in schools *other than* their children's schools. Yet the media successfully leverage the myth of failed schools to reinforce for the public the notion that economic inequality and stagnant personal economic growth are the result of schools and the education system, and specifically not that of capitalism.

In fact, despite a steady level of satisfaction with local schools, Gallup and PDK noted that there has been a steady decline in public perception of the state of schooling in the United States (broadly, not locally) since 1985, when the survey began. Coincidentally, 1985 was the year in which the Reagan administration released *A Nation at Risk* (ANAR), which decried the state of schooling across the nation. The release of ANAR not only took advantage of long-held assumptions that schools in the United States were not up to par with those of our adversaries (a sentiment that became widespread following the launch of Sputnik); it also opened the door to neoliberalism in education. The assumption then was—as it is now—that those within the field of education had failed and could not be trusted to reform education (Goldstein, 2014).

A 2011 article written by education reformer Joel Klein opens with the following editorial note:

> Who better to lead an educational revolution than Joel Klein, the prosecutor who took on the software giant Microsoft? But in his eight years as chancellor of New York City's school system, the nation's largest, Klein learned a few painful lessons of his own—about feckless politicians, recalcitrant unions, mediocre teachers, and other enduring obstacles.

Appearing in the semi-news publication *The Atlantic*, this statement promotes a few general conclusions: (1) schools in New York (and the United States by extension, as New York is the largest state) have failed; (2) incompetent politicians have not held the system accountable; (3) unions are obstacles to reform; and (4) teachers are, generally, mediocre at best. But what is also promoted is the idea that educational reform—or a revolution (which can rely on an understanding that there is an offensive and defensive component)—ought to be led by those outside of education. Klein, in short order, picks up the editorial thread of mediocrity by actually citing *A Nation at Risk*.

The way in which the media discuss and present education dramatically shapes the public perception of schools. The presentation of failed schools establishes the discursive environment whereby voters believe that while their local schools are doing well, they have failed writ large. If the media are able to convince their audiences that schools have failed, they are in a position to provide solutions. Accordingly, the "media's coverage of education plays a pivotal role in shaping, reinforcing, and normalizing contemporary discourses of education policy, particularly around school reform and teacher quality..." (García, 2015, p. 2). The neoliberal solution (deregulation) in search of a problem (government-controlled schools) must establish a need prior to making a sale. A common tactic in sales marketing is the short "elevator pitch," where the seller engages a prospect with "You know how X is a problem? Well, I sell Y to fix that." The "X" is presented as a commonsensical and universally understood problem, whether the prospect agrees or not. The problem is presented as indisputable, and the seller wastes no time in discussion of whether or not the problem is actually a problem, or if it even exists at all. Simply put, the goal is to establish the common belief that "X" is a problem and that the prospect is in clear need of the "Y" product. Within the education universe, the "X" is the simple lie that schools have failed, and the "Y" product is, within the neoliberal imaginary, deregulation and privatization. The presentation of "X = failed schools" and "Y = privatization" often benefits from demagoguery because, according to Patricia Roberts-Miller,

> Demagoguery is about identity. It says that complicated policy issues can be reduced to a binary of us (good) versus them (bad). It says that good people recognize there is a bad situation, and bad people don't; therefore, to determine what policy agenda is the best, it says we should think entirely in terms of who is like us and who isn't. (2017)

The media, in an effort to continue to sell the "manufactured crisis" of failed schools, must tell their national audiences a story of failure in order to bolster the belief that there is a need for reform. "Fox and Friends" on the Fox News channel—which is purportedly President Trump's favorite "news" program—regularly runs a segment on schools. The segment is titled "Trouble with Schools" and often utilizes an animated graphic played over the sharp sound of metal grinding against metal as a locker door falls off its hinges. The segments consistently discuss schooling from the viewpoint and seemingly commonsensical perspective that schools are woefully failing. The visual representation of schools falling apart is the network's way of eliciting a visceral reaction from its audience while reinforcing the general consensus of national school failure. The viewer is not presented with alternative information, and the assumption of failure is taken as a fact not to be questioned. "The terms of the debate [over educational policy] that [the media] represent are often determined by politicians' interpretation of the problems. In this sense, then, it is not only the media but also how the problems are presented by the candidates themselves that misrepresent educational problems" (Gerstl-Pepin, 2002, p. 50).

Political Ideologies in the Media

Control over the media (who owns it, who funds it, what stories are acceptable and which are not) is an ongoing battle dating back over 50 years, as we discussed in Chapters Two and Three. The goal of right-wing organizations and philanthropists has been to capture the media market. Their strategy is to begin with college newspapers, grow to local news networks, establish national cable media outlets such as Fox News, and produce biased documentaries such as those made by Dinesh D'Souza. Herman and Chomsky (2002) explore the notion of manufactured consent as a method by which the dominant powers mobilize the media to control society through propaganda. In their view, this represents a threat to democracy. According to Chomsky, "the press is owned by wealthy men who have every interest in not allowing certain ideas to not be suppressed…" (Wubbena, 2015, p. 5).

In their discussion of maintaining a democracy, Levitsky and Ziblatt (2018) suggest that there are two fundamental expectations: mutual toleration and forbearance. They suggest that, with the help of Fox News, Republicans began to undermine the idea of mutual toleration by likening Democrats to terrorists who lack patriotism and are fundamentally anti-American. Patricia Roberts-Miller likewise noted that the media consistently demonized dissent directed at the War on Terror (2017). And while they do not make overt connections to Fox News's Sean Hannity's insistence that there is a "Deep State" at work to undermine Trump, Levitsky and Ziblatt do examine the ways in which Senator Joseph McCarthy purported to have lists of embedded communists set on undermining the U.S. government. Covered on television and across newspapers, the McCarthy hearings created an environment in which the average American could begin to question the concept of mutual toleration through being swayed by the fake news of the time, as delivered by media outlets.

García (2015) argued that educational portrayals in the media, namely in long-form films and documentaries, "naturaliz[es] the neoliberal agenda for education as lived reality, its assumptions [of capitalist realism] slowly permeate society and shape and frame the contemporary policy debates and public discourses on public education" (p. 6). According to García, the presentation of educational processes in film begin with the assumption that neoliberalism is natural and the best course of action when implementing and reinforcing educational and social policy. The presentation of educational processes and policies in the media are, as discussed, situated in the assumption that schools have failed. Yet Malin and Lubienski (2015) found that the majority of "experts" discussing educational policy across media platforms are not experts in education; rather, they are members of ideological organizations pushing for privatization. When it comes to education conversations on media platforms, those conversations have suffered from the media's insistence on providing platforms for ideological reformers and not actual experts. When families see a news report about the failing state of education across the country as presented by an individual affiliated with an organization seeking to privatize education, the media representation skews the audience's understanding.

While the Pew Research Center reports that half of all Americans got their news from television (both local and national) in 2017, that figure is markedly down over recent years. However, while there has been a steady decline in television news viewership in favor of getting news from social media platforms, local television news is still the most-consulted medium. (See Table 8.1).

Broadly speaking, while news on social media has proliferated over the past decade with the rise of platforms such as Facebook,

Table 8.1. Where People Get Their News.

SOURCE	2016	2017	CHANGE
*Television	57%	50%	−7
Online	38%	43%	+5
Radio	25%	25%	0
Print Newspapers	20%	18%	−2
**Social Media	62%	67%	+5
Local Television News	46%	37%	−7
Cable News	31%	28%	−3
Network Television News	30%	26%	−4

Note: Data aggregated from Gottfried & Shearer, 2017; Matsa, 2018; Shearer & Gottfried, 2017.

* Television is given as a broad category by the Pew Research Center when not disaggregated across the categories of local, cable, and network television news.

** The Pew Research Center notes that its social media category should be understood as where surveyed individuals get some of their news, as only 20% do so "often."

Twitter, YouTube, and others, local television news remains the regular source of news for most Americans.

Because the majority of Americans get their information from local television news, what becomes important is consideration of who owns the majority of that news medium. In the spring of 2018, a viral video of dozens of reporters across the United States delivering the exact same script went viral. The reporters were all employees of local broadcast stations owned by the Sinclair Broadcast Group (SBG). SBG is a hyper-conservative media group that controls 40% of all local news media and is heavily connected to Donald Trump (Matthews, 2018). The reporters at 173 local stations, all reading from an identical script, warned viewers of "the troubling trend of irresponsible, one-sided news stories plaguing our country" (Domonoske, 2018). As has been suggested, the goal of the scripted announcement was to work with Trump to undermine public perception of mainstream media. The consolidated control of local television news by SBG represents a real threat to democracy, because

> most voters increasingly use the media as their primary source of information, their role in electoral politics is key to the functioning of our democracy. If one believes in the ideal of participatory democracy in which voters are able to make informed decisions about candidates, then the information the media present to voters is an integral component to the operation of democracy. (Gerstl-Pepin, 2002, pp. 37–38)

Outside of local television, social media sites and news platforms have introduced new ways of delivering, creating, and receiving media information. Like confirmation bias, a growing body of research is finding that many use social media platforms to reinforce their own ideologies and, in turn, reinforce a network of echo chambers (Brewer & Wallis, 2015; Stafford, 2016; Williams, McMurray, Kurz, & Lambert, 2015).

How We Use News

As mentioned above, the rise of social media and the proliferation of its use in the delivery of news has dramatically increased over the past decade. The power of social media in spreading news (or "fake news") during the 2016 presidential election remains an ongoing point of contention and investigation. And while all intelligence agencies in the United States maintain that there were official efforts on the part of Russia to leverage social media to wield influence over the outcome of the election, social media have increasingly become a place where individuals and organizations share information and news. And while much of our interaction on social media platforms like Facebook and Twitter operates generally within echo chambers (Boutyline & Willer, 2016; Brewer & Wallis, 2015; Colleoni, Rozza, & Arvidsson, 2014; Goldie, Linick, Jabbar, & Lubienski, 2014), the proliferation of misleading or false news has become a real threat to information gathering. For example, right-wing ideologues opposed to Hillary Clinton created and promoted a widely followed, false story about an underground child sex trafficking ring in the basement of a pizza parlor in Washington, D.C. The conspiracy theory, which came to be known as "Pizzagate," suggested that Clinton and John Podesta were directly involved in the illicit activity. The "news story" spread like wildfire across social media to the point where a Donald Trump supporter entered the restaurant with an assault rifle to "investigate" (Griffin, 2016). Other peddlers of right-wing fake news include Alex Jones of InfoWars. Jones, who promoted the Pizzagate fraud, consistently tells his listeners and readers that mass shooting events such as the one at Sandy Hook Elementary School in Newtown, Connecticut, which took the lives of 20 children and 6 educators, are false-flags or fake news that lend support to a government effort to confiscate guns. Jones's conspiracy theories have resulted in a slurry of death threats and intimidation tactics directed toward the parents who lost children in the massacre, as consumers of Jones's theories not only buy into his "info" or "news," but use that false information to inform illicit activity. Jones and others like him have found voice across a myriad of media platforms (radio, internet, and social media). In short, the rise of news and fake news across social media and the ability to spread false information across many platforms demand that we understand how the platforms are used and how they ought to be used. In August 2018, Facebook and YouTube removed Alex Jones's various pages associated with InfoWars, claiming that the content violated their user agreement and constituted threats (Rosenblatt, 2018).

In a large-scale survey, the Reynolds Journalism Institute found that individuals who self-identified as liberal were far more likely to be more trusting of what are generally understood as official news media than those who self-identified as conservatives (Kearney, 2017). Additionally, they found that White respondents were more likely to believe and trust news media information as compared to non-Whites. Liberal trust in the media remained steady across the age range 18–79, while conservative trust in the media steadily eroded across the same age range. Respondents were asked to list three sources of news they considered trustworthy and three that they considered untrustworthy (see Table 8.2). Other resources include the Media Bias/Fact Check website, which catalogues over 2,500 media sources and examines them for political leaning, bias, and fact reporting (Media Bias/Fact Check, n.d.).

Since the election of Donald Trump in 2016, hate crimes have increased dramatically (Bauman, 2018). Additionally, the far right has leveraged social media to further its attacks on those who do not align with their ideological perspective of the world. Some of these attacks have created false narratives about professors in an attempt to get them fired for seemingly not being adherents to far-right-wing philosophies of capitalism. White supremacists have even leveled death threats against professors for their perceived criticism of Trump and capitalism (Cuevas, 2018). Further, Donald Trump himself has suggested that the media are the enemy of the people, and the power of the media and social media has propelled that animus into actual violence and the threat of more

Table 8.2. Least and Most Trusted Sources of News

LEAST TRUSTED (LEAST TRUSTWORTHY AT TOP)	MOST TRUSTED (MOST TRUSTWORTHY AT TOP)
Occupy Democrats*	Atlantic
Buzzfeed	USA Today
Breitbart	New York Times
Social Media	Kansas City Star
Trump	Seattle Times
Infowars	Time
Yahoo	Washington Post
Internet	Denver Post
Huffington Post	Associated Press
Blaze	Politico
Fox	Local
Limbaugh	Dallas Morning News
ABC	LA Times
MSNBC	Wall Street Journal
Drudge Report	Guardian
NBC	PBS
CNN	NPR
CBS**	BBC
	Reuters
	Public Television
	Economist***

Note: Adapted from Kearney (2017).
* Occupy Democrats is listed as the most untrustworthy.
** Kearney depicts CBS as only slightly untrustworthy.
*** The Economist is listed as the most trustworthy.

violence against anyone who does not adhere to Trump's agenda (Miller, 2018). Turning Point USA (TPUSA) is a non-profit organization whose "mission is to identify, educate, train, and organize students to promote the principles of freedom, free markets, and limited government" (Turning Point USA, n.d.). Leveraging the power of social media, TPUSA purposefully engages in on-campus arguments in an attempt to lure in "angry liberals" on campus—namely professors—so that they can video the incident and post the videos on social media as evidence of the far-left "socialist" and "Marxist" state of American colleges and universities (This American Life, 2018). Their videos, heavily edited, receive tens of thousands of views. Additionally, TPSUSA maintains the "Professor Watchlist" in an effort to "expose and document college professors who discriminate against conservative students and advance leftist propaganda in the classroom" and inform students and parents of the "names of professors that advance a radical agenda in lecture halls" (Professor Watchlist, n.d.). TPUSA is heavily connected to the Koch brothers and with Donald Trump (DESMOG, n.d.) and has a history of racial bigotry (Kelley, 2018). Ongoing funding for the social media efforts led by TPUSA include the Ed Uihlein Foundation (which has heavily supported Wisconsin Governor Scott Walker and the Tea Party Patriots Citizens Fund), Illinois Governor Bruce Rauner, Home Depot co-founder Bernie Marcus, the Henry and Lynde Bradley Foundation, and the Richard and Helen DeVos Foundation (relatives of Betsy DeVos through marriage) (Kotch, 2017). Campus Reform is likewise a right-wing organization that leverages social media to expose what it considers to be a liberal bias on college campuses (Campus Reform, n.d.).

Other right-wing funded media websites that find a foundation in neoliberal ideology and promote the myths of education reform include The 74 and EducationPost (Schneider, 2016, 2017). These new forms of online media seek to shape the conversation about education reform. What appears online in terms of school reform is of interest, given the role that the media and internet play in how Americans develop opinions. For example, the search term "school voucher" reached its highest level in 10 years in February 2017 (Google Trends, n.d.). While there is no way to know for certain, it is entirely possible that the media coverage of Betsy DeVos's confirmation hearing in the month prior and her final confirmation drove the spike in searches for the term. In fact, the single largest day for searches of "school voucher" occurred on February 7, 2017, the day that DeVos was confirmed. The highest concentration of searches occurred in Indiana, and "Betsy DeVos" is a related query. If the media and websites that individuals land on are dominated by those who are funded by right-wing, pro-reform philanthropists, then the information is decidedly skewed in favor of privatization.

The concentration of local television news under the Sinclair Broadcast Group is not an isolated event. Consolidation of larger network news outlets has been ongoing for decades. As Chomsky suggested, power and control over the media are becoming ever more concentrated into fewer groups (Herman & Chomsky, 2002). In total, there are five companies that effectively control the entire media market. Comcast is the largest parent company across the broad media categories, with a market capitalization of $155,200,000,000. By comparison, the other market capitalizations are Disney with $147,900,000,000, TimeWarner with $64,600,000,000, 21st Century Fox with $47,100,000,000, CBS with $25,100,000,000, and Viacom with $14,700,000,000 (*Wall Street Journal*, 2016). In total, the major networks and their parent companies' combined capitalization is valued at just under $455 billion. At the time of this writing, the Justice Department under the Trump administration approved a bid by Disney to purchase 21st Century Fox for $71 billion (Lee & Kang, 2018). The move will reduce the total number of parent companies from five to four.

The problem as it relates to the concentration of power over media is that it can become a tool for propaganda, fake news, and partisan bias. The European Association for Viewers Interests (EAVI), an organization focused on media literacy, developed a taxonomy of misleading news beyond the catchall "fake news" that has become so prolific since the 2016 presidential election in the United States (EAVI, n.d.). The ten types of misleading news are detailed in Table 8.3.

The scripted segments across all Sinclair Broadcast Group stations have been described as right-leaning material that is presented in such a way that it appears to be news. Often, these segments have been explicitly pro-Trump and have helped spread many of

Table 8.3. Types of Misleading News

TYPE	CHARACTERISTICS	IMPACT	MOTIVATION
Propaganda	Used by governments and corporations to manage values and knowledge	Neutral	Passion, Politics/Power
Clickbait	Eye-catching, sensational headlines; content may not reflect headline	Low	Money, Humor/Fun
Sponsored Content	Made to look editorial, difficult to immediately discern that it is an advertisement	Low	Money
Satire/Hoax	Humor, social commentary	Low	Humor/Fun
Error	Mistakes published by reputable news organizations (corrections often follow)	Low	(Mis)Inform
Partisan	Ideological interpretation of facts; uses facts to further confirm bias	Medium	Passion, Politics/Power
Conspiracy Theory	Non-falsifiable, evidence contrary to conspiracy is regarded as proof of the conspiracy, rejects experts	High	Passion, (Mis)Inform
Pseudoscience	Anti-vaccination, climate change denial	High	Politics/Power, Money
Misinformation	Mix of factual and false information, false or party-content	High	(Mis)Inform
Bogus	Entirely fabricated, meant to intentionally mislead, bots, motivated by politics and/or ad revenue	High	Politics/Power, Money

Note: Adapted from EAVI (n.d.).

Trump's own manufactured fake news stories (Zurawik, 2017). Applying EAVI's taxonomy, the SBG segments could be classified as propaganda, partisanship, and/or misinformation.

Understanding that the push to reform education by reimagining it as a private good that is best overseen and delivered through private control requires the ongoing cultivation of the myth that schools have failed. The media, in all forms, serve as the method of maintenance of that myth through the production of distorted information about schools, about teachers, and the need to place them in private hands. The aim of such reforms—funded almost entirely by right-wing venture philanthropists—is to deregulate education and, often as a result, to increase personal profits. These reformers have sought to take control of all facets of news media, from college newspapers to local television to social media. The aim is to shape the narrative. And having the ability to shape that narrative, much in the way that a salesman gives an elevator pitch, establishes the desired reality in which a product can be sold. Without a doubt, when it comes to education and the media, the product being sold is privatization.

References

Bauman, D. (2018). *After 2016 election, campus hate crimes seemed to jump. Here's what the data tell us.* Retrieved August 7, 2018, from https://www.chronicle.com/article/After-2016-Election-Campus/242577

Berliner, D.C., & Biddle, B.J. (1995). *The manufactured crisis: Myths, fraud, and the attack on America's public schools.* Reading, MA: Addison-Wesley.

Boutyline, A., & Willer, R. (2016). The social structure of political echo chambers: Variation in ideological homophily in online networks. *Political Psychology, 38*(3), 551–569.

Brewer, T.J., & Wallis, M. (2015). #TFA: The intersection of social media and education reform. *Critical Education, 6*(14), 1–18.

Campus Reform. (n.d.). *About.* Retrieved August 1, 2018 from https://www.campusreform.org/about/

Colleoni, E., Rozza, A., & Arvidsson, A. (2014). Echo chamber or public sphere? Predicting political orientation and measuring political homophily in twitter using big data. *Journal of Communication, 64*, 317–332.

Cuevas, J. (2018). *A new reality? The far right's use of cyberharassment against academics: A firsthand account by a targeted faculty member.* Retrieved July 1, 2018, from https://www.aaup.org/article/new-reality-far-rights-use-cyberharassment-against-academics-.W2metC2ZNTY

DESMOG. (n.d.). *Turning point USA (TPUSA) background.* Retrieved August 1, 2018, from https://www.desmogblog.com/turning-point-usa

Domonoske, C. (2018). *Video reveals power of Sinclair, as local news anchors recite script in unison.* Retrieved July 1, 2018, from https://www.npr.org/sections/thetwo-way/2018/04/02/598794433/video-reveals-power-of-sinclair-as-local-news-anchors-recite-script-in-unison

EAVI. (n.d.). *Infographic: Beyond fake news—10 types of misleading news.* Retrieved January 1, 2018, from https://eavi.eu/beyond-fake-news-10-types-misleading-info/

Ford, D., Porfilio, B.J., & Goldstein, R.A. (2015). The news media, education, and the subversion of the neoliberal social imaginary. *Critical Education, 6*(7), 1–24.

García, J. (2015). Learning from bad teachers: The neoliberal agenda for education in popular media. *Critical Education, 6*(13), 1–18.

Gerstl-Pepin, C.I. (2002). Media (mis)representations of education in the 2000 presidential election. *Educational Policy, 16*(1), 37–55.

Goldie, D., Linick, M., Jabbar, H., & Lubienski, C. (2014). Using bibliometric and social media analyses to explore the "echo chamber" hypothesis. *Educational Policy, 28*(2), 281–305.

Goldstein, D. (2014). *The teacher wars: A history of America's most embattled profession.* New York: Doubleday.

Google Trends. (n.d.). *School voucher.* Retrieved August 1, 2018, from https://trends.google.com/trends/explore?date=today%20 5-y&geo=US&q=school%20voucher

Gottfried, J., & Shearer, E. (2017). *Americans' online news use is closing in on tv news use.* Retrieved July 1, 2018, from http://www.pewresearch.org/fact-tank/2017/09/07/americans-online-news-use-vs-tv-news-use/

Griffin, A. (2016). *What is Pizzagate? The Hillary Clinton conspiracy theory that led to a man opening fire in a restaurant.* Retrieved July 1, 2018, from https://www.independent.co.uk/life-style/gadgets-and-tech/news/pizzagate-what-is-it-explained-hillary-clinton-paedophile-conspiracy-gunman-fake-news-a7456681.html

Herman, E., & Chomsky, N. (2002). *Manufacturing consent: The political economy of the mass media*. New York: Pantheon.

Kearney, M.W. (2017). *Trusting news project report 2017*. Columbia, MO: Reynolds Journalism Institute. Retrieved from https://www.rjionline.org/downloads/who-trusts-and-pays-for-the-news-heres-what-8728-people-told-us/

Kelley, B.J. (2018). *Turning Point USA's blooming romance with the alt-right*. Retrieved August 1, 2018, from https://www.splcenter.org/hatewatch/2018/02/16/turning-point-usas-blooming-romance-alt-right

Klein, J. (2011). *The failure of American schools*. Retrieved July 1, 2018, from https://www.theatlantic.com/magazine/archive/2011/06/the-failure-of-american-schools/308497/

Kotch, A. (2017). *Who funds conservative campus group Turning Point USA? Donors revealed*. Retrieved August 1, 2018, from https://www.ibtimes.com/political-capital/who-funds-conservative-campus-group-turning-point-usa-donors-revealed-2620325

Kumashiro, K. (2012). *Bad teacher! How blaming teachers distorts the bigger picture*. New York: Teachers College Press.

Lee, E., & Kang, C. (2018). *Justice Dept. approves Disney's purchase of Fox assets*. Retrieved August 7, 2018, from https://www.nytimes.com/2018/06/27/business/media/disney-fox-antitrust-comcast.html

Levitsky, S., & Ziblatt, D. (2018). *How democracies die*. New York: Crown.

Lopez, S.J. (2010). *America's views of public schools still far worse than parents'*. Retrieved February 1, 2018, from http://news.gallup.com/poll/142658/americans-views-public-schools-far-worse-parents.aspx

Malin, J.R., & Lubienski, C. (2015). Educational expertise, advocacy, and media influence. *Education Policy Analysis Archives, 23*(6), 1–32.

Matsa, K. (2018). *Fewer Americans rely on tv news; What type they watch varies by who they are*. Retrieved July 1, 2018, from http://www.pewresearch.org/fact-tank/2018/01/05/fewer-americans-rely-on-tv-news-what-type-they-watch-varies-by-who-they-are/

Matthews, D. (2018). *Sinclair, the pro-Trump, conservative company taking over local news, explained*. Retrieved August 1, 2018, from https://www.vox.com/2018/4/3/17180020/sinclair-broadcast-group-conservative-trump-david-smith-local-news-tv-affiliate

Media Bias/Fact Check. (n.d.). *About.* Retrieved August 1, 2018, from https://mediabiasfactcheck.com/about/

Miller, H. (2018). *C-SPAN caller threatens "to shoot" CNN hosts Brian Stelter and Don Lemon.* Retrieved August 7, 2018 from https://www.huffingtonpost.com/entry/c-span-cnn-brian-stelter-don-lemon_us_5b674492e4b0fd5c73dacf89

Professor Watchlist. (n.d.). *About us.* Retrieved August 1, 2018, from https://www.professorwatchlist.org/about-us/

Roberts-Miller, P. (2017). *Demagoguery and democracy.* New York: The Experiment.

Rosenblatt, K. (2018). *Facebook, YouTube and Apple remove Alex Jones and Infowars from their platforms.* Retrieved August 8, 2018, from https://www.nbcnews.com/tech/tech-news/facebook-removes-four-pages-belonging-infowars-alex-jones-n897861

Schneider, M. (2016). *About "Education Post, the Nonprofit"—including its anonymous donor.* Retrieved August 2, 2018, from https://www.huffingtonpost.com/mercedes-schneider/about-education-post-the-_b_9769482.html

Schneider, M. (2017). *In 2015, The 74 media was overwhelmingly funded by litigious, union-busting, Partnership for Ed Justice.* Retrieved August 2, 2018 from https://deutsch29.wordpress.com/2017/10/10/in-2015-the-74-media-was-overwhelmingly-funded-by-litigious-union-busting-partnership-for-ed-justice/

Shearer, E., & Gottfried, J. (2017). *News use across social media platforms 2017.* Retrieved July 1, 2018, from http://www.journalism.org/2017/09/07/news-use-across-social-media-platforms-2017/

Spring, J. (2010). *Political agendas for education* (4th ed.). New York: Routledge.

Spring, J. (2011). *The politics of American education.* New York: Routledge.

Stafford, T. (2016). *How to check if you're in a news echo chamber—and what to do about it.* Retrieved July 1, 2018, from https://theconversation.com/how-to-check-if-youre-in-a-news-echo-chamber-and-what-to-do-about-it-69999

This American Life. (2018). *My effing First Amendment*. Retrieved August 1, 2018, from https://www.thisamericanlife.org/645/my-effing-first-amendment

Turning Point USA. (n.d.). *About Turning Point USA*. Retrieved August 7, 2018, from https://www.tpusa.com/aboutus/

Wall Street Journal. (2016). *Chart: Media behemoths*. Retrieved August 1, 2018, from https://www.wsj.com/livecoverage/att-timewarner-senate-hearing/card/1481127262

Williams, H.T.P., McMurray, J.R., Kurz, T., & Lambert, F.H. (2015). Network analysis reveals open forums and echo chambers in social media discussions of climate change. *Global Environmental Change, 32*, 126–138.

Wubbena, Z.C. (2015). Breathing secondhand smoke: Gatekeeping for "good" education, passive democracy, and the mass media: An interview with Noam Chomsky. *Critical Education, 6*(8), 1–9.

Wubbena, Z.C., Ford, D., & Porfilio, B.J. (2016). *News media and the neoliberal privatization of education*. Charlotte, NC: Information Age Publishing.

Zurawik, D. (2017). *Sinclair Broadcast Group is finding out how harsh the national spotlight can be*. Retrieved August 2, 2018 from http://www.baltimoresun.com/entertainment/tv/z-on-tv-blog/bs-fe-zontv-sinclair-trump-20170705-story.html

Chapter Nine

FOUNDRY10:
AN EXAMPLE OF PHILANTHROPY BUILDING SCHOOL AND COMMUNITY PARTNERSHIPS
by Lisa Castaneda

Preface

In the previous chapters we examined several examples of how Big Philanthropy impacts the U.S. education system, often serving the interests of an elite few. This chapter, written by Lisa Castenada, describes how the philanthropic foundation foundry10 is working in a different way within communities to impact education in localized and meaningful ways. The chapter shows how philanthropy can be done in a way that includes the voices of community members in a true ground-up strategy, rather than the "AstroTurf" strategies employed by the Koch brothers, the SPN, and organizations such as ALEC. As detailed in this chapter, many of foundry10's projects come from within the classroom itself, with the initial impetus for projects coming from students' ideas and educators' experiences. Foundry10's approach to doing educational philanthropy is best summarized in this statement: "We believe that educators working directly with students know and understand the needs of their students in ways that we, as outsiders, cannot." Educators may find this example useful for searching out and collaborating in different ways with educational philanthropy foundations in their own local school contexts.

Philanthropic educational foundations often have similar origin stories: a wealthy benefactor wishes to deploy funds to help improve education in some measurable way. Our story at foundry10 begins in a somewhat similar manner but diverges quickly from the traditional model into something that functions very differently from most philanthropic organizations. We are a philanthropic educational research organization co-founded by myself, a former teacher, in partnership with a successful programmer and businessman named Gabe Newell. In this chapter I share a bit about our origins and organizational structure/philosophy and then move on to some concrete examples of how our approach to philanthropy involves a collaborative partnership with educators. Through stories and examples, it is my hope that others may feel inspired or compelled to expand their thinking about what educational philanthropy has the potential to be.

Our Story

After spending a short time in the corporate world, my passion for education led me to a teaching certification program and, ultimately, a master's in education. While working toward the master's degree, I became increasingly concerned with the gap between research in academia and its application in the classroom. As I gained exposure to educators from other communities, my concerns about the inequity of the educational experience in the Greater Seattle area steadily deepened. In both sharing and listening to the stories about the ways in which educational philanthropies intersected with local schools, I felt a sense of unease about educational philanthropy's ability to sometimes be invasive rather than supportive of my peers' work with children. At this point in time, a parent at the school in which I was teaching approached me to discuss the idea of teaming up to do work involving both research and philanthropy in education. As we discussed the challenges inherent in the educational system, the two of us decided that co-founding an educational research organization that would operate philanthropically, with a focus on creating value directly for kids, would be a useful endeavor. Thus, in the spring of 2013, Gabe Newell and I co-founded what would come to be known as foundry10, with the idea that it would be an active, collaborative research organization that emphasized community voices. He would provide the funding for the organization, and I would direct the operations, hiring, and initiatives that we would ultimately develop.

Gabe and I wanted to take an agile, child-centered approach to the generally slow process of advancing education. He felt that the best way to do that was to empower someone who had educational experience as the primary architect of that structure. Though his experience within the software and business world would prove invaluable in terms of my own understanding of how to build an organization, my expertise with children, teachers, and learning would form the basis of all decisions in terms of how we functioned and utilized our resources. My experience as an educator has a direct influence on the organizational decisions I make, particularly with regard to student/teacher interactions.

Our Structure and Our People

In terms of how we function, we have an intentionally broad list of areas on which we prefer to focus. We often form collaborative connections with others through the work we have done in related communities that is focused on similar questions or concerns. Then, based on our partners' experiences in their community and our knowledge in those areas, we co-design something that we all believe will create value for children. At that point, if the idea is something that will require funding in order to implement it, we work to make that portion of the process as straightforward as possible for our partners. Our philanthropic endeavors don't follow the traditional grant structure and are not one-size-fits-all. We believe that educators working directly with students know and understand the needs of their students in ways that we, as outsiders, cannot. And we know that because we are independent researchers, we bring a knowledge and experience that classroom teachers may not possess to help design and implement ideas.

We believe that one of the primary considerations when structuring a philanthropic endeavor should be the experience that those in leadership have with the cause they are designed to support. Foundry10 is a philanthropic educational research organization whose goal is to undertake research that will create value for kids and teachers. The philanthropic portion is key in that the programs, projects, and research we engage in are not limited by the financial constraints that permeate the education field as a whole; we provide charitable donations (or in-kind donations) to schools as part of our work in nearly every project or program. Our projects often start quite small with community-level partnerships, and, if it seems like something that might be interesting to more people, we find avenues to share the findings and help others try variants of those ideas.

Our research questions are derived in conjunction with the educators we work with so that they address concerns in the field. In fact, several projects were initiated as the result of students reaching out to us with ideas that originated in their own classrooms, where research questions find articulation through such conversations. Whenever possible, we prefer to work directly at the classroom or school level to help ensure that programs are linked to people who are enthusiastic and directly connected to children. If a connection comes to us from a district or administrative level, we try to loop teachers into the process as quickly as possible to keep it grounded in practice.

Foundry10 operates within a relatively flat organizational structure, thus empowering all employees to start projects, form collaborations with outside parties, make decisions, and pursue ideas. We believe that this organizational structure allows for diverse thinking and true opportunities for equity. There is no "work your way up" in order to have a voice here. To do that would diminish the potential of individuals to show how their knowledge and lived experience within the educational paradigm can be of use to the communities in which we collaborate.

Foundry10 employees range in academic experience from current high school students to people with PhDs, as we believe it is important to capture a wide spectrum of educational experiences to help us further connect with the lived experiences of those we serve. The emphasis here is on placing individuals with a range of experiences in meaningful, empowered roles. If we cannot hear, acknowledge, and act upon the voices within our group, how can we possibly expect to hear, acknowledge, and act in concert with the voices in the communities we are trying to serve?

Our goal, structurally, is to create an environment where things happen (hence the name foundry10, a foundry being a place where things are created; we didn't want to be a place where people just thought and did not take action). Though we ground our work in theory and research, we see ourselves as a place of action within communities where we invest time and energy to connect with people on a real, human level.

One aspect of traditionally hierarchical structures within educational philanthropy that can be so frustrating is that as people reach the top of the hierarchy, they are often many years removed from working directly with children. This is a challenging place in which to effectively operate, particularly in data- and research-focused organizations where there is a great deal of pressure to provide standard metrics of success. The further removed from actual contact with children one becomes, the easier it is to see programs and projects as numbers, money spent, and metrics either met or missed. At foundry10, all employees are asked to maintain regular interactions with children in the course of their work. These interactions vary depending on role. For some employees, that takes the form of teaching a program in the community; for others, it involves mentorship of youth through one of our on-site programs. Some spend time in classrooms collaborating on programs with teachers, and still others actively mentor and engage with youth employed by the organization. We feel that this point cannot be emphasized too strongly. If educational philanthropists truly want to be in touch and mindful of the work they are doing to help children, we believe they absolutely must spend regular time with the children they are working to serve.

Case Example #1: Partnering with Educators

Educators are often asked (or in some cases told) to implement programs in their classrooms either because of a new curriculum adoption, a new staff member, or perhaps a grant that the school has received. This is sometimes done with little or no regard or recognition of the teachers' knowledge of their own student population and the relative usefulness of any such intervention. We insist on collaborative connections with teachers for three reasons. First, it allows us to learn from the individuals we are working with so that we can share such knowledge with future collaborators. Second, though we may have ideas about what would make for interesting educational endeavors, we understand very well that the people who know their students best are the ones who spend every day with them. Third, by collaborating with the teacher directly, the program we create is more sustainable in that classroom and school community.

An example of how this works came from a principal in a local district who was interested in developing a spring break intervention. We interacted with her while running a different summer school dramatic arts intervention that used her district's building. The principal was inspired by the summer program as she watched it unfold and asked if we could sit down and brainstorm a way to shorten the format, apply it to kids struggling in math (the summer program focused solely on reading), and provide opportunities for kids to learn during spring break. The school is Title 1 and has a struggling student population. After an initial conversation with the principal, we said that teacher buy-in was essential in order to move ahead, especially considering that this would be a spring break program. She began to talk informally to teachers about the idea, and once she had several teachers who expressed interest, we began the process of determining both the research questions we would investigate collaboratively and the metrics we would use to gauge the project's success.

As the project evolved in conversations with the teachers and the principal, we saw that the school team was strongly motivated to try a different approach that allowed for more flexibility, creativity, and support for families during spring break (which can be a particularly tough time for the working poor in terms of feeding their children and finding childcare). We agreed that the program would likely create value in terms of student learning but wanted to help ensure that there really was an aspect of dramatic arts integrated into the core curriculum they wanted to design. Discussions began to expand to include our drama specialist and network of teaching artists. We would provide the personnel, and initial determinations were made about how the school would likely select student participants. With the heavy arts component, we felt confident that there would be creative value in addition to providing stability for kids and offering additional curricular exposure outside of standard school hours. The school was interested in improving students' math test scores, which we agreed would be beneficial for children, but we were also interested in student subject-area interest, motivation, and sense of self-efficacy. Working with the school, we devised a plan to enable us to gather an array of qualitative and quantitative data that would meet the needs of both groups. We hoped that student scores would improve, but we were equally concerned that student motivation and interest increase. Each step was collaborative, and teachers were compensated by foundry10 for the planning and meeting times as part of the funding we provided. We also assisted the school in finding additional funding sources to further offset the costs of the program.

As the start of the program approached, the principal and teachers realized that although they had earmarked spaces for certain kids who were really struggling in math, there was an additional subset of students who were not struggling in math but were homeless and, quite literally, had nowhere to go during spring break. The teachers and principal felt it was appropriate—and indeed necessary—to alter the program slightly to meet the needs of that group of students as well. The school felt that the inherent value of having a place to be, with peers, breakfast and lunch provided, and the opportunity to engage with dramatic arts and music in a safe setting was invaluable for the homeless students, even if they did not need the math intervention, and was the correct choice for their community. We had no problem with the alteration, but we realized that some of the measures of success might shift. Now we had students who had no need of math remediation occupying a few spots.

As an organization, we make decisions that benefit children directly, even if that means the metrics at the end might not look the way we initially thought they would. Through continued dialogue with school personnel, we understood why they made the decisions they did and were pleased that they felt empowered to do what needed to be done to be responsive to their community. This program has now run for several years, and the joint collaborative effort has continued to be refined and iterated each year.

Case Example #2: Student-Initiated Projects

We often feel as though there is a lack of attention and funding for vocational programs, even though they can create enormous value for students. Because of this and our regard for the way in which students pursue areas of interest such as automotive technology as career paths, we went into the community and began observing programs and talking with teachers and students. We learned about schools in our community that were very interested in doing some kind of special, larger automotive project but lacked the necessary funding to do so. We wanted to better understand the type of student learning that might occur with a larger, focused auto project.

It was important to us that students generate an idea that was exciting to them rather than be told by us to do something. Students researched potential auto projects with their teachers and presented multiple ideas to us based on their interests. At one school, we funded an A/C electric dragster, a type of car that had never been built by students prior to this project. It was an extremely advanced project, but the students felt confident that with some outside expert assistance they could pull it off. Their teacher ultimately became certified to race the dragster (since the district would not allow students to drive it) and set a world record with students serving as the pit crew.

At another school, students put together a very creative presentation about how they would build Model T kit cars with a hybrid/V8 conversion. We donated the equipment and ultimately the project (which was rebuildable, so the cars could be used year after year) became the foundation for a third-year advanced automotive class. The teacher had wanted to have a larger project for third-year students so that he could build out a curriculum, and this project helped form the basis of that program. A third school opted to work with specialized electronic circuit boards because students wanted to better understand automotive electronics (which is becoming increasingly important and is the focus of little or no instruction at the high school level).

In all cases, we were able to gather interesting data about student learning, exposure to advanced technology, and career paths in vocational programs. Students were exposed to projects rarely attempted at the high school level and were able to leverage their classwork for resumes and on auto training program applications. We saw the students' interest and curiosity, we worked with the schools, and we provided the opportunity to explore projects of interest that would also be valuable and relevant to their future plans. Again, we believe that educational philanthropy is not about us imposing our values and metrics on other people; rather, it is about working together to consider what is beneficial for a particular group of children and then finding ways to check in and ensure that we did, indeed, create a worthwhile experience.

Case Example #3: School-Initiated Projects

As I constructed this chapter, a teacher involved in one of our technology programs was facing several structural challenges at her school. She reached out to us in frustration because she needed help, and her school's IT position no longer existed; the person had left, and the district had not replaced him due to structural issues within the district itself. She didn't want to be a burden on us but felt that she was going to have to drop parts of the program plan because she was unable to solve the difficult and time-consuming tech challenges without support. Because of the way we function, we were able to get one of our technical team members on a plane to go out to her classroom and help her. By providing her with assistance, we also helped to ensure that the children who were meant to benefit from the program had a greater likelihood of engaging with the technology as intended. Things ultimately came together quite well because we were able to ensure that the project functioned in a way that worked for her. This was an inner-city school with a large population of students who were truly interested in art. Doing virtual art became quite popular among the students. They found a new way to express their artistic interests, and the teacher witnessed an increase in both community building and student interest in ways of using technology to increase artistic expression. The teacher had connected with us because she was interested in bringing an advanced technology into her classroom in a way that supported her work as an art teacher. We worked with her to provide the tools and some support to help her get the program she had imagined off the ground.

Another example of teachers initiating projects with us comes from a particular experience we had working with an elementary school to implement a comprehensive after-school program. The teachers asked if we could assist in designing and funding the program, and we said that if they would be willing to survey their students and teachers about what should be offered as after-school programming, we would be glad to team up. There was a great deal of interest, and amid a plethora of ideas (hip-hop dance, science club, archery, dramatic arts, and others), one of the things the students and teachers were most excited about was after-school kickball. We were a bit surprised, since we generally had not provided any funding for things such as kickball (people are usually much more interested in STEM subjects or art). We funded it and asked the teachers and students to give us feedback about the program. To our great surprise, kickball was the most popular offering, as the school structured it to be a community-building experience. Younger children were paired with older buddies so that students of different ages and grades could play and learn the game together and form connections. Kids loved it, teachers were excited, and it altered the way children interacted with each other after the program.

Though these are small examples, they illustrate the value in taking a step back to listen and learn from the needs/wants of a community. Importantly, we did not decide to form a committee on kickball education and then try to spread this program across the nation in every school. We recognized that the most valuable take-away from that experience was that, once again, a school was listening to its community and saw an opportunity to connect and use resources to do something for its unique population. It was an example to us of how we need to be humble and open, and that the best ideas are often not things that would be useful on a mass scale, for all students.

Elements We Find Helpful in This Type of Philanthropy

Our approach to philanthropic work in education has its foundation in the following ideas, which we think could be incorporated into other organizations and add value to the work they do:

- Staying grounded in student and teacher voice. It is easy, in any philanthropy, to let the good feelings of acting cloud the view of what value could and should be created. Focusing on listening to the groups most affected—teachers and students—as much as possible and working collaboratively helps us to better reflect on whether or not a program is optimally meeting the need for which it was created.

- A commitment on the part of everyone involved to look more broadly at metrics, focusing on the value we create for students versus relying on standard mechanisms for metrics such as test scores or being hyper-focused on one area, such as STEM.
- An organizational staff that represents a diverse array of educational backgrounds and experiences. If we only invite people for whom the system has worked well, we are dismissing the ideas of many who may have much to share.
- Partnerships that are not simply tied to a fixed amount of funding but are connections for creating value directly for children. Whenever possible, allowing some flexibility in budgeting to account for potential problems and to ensure that projects really do what was intended.
- Regular interaction with the student populations we serve is vital, at all levels of the organization. An organization that is designed to serve the needs of children does this best by having employees who regularly interact with children and see their work in action.
- Truly collaborative design between our team and the communities we serve, with an emphasis on shared expertise. By bringing multiple voices to the table, we can design stronger programs and research projects that resonate within the community and provide external validity to the studies we undertake.
- An iterative approach to projects and programs. Building and developing programs year-over-year in coordination with the communities we serve relieves some of the pressure to get everything perfect the first time and gives us the flexibility to improve the program the next time.

Concluding Thoughts

In order to help children develop into creative, compassionate, and interesting adults, we need to provide them with the opportunity to engage in a range of activities and to have positive experiences that may not directly translate into improved test scores. When philanthropic organizations put all of their weight on student performance of academic tasks, they are forcing students, teachers, and administrators into a funnel. The pressure on all of those groups to "perform" well in order to maintain funding—or even apply for funding—is counterproductive. Interesting and capable people don't just magically develop because their test scores were strong.

What we hope to illustrate in our work is that through a diverse staff, open and flexible structure, and genuine collaboration with outside groups and individuals, our philanthropic work has expanded in ways we never would have imagined. We invest in people and provide them the opportunity to create interesting things for children, and we make a really huge effort to share our work. We make available our data sets, our programs, our projects—everything we learn from all of the programs and research. Though we publish in academic journals, we also make it a point to present and co-present at teacher-focused events, write popular press pieces, and share data with schools so that they can use it to further develop their own projects and programs.

Yet showing success is important. One of the great challenges of educational philanthropy is balancing money, data, outcomes, and children. In order to do so effectively, an organization must be knowledgeable in all those areas. As researchers, we know that data can say what we want them to say, and that statistical significance does not necessarily translate into educational significance. People who work in schools know their students in ways that we, even as educators ourselves, do not, and to ignore those voices when trying to do good in communities is an egregious mistake. As stewards of the money we have been entrusted with for the benefit of children, we have a fiscal and ethical responsibility to do so wisely. We encourage those in power in other organizations to be open to accepting the fact that the collective wisdom of the larger group of people with whom we collaborate will help us to make better, more interesting choices. We cannot impact the educational landscape by choosing to hear only the voices of the people who went to graduate school. We cannot invite a community member to have brunch with us and then speak as though we understand the true needs of a diverse group of individuals.

Though we are certainly newer to the scene and perhaps smaller players in the field of educational philanthropy than others, we feel like we are filling an overlooked niche. While not all of the facets of our organization are obtainable by others, we believe that there is space in many other organizations to reflect upon the diversity of their staff, the empowerment of their employees, how they collaborate with external partners, their own interactions with children, and the metrics they use to gauge success. Educational philanthropy is important work, and many schools and community groups would not have the opportunities they have enjoyed without it. As a collective group, we must consider how we use what we have to empower and build up communities of learners and how we connect with those communities in a humble and responsive way.

Chapter Ten

COLLECTIVE RESISTANCE:
RESOURCES FOR CHANGE

In the previous chapters, we have aimed to document and contextualize the impact of philanthropy on educational systems in the United States. We have explored the details of how Big Philanthropy has been used as a tool to fuel a conservative ideological war on public education for many decades, how the *Citizens United* ruling has reduced the power that ordinary citizens have by allowing special rights to resource rich corporations, and how organizations like ALEC are facilitating private industry to gain influence in the drafting of model education policy with state legislators. We have also tracked the activities of Big Philanthropy in higher education (such as those of the Charles Koch Foundation), surveyed the current ideological landscape as it impacts educational policy, and documented the various roles that the media play in influencing public opinion in regard to education. Finally, we have offered an alternative vision of the role of philanthropy in education with the case study of foundry10, an educational philanthropic organization that works from within communities to suit their needs, rather than dictating policy and action from the top down. In this final chapter, we aim to provide educators and concerned citizens with resources and suggestions to help them to stay informed about the role of philanthropy in their local education communities and what actions they can take to better serve the educational needs of those communities. Resources and suggestions for collective action listed below for each chapter and topical area.

Chapters Two and Three:
Chapter Two: "The Haves and the Have Mores:" Fueling a Conservative Ideological War on Public Education [reprinted]; and Chapter Three: "The Haves and the Have Mores": An Update, 2005–2008

We encourage readers to use databases such as Foundation Directory Online (https://fconline.foundationcenter.org/), sometimes available through university libraries or by subscription, or free sites such as Conservative Transparency (http://conservativetransparency.org/) to track the funding of Big Philanthropy. Chapters Three through Ten (below) provide additional resources to further explore specific components of the conservative strategies.

Chapter Four:
Citizens United and the Disuniting of the United States

In the wake of the *Citizens United* ruling, the resources below can be used by educators to stay informed and take action in their communities.

Educators and concerned citizens can choose to join or organize a local group of Move to Amend. Move to Amend advocates adding a 28th Amendment, which would assert that rights provided by the Constitution are rights of natural persons only; therefore, corporations do not have constitutional rights. This amendment would address the ways in which campaigns can be financed (https://movetoamend.org/wethepeopleamendment).

Working with existing organizations concerned with the impact of *Citizens United* on education policy is another good way for educators and concerned citizens to get involved. Join and get involved with Common Cause, which is working to combat ALEC, to end gerrymandering, and to overturn *Citizens United* (https://www.commoncause.org/). Free Speech for People is another organization that is working to end Super PACs, advocating for the adoption of the 28th Amendment, and challenging foreign influence over U.S. elections (https://freespeechforpeople.org/).

The site Reclaim Democracy offers additional readings and lists organizations and actions people can take (http://reclaimdemocracy.org/who-are-citizens-united/).

Chapter Five:
Hidden Strategies State by State:
The History and Work of the American Legislative Exchange Council (ALEC), 1973–2018

As discussed in Chapter Five, the American Legislative Exchange Council's (ALEC) "bill mill" activities used to be hidden from public view. However, since at least 2002, ALEC's activities have been brought to light in public discourse by various media sources. Educators and concerned citizens may find it useful to take the time to "get to know ALEC" and what activities the council is taking that might impact their communities. Various media sources have brought ALEC to the American public's attention, including websites, online videos or newscasts, and articles (print and online) or blog posts, and these can be used to familiarize yourself with the history of ALEC and its most recent activities. Our curated list of websites that track and represent ALEC's activities (http://bit.ly/ALECWEBSITES), informational video sources describing ALEC's activities (http://bit.ly/ALECVIDEOS), and online articles and blogs referencing ALEC's activities (http://bit.ly/ALECARTICLES) can be found using the aforementioned permanent links. Depending on the level at which educators teach, they may use these resources as teaching tools to educate their students about organizations like ALEC and to explore how Big Philanthropy can seek to influence policies that affect their educational lives and beyond.

Educators may find it useful to reach out to local and state-level progressive grassroots organizations. For example, in the State of Georgia, the organization Better Georgia (http://bettergeorgia.org/) provides information and resources for citizens on a variety of political issues that are particular to the state, including issues related to education. Better Georgia is free to join and offers members newsletters and emails about current political issues. Better Georgia has also dedicated a page to tracking ALEC's activities (http://bettergeorgia.org/category/government-accountability/alec/). If you are unable to locate a similar resource in your state, you may consider starting your own network or reaching out to an organization in another state for additional information.

Chapter Six:
Philanthropy Goes to College: Tracking the Money

In our chapter on the impact of Big Philanthropy on institutions of higher education, we explored the importance of tracking the money that flows into universities in order to highlight any threats to academic integrity that might arise as a result of philanthropic donors who use their financial gifts as a way to leverage influence within universities. In order to combat this phenomenon, we encourage educators and concerned citizens to connect with and use resources provided by existing organizations that track the money (and possible strings attached) flowing into institutions of higher education. In cases where it is appropriate, educators and concerned citizens can help encourage universities to "resist the gift" if the gift comes with strings attached.

The organization UnKoch My Campus publishes articles and reports related to the Koch brothers' influence in higher education. You can join their mailing list, donate, and/or learn more about how to connect with the organization to protect your local campus (http://www.unkochmycampus.org/). On the UnKoch My Campus website, educators can learn more about the Association for Private Enterprise Education (APEE), a network of college professors dedicated to promoting Charles Koch's "integrated strategy," including leaked recordings and transcripts of a 2016 conference program (http://www.unkochmycampus.org/kochileaks/) and a list of conference participants by university. This archive also lists the names of presenters and representatives from ALEC and the SPN who attended the conference (https://ia801209.us.archive.org/17/items/APEETracker2016/APEE%20Tracker%20-%202016.pdf).

Chapter Six tracks the tremendous influence of the Charles Koch Foundation on universities. If you are curious about whether Koch has given money to a university near you, check out Greenpeace's Polluterwatch, Charles Koch University Funding Database for information on Koch Foundation funding to universities between 2005 and 2015, sourced from IRS 990 tax filings (http://polluterwatch.org/charles-koch-university-funding-database).

Another great resource for becoming more informed on the impact of Big Philanthropy on higher education is the work, websites, and wiki pages curated by the Center for Media and Democracy. The Center for Media and Democracy's SourceWatch Wiki page tracks corporations and PR spin, tracks ALEC's model bills and activities, tracks studies disseminated by the State Policy Network, and tracks Koch money and influence (https://www.sourcewatch.org/index.php/SourceWatch). The Center for Media and Democracy's PR Watch which leads investigations, public information requests, and lawsuits that inquire into the influence of money on politics, law, and democracy (https://www.prwatch.org/cmd/index.html). Within this site, you can search specifically for articles and resources related to education (https://www.prwatch.org/topics/education).

Chapter Seven:
Ideological Bedfellows: Elevating the Individual over the Collective Good in Education

While our chapter on Ideological Bedfellows paints a gloomy picture of the landscape across educational policy, there are organizations that are fighting against the insular power that reformers have developed. We've chosen to list these organizations online in an effort to maintain an active list that can be updated over time. Our curated list can be found using this permanent link (bit.ly/ResistanceOrgs). Because the list is live, we would like to hear from you about existing or new organizations as they being their work fighting against the privatization of education.

Chapter Eight:
The Megaphone Behind the Myth: The Media's Role in Shaping Public Discourse about Education Reform

As educators and citizens, we believe that the best course of action when curating where you get your news (and the types of news you pass along to your students) is to understand where the information comes from, what bias might exist, and whom might the distortion benefit. In the era of fake news, it is important to have tools to determine the reliability of news sources and stories. As citizens, we must be vigilant against media threats to our democratic ideals. And as educators, this effort begins with you.

This site provides a useful inventory of just about every misleading news/media/social media website and categorizes it as bias, fake, conspiracy, unreliable, satire, hate, clickbait, political, rumor, etc. As an online source, it is able to be updated and therefore timeless (bit.ly/FalseMisleadingMedia).

For a good listing of think tanks and policy institutes from across the political spectrum, see http://bit.ly/ThinkTanksPolicyInstitutes.

Conclusion

In order to create positive change in response to the pervasive and organized ideological "war of ideas" perpetuated by the right in the United States, educators and concerned citizens must take substantial coordinated action to maintain their power within U.S. educational policy and practice. As mentioned throughout this book, this can be a daunting undertaking when educators feel they are merely one voice against a clamor of massive resources and organization. Our primary aim in this chapter was to provide resources and tools to help educators connect with other individuals and organizations within their communities in order to gain strength in numbers and in collective action.

The goal of using these resources to take collective action can be accomplished by taking steps to learn, organize, and take collective action. This book is a step toward becoming more informed. Educators and concerned citizens can begin by utilizing the resources in this chapter and throughout the book to educate themselves about the current educational landscape. We offer the following suggestions for further learning, resistance, and collective action.

1. Read.
   - Read factual and reputable news sources such as newspapers that emphasize fact-checking and ascribe to journalistic ethics and standards (i.e., *The New York Times*, *The Washington Post*, etc.).
   - Read widely and critically of other media sources to understand the spin that is being put on news sources for political gain. Ask yourself and encourage others to ask critical questions of the texts.
   - Share your readings with others and join forces with other educators, citizens, and progressive or grassroots organizations (such as those we have listed in this book) to work against individualistic efforts to dismantle public education.
2. Take Political Action.
   - Help register people to vote.
   - Consider running for office.

- Write your members of Congress on both sides of the aisle. Consider writing postcards, or joining with other educators to have a "postcard writing party."
- Get involved in local and state politics.
- Find out about the impact of ALEC and the State Policy Network (SPN) in your state and take action to push back.
- Track the money flowing into various educational institutions and question the possible strings attached to these donor agreements.
- Get involved with existing organizations or form new groups to represent particular community interests.

While this is only a partial list, we hope that it will serve as a starting point to help encourage educators and concerned citizens to use the power of their collective voice to take action and make positive changes to educational systems in the United States. It is only through questioning and having the courage to speak out collectively against unjust systems that the people of the United States can assure that the democratic process is preserved when it comes to making decisions and creating policies that impact our public schools and the children and adults who occupy them.

AUTHOR BIOS

KATHLEEN DEMARRAIS is a Professor in the Department of Lifelong Education, Administration, and Policy at the University of Georgia. With a background in sociology and anthropology of education, she serves as a qualitative methodologist in UGA's Qualitative Research Program. She has a long history of teaching qualitative research methods courses and mentoring doctoral students. Her research focuses on qualitative methodologies, critical qualitative research, qualitative pedagogy, and the teaching of qualitative research methodologies. A key research strand includes the history and funding of conservative philanthropists in the United States and their impact on educational policy and practice. In addition to numerous articles and book chapters, her books include *Foundations for Research: Methods of Inquiry in Education and the Social Sciences* (with S. Lapan), *Inside Stories, Educating Young Adolescent Girls* (with P. O'Reilly & B. Penn), *The Way Schools Work: A Sociological Analysis of Schooling* (with M. LeCompte), *Life at the Margins: Profiles of Diverse Adults* (with J. Merrifield, D. Hemphill, & B. Bingman), and *Teach for America Counter Narratives: Alumni Speak Up and Speak Out* (with T.J. Brewer).

T. JAMESON BREWER, Ph.D., is an Assistant Professor of Social Foundations of Education at the University of North Georgia. His teaching experience spans the middle school, high school, undergraduate, master's, and doctoral levels. Broadly conceptualized, his research focuses on the impact of privatization and marketization of public education by way of school vouchers, charter schools, alternative teacher certification, and homeschooling. His forthcoming books include *Becoming a Teacher in an Age of Reform: Global*

Lessons for Teacher Preparation and the Teaching Profession (with C. Lubienski) and *Teach for All Counter-Narratives: International Perspectives on a Global Reform Movement* (with K. deMarrais and K. McFaden). Follow him on Twitter: @tjamesonbrewer

BRIGETTE ADAIR HERRON is a Ph.D. candidate in the Department of Lifelong Education, Administration, and Policy at the University of Georgia. She is from Athens, Georgia, and holds a bachelor's degree in Anthropology, a master's degree in International Policy, and graduate certificates in Women's Studies, Interdisciplinary Qualitative Studies, and Global Health from the University of Georgia. Her scholarly research interests include global perspectives on justice-oriented feminist pedagogies in adult and higher education, examining the influence of philanthropy and dark money on curriculum and pedagogy in higher education, and teaching qualitative research methodology.

JAMIE C. ATKINSON is an Assistant Professor in the Department of Reading, Foundations, and Technology at Missouri State University, where he also serves as the Program Coordinator for the Masters Arts of Teaching Program. Jamie's research focuses on how sociopolitical dynamics and ideologies combine to drive state-level educational policymaking. This work includes examining the rapid rise of neotribalism and how political ideologues utilize education policy and curriculum as a tool to divide. An additional aspect of his work focuses on the use of critical self-analysis and personal narratives—critical autoethnographic approaches—to develop future educators' philosophical understandings. More generally, Jamie examines sociopolitical, historical, and philosophical foundations contributing to critical democratic understandings in teacher education. His teaching experience spans middle and high school, undergraduate, and graduate levels. Jamie's most recent journal article has been published in the journal *Democracy and Education*.

JAMIE B. LEWIS is an Associate Professor and Chair of Studies in Educational Foundations at Georgia Gwinnett College who began her professional career as an attorney and practiced law in Knoxville, Tennessee. She earned her Ph.D. in Social Foundations at the University of Georgia. Jamie's scholarship focuses on the impact of power and privilege on educational practices and policies, as well as the examination of the sociocultural contexts of education. Her dissertation was a legal history of segregated education in Kansas between 1888 and 1954, in which she was able to combine her interests in law, sociocultural contexts, history, and the ways in which power and privilege impact educational practices and policies. Her current research explores how political connections between philanthropists and federal and state governments inform educational policies and practices such as the Charter School Movement, Trigger Laws, Every Student Succeeds Act, ALEC, and the Supreme Court's *Citizens United* decision.

JOHN DAYTON is a Professor of Education Law and Policy at the University of Georgia and Adjunct Professor of Higher Education. He serves as Editor-in-Chief of the *Education Law & Policy Review* and Director of the Education Law Consortium (see www.edlawcon.org), a non-partisan pro bono research group dedicated to advancing knowledge and practice in education law. Professor Dayton is an internationally recognized expert on law and policy, with experience in public and private legal practice. He has served as a judicial clerk and as a public school educator and program director. Professor Dayton holds both a law degree and a doctoral degree in educational administration and policy from Indiana University. He has taught law and policy courses for three decades, including education law, higher education law, special education law, medical law, and professional ethics. Dr. Dayton was awarded the Glickman Award for excellence in research and teaching. He is a member of the prestigious University Teaching Academy and serves on the editorial boards of leading scholarly journals in education law, policy, and finance. Dr. Dayton is the author of over 100 law review articles, books, and other publications on law and policy. He is an internationally recognized author and speaker on law and policy issues.

LISA CASTANEDA has a Master's degree in education and is a cofounder and the CEO of foundry10, a philanthropic educational research group. After teaching grades K–8 for ten years, Lisa jumped at the opportunity to start a philanthropic organization that was charged with expanding the ways in which people think about learning. The unique organizational structure of foundry10 is influenced by Lisa's years of experience in education and her desire to work collaboratively with educators, community members, and researchers in an authentic and useful way. Her primary areas of focus are organizational development, technology in schools, professional development and sustainability of programs, and vocational learning. Lisa's work has been featured in a variety of publications across several domains, and she actively shares her work at both educational and research-oriented conferences.

INDEX

50CAN, 250-251
74, the, 274
990s, IRS, 49, 93, 98-99, 101, 103, 106, 147-148, 195, 301
A Nation at Risk (ANAR), 238, 245, 265
Accountability, 245-247
  hyper-accountability, 237
  in education, 3, 17, 19, 22, 26, 46, 76, 140-141, 152, 163-165, 238, 245-247, 250
  in campaign ads, 133
Adolph Coors Foundation, 64
Allegheny Foundation, 48, 147-148. *See also* Scaife Family Foundations
American Creed, 126, 130
American Enterprise Institute, 43, 50, 52, 62-63, 70, 104, 184, 187
American Legislative Exchange Council (ALEC), 139-169, 187, 203-204, 243, 248, 250, 252-254, 263, 283, 297-304
  alumni, 159-161
  core programs and projects, 162-168
  future plans, 166-168
  history of, 139-149
  leadership structure, 149-150
  membership, 149-161
  model bills and legislation, 141, 149, 163-169, 301
  policy centers, 167
  sources of funding, 144-149, 167
  task forces, 149, 151-152
American Opportunity Foundation, 49
Americans for Prosperity, 104, 150, 187, 203

Annie E. Casey Foundation, 40, 142
Anschutz Foundation, 142, 148
Arthur Rock, 251
Association of Private Enterprise Education, 200, 207
Astroturfing, 142
  strategies, 283
Austin v. Michigan, 119, 124
Austrian economics, 188

Barron, Eric, 199-203
Bastiat Society, 207
BB&T, 198-201, 205-206, 213-217. *See also* BB&T Foundation
Bellamy, Ray, 197, 202
Benson, Bruce, 198-200
Bennett, William, 48, 59, 67-68. *See also* Empower America
Big Philanthropy, 142, 167-168, 231, 283, 297-301
Bill of Rights, 126-127
Bill and Melinda Gates Foundation (Gates Foundation), 142, 144, 146-147, 250-252
Bipartisan Campaign Reform Act (BCRA), 117
Bossie, David, 118
Bradley, Lynde and Harry, 38, 41-42, 44-47, 49, 53, 58-60, 63-68, 70, 79, 93, 101, 103, 107, 145, 147-148, 191, 274. *See also* Lynde and Harry Bradley Foundation
Brandeis, Louis, 115, 135
Broad Foundation, 250-251
Brown v. Board of Education, 24, 184, 187

309

Buchanan, James McGill, 184-187, 191-192
Buckley v. Valeo, 117-118
Bush, George, H. W., 10
Bush, George W., 31, 47, 60, 82, 130
  administration, 32, 70, 82
  base, 53
  campaign, 67
  white house, 48
Bush, Jeb, 141

Campaign finance, 115-117, 120-121, 124, 134
Capitalism, 3-5, 15, 17, 23, 44-45, 190-191, 206, 213-216, 217, 264, 272
  American, 190
  democratic, 45
  laissez-faire, 44
  Professor of, 206
  Programs of, 216
  study of, 213-215
  unregulated, 191
Capitalist, 4, 9, 15, 91, 174, 190, 214, 239, 268
  economy, 4, 239
  ideas, 190
  realism, 268
  system, 9, 15, 174, 214
  wealthy capitalists, 91, 109
Carter, Jimmy, 131
Castle Rock Foundation, 64, 107, 144
Catholic Schools, 38, 178, 180, 219
  Catholic University of America, 178, 180, 219
Cato Institute, the, 43, 63, 69-70, 75, 85, 104, 187, 213, 216
Center for Education Reform (CER), 47, 69, 148
Center of Study for Public Choice, 187
Charles Koch Foundation (CKF), 101, 103, 107, 145, 147-148, 168, 175, 177-181, 196-212, 215, 217, 220, 297, 301. *See also* Charles G. Koch Foundation

Charles G. Koch Foundation, 63, 75, 92, 103, 107, 144, 147, 175
Charter Schools, 16-17, 23, 26-28, 38-39, 47, 52, 68-69, 76-77, 100, 109, 148, 163-165, 237-238, 241, 243-245, 247, 250-254, 262, 305. *See also* Schools
  charter network, 251
  Charter School Act of 1998, 77
  Charter School Growth Fund, 252
  Charter School Resource Center, 76
  laws, 163
  movement, 69
  Next Generation Charter Schools Act, 164
Chodorov, Frank, 36, 54-58, 61, 80
Churchill, Winston, 130
Citizens United, 92, 110, 115-134
Citizens United v. FEC, 91, 120-121
Citizens for a Sound Economy, 68, 187
Civil Rights, 240,
  language of, 251
Civil Rights Movement, 184, 185, 255
Claude R. Lambe Foundation, 63, 188
Clinton, Hillary, 119, 271
Clinton Foundation, 248
Club for Growth, the, 187
Collegiate Network, 43, 50, 58-61
Comcast, 275
Common Core State Standards (CCSS), 19, 142
Competitive Enterprise Institute, 187
Coors, Holland "Holly", 64
Coors, Joseph, 64,
Coors, Peter, 144
Corporations are people, 116

Dark Money: The Hidden History of the Billionaires Behind the Rise of the Radical Right, 184
Democracy, 7-8, 26, 33, 91, 95, 115-117, 125, 127, 130-134, 267-268, 270, 299
  American, 125, 131
  dismantling, 95

INDEX

Democracy, *cont.*
  Reclaim Democracy, 299
  threat to, 267, 270
Democracy in Chains, 184
Democracy Reform Act, 134
Democrats for Education Reform (DFER), 249, 252
DeVoe L. Moore Center, 200-202
DeVos, Betsy, 16-17, 109-110, 242-243, 274-275
DeVos Urban Leadership Initiative, 93, 108
Disney, 275,
Donors Capital Fund (DCF), vii, 95, 101-105, 109-110
Donors Trust (DT), vii, 95, 101-105, 109-110, 148
Donor-advised funds, 101-102, 104, 109, 148
Doris and Donald Fisher Fund, 251
D'Souza, Dinesh, 61-62, 267

Earhart Foundation, 41, 53, 58, 63, 93, 107
Education, vii-viii, 3-6, 11, 13-28, 31-36, 38, 40, 46-49, 52, 56-84, 91-106, 109-110, 132, 140-142, 148, 151-152, 154, 162-169, 177, 181-183, 192, 197, 202-204, 206, 210, 215, 220, 229-232, 237-255, 261-277, 283-303
  activities, 40, 98, 167, 220
  as public good, 109
  career and technical, 17
  civics, 98, 132
  collective good in, 93, 237, 301
  colleges of, 244-246, 250
  democratic, 28
  deregulate, 277
  economic, 3, 195
  higher education, 21, 50, 68, 71, 141, 164-165, 168, 181-182, 184-185, 192, 197, 202-204, 206, 210, 230-231, 297, 300-301
  K-12, 67-68
  K-16, 15

Education, *cont.*
  legislation, 169, 242, 297
  marketplace, 248, 250
  materials, 192
  model bills, 140, 164-166
  neoliberalism in, 3-6, 94, 101, 244, 261, 265
  online, 21
  organizations, viii, ix, 76, 83
  P-12, 163-165, 168
  P-16, 32, 83
  policies, vii, 16, 21, 23, 28, 31-32, 50, 63, 67, 70, 75, 83, 109, 111, 148, 166, 266-268, 297-298, 301, 303
  pre-k, 75
  private, 163, 185, 241
  privatization of, 16, 22, 71, 106, 185, 241, 248, 269, 302
  programs, 81, 177
  public, 15, 57, 80, 83, 91, 93-94, 106, 109, 140-142, 163-164, 165, 246, 268, 303
  reforms, vii, ix, 16-17, 69, 75-76, 93-94, 237-238, 241-255, 261-265, 274, 277, 302
  reform network, 247-255
  religious, 52
  savings accounts, 17, 163
  sex education, abstinence-only, 21-22
  science, 238
  State Board of Education, 164-165
  STEM, 238
  task force, 140, 151-152, 154, 253-254
  teacher education, 84, 141, 244-245
  United States Department of (USDOE), 71, 154, 250
Education Reform Now, 249-250, 252
Education savings accounts, 17, 163
Education Teacher Performance Assessment (ETPA), 141
Educational philanthropy, 283-285, 287-288, 291, 295-296
EducationPost, 274
Electoral College, 115

Eli and Edythe Broad Foundation, 142
Enactus, 201
Empower America, 67-68, 82. *See also* Bennett, William
ExxonMobil, 144-145, 147, 150

F. M. Kirby Foundation, 41, 93, 107,
Facebook, 269, 271-272
Fake News, 94, 268, 271-272, 275, 302
Fahrenheit 9/11, 31
Federal Election Campaign Act of 1971, 117
Federalism, 139, 151, 155, 159, 162, 168
  anti-, 13
Fink, Richard, 187-189
First Amendment, 117-123, 128-129, 165
Florida State University (FSU), 181
  Economics department, 195
  FSU Progress Coalition, 198
  Florida State University Foundation, 181
    establishment of, 195
  resistance, 200
  Students for Healthcare Reform, 201
Foreign interference, 127
Forming Open and Robust University Minds (FORUM) Act, 164-165
Foundation for Excellence in Education (FEE), 141
Four Sisters, 41
Fox News, 78-80, 268, 273
  Letterman, David on, 83
  Fox and Friends, 267
Free Congress Foundation (see American Opportunity Foundation), 49, 63-64
Free market, viii, 4-5
  ideology, 175, 177-178, 216, 220
  free-market nationalism, 17, 142
  and education, 22, 52, 243
  O'Connell, Frank memo, 42
  Chodorov on, 54-56
  conservative think tanks, 63, 67, 73, 206

Free market, *cont.*
  and ALEC, 159-168
  philanthropists, 174-175
  scholars, 183-184, 192, 213
  free society, 190-191
  Benson, Bruce, 198
  curriculum, 200, 240
  Students for Healthcare Reform, 201
  and entrepreneurism, 238
Free speech, 50, 116-122, 127-129, 163. *See also* Citizens United; FORUM Act
Freedom Works, 68-69, 187
Friedman, Milton, 16, 61, 237
Friedmanism, 237-238, 242, 245

Gates, Bill, 40
Gates Foundation (Bill and Melinda Gates Foundation, the), 40, 142, 144, 146, 250-252
General Motors Foundation, 146-147
George Mason University, ix
  foundation, 182
  history of Koch's involvement, 176-180, 184-192
  Buchanan, James McGill, 184-187
  Institute of Humane Studies (IHS), 104, 179, 181, 182, 188-189
  law school, 183
  Center for Study of Public Choice, 49
  Mercatus Center *see* Mercatus Center
  student resistance, 194-195
  Transparent GMU, 195
Georgia Public Policy Foundation, 76-78. *See also* SPN
Gleason Family Foundation, 145, 147-148
Goldwater Institute, the, 75, 142
Great Schools Tax Credit Program Act, 164
Great Society, the, 129

Hayek, F. A., 188

INDEX 313

Heritage Foundation, the 40, 43, 46, 48, 50, 63
  Fuelner, Edwin Jr. 58
  history of 64
  student leader development 65-66
  Bennett, William 67-68. *See also* Empower America
Homeschool, 241, 247

Independent Institute, 43, 183, 206
Intercollegiate Society of Individualists (ISI), 55, 58
Intercollegiate Studies Institute, 43, 48-50, 58
Institute for Educational Affairs (IEA), 37, 42, 46, 59
Institute for Humane Studies (IHS), 104, 179, 181, 182, 188-189
  history of, 191-192
  talent pipeline, 202
  funding for, 218
IRS Tax Codes, 95
  501(c)(3), 96
  501(c)(4), 96-97

James Madison Institute, 201-203
Jaquelin Hume Foundation, 146-147
Jefferson, Thomas, 10, 61
Jeffersonian Project, the, 162
John Birch Society, 44, 185
John Locke Foundation, 207
John M. Olin Foundation. *See* Olin, John M.
Jones, Alex, 160, 271-272
Joyce Foundation, 142
JM Foundation, 63

Koch,
  Charles G., ix, 53, 94, 103, 184-185, 188
  David H., 63, 175
  Fred, 185
  funding of universities and colleges, 220-230
  Koch Cover-Up Bill, 203

Koch brothers, 250, 252-253. *See also* Koch
Koch Family Foundation
Kristol, Irving, 6, 37, 46, 79
Kristol, William, 60

Laura and John Arnold Foundation, 142, 250-251
Limited government, 5, 42, 45, 61, 63-65, 101-102, 118, 166, 168, 216, 273
Lumina Foundation, the, 145, 147
Lynde & Harry Bradley Foundation, 38, 41-42, 44-47, 49, 53, 58-60, 63, 68, 70, 79, 101, 103, 107, 145, 147-148, 191, 274
Lopez, Ed 209
  Koch organizations 206
  Center for Study of Free Enterprise, 209-210
  Strategy Document 212. *See also* School choice

Marcuse, Herbert, 34
MacLean, Nancy, 184-188
Mayer, Jane, 109, 184, 197
McCarthy, Joseph, 265
McConnell v. FEC, 119-122, 125, 129
McCutcheon v. Federal Election Commission, 132
Memorandum of Understanding (MOU), 195
Mercatus Center, 74, 176, 179, 181
  Koch funding for, 182
  history of, 188
  political economy, 188-191
Meritocracy, 17, 239-240, 246-248, 251
Michael and Susan Dell Foundation, 142, 251
Miller, Kent S., 197, 202
Moore, Michael, 31
Moral Foundation of Capitalism (MFOC) Program, 216-217
Myrdal, Gunnar, 126

Nader, Ralph, 34

National Council for Teacher Quality (NCTQ), 250
National Voter Registration Act (Motor Voter Act), 186
Neoconservative, 6, 9
  post-neoconservative, 14-16
Neoliberal, 15, 17, 93, 110, 140, 142, 163, 266
  agenda for education, 3-6, 94, 101, 244, 261, 265
  ideas, 22-23, 25-26, 250, 262
  ideology, 14, 110, 231, 238-240, 245, 254, 274
  knowledge regime, 141
  language, 26
  policies, 16, 21, 28, 148
  political project, 261
  reform, 244
  thought, 13
  neoliberals, 11-12, 15, 17, 28
Neoliberalism, 3-6, 244, 265-266, 268
  definition and history of, 4-6
  as a form of governmental reason, 5
  in education, 3, 244, 265-266, 268
New Deal, 10, 38, 129, 132
NewSchools Venture Fund (NSVF), 250
Next Generation Charter Schools Act, 164
Nixon, Richard M, 33, 37, 46

Oligarchy, 91, 115-116, 130-131, 134
Olin, John M. (John M. Olin Foundation), 38-39, 45
  four sisters, 41
  history of, 41-42
  funding initiatives, 43-44, 58-59, 67
  Joyce, Michael, 46
  see Philanthropy Roundtable
  American Enterprise Institute, 62-63
  Empower America, 68
  Piereson, James, 81
  Intercollegiate Studies Institute, 43
  Donors Trust, 103

One person one vote, 116

Partnerships for Student Success, 164
Pearson, 141
Pence, Mike, 187
Philanthropic educational research organization, 286
Philanthropy Roundtable, the, vii-viii, 91
  history of, 37-38
  educational programming, 39-40
  members, 53
  see Powell Memo (Powell Manifesto)
  guiding principles, 100
  Meyerson, Adam, 101
PhRMA, 144, 150
Pioneer Institute, the, 142
Political
  advocacy, 41, 67
    Citizens United, 119
    education reform network, 249
  corruption, 117, 119, 127, 130
  gerrymandering, 133
  process, vii, 40, 116, 127-129, 133-135
  speech, 120-123
Powell, Court Justice Lewis F. Powell, Jr, 33
Powell Memo, the (also Powell Manifesto), 33-37, 64, 71, 173-174
  "The Haves and the Have Mores", 91. *See also Citizens United v. FEC*
Private enterprise, vii, 42-45
Progress Florida, 200
Public Choice Society, 207

Rand, Ayn, 198-200,
  Ayn Rand Institute, 216
Randolph Foundation, the, 38
Rasmussen, David W., 202
Radical Right, 109, 190
  philanthropic giving, 184. *See also Democracy in Chains*

INDEX

Reagan, Ronald, 6-7, 13, 130. *See also*
　A Nation at Risk (ANAR)
　neo-Reagan, 8
　Reagan administration, 187
　Joyce, Michael S., 47-48
　Feulner, Edwin Jr., 58
　Bennett, William, 67
　Kirkpatrick, Jean, 82
　George Mason University, 187
　Cowen, Tyler, 190
　Reaganomics, 238
Rehnquist, William H., 33
Reich, Charles, 34
Resistance, 193, 220, 302
Resisting the gift, 230-232
Return on investment (ROI), 178
Reynolds v. Sims, 116
Richard and Helen DeVos (Amway) Foundation, 41, 80, 103, 274. *See also* DeVos Urban Leadership Initiative, 93, 108
　Amway pyramid scheme, 80
　Donors Trust, 103
　TPUSA, 274
Richardson, Grace Jones, 51
Richardson, Lunsford, 51
Robertson Foundation, 250-251
Rove, Karl, 47

Scaife Family Foundations
　Sarah Scaife Foundation, 48, 50, 53, 63, 93, 108, 191
　Allegheny Foundation, 48, 147-148
　Carthage Foundation, 48-49, 53, 59, 63
　Scaife Family Charitable Trust, 186
Scaife Foundations. *See* Scaife Family Foundations
Scaife, Richard Mellon, 48, 144, 168
Scalia, Antonin
　Antonin Scalia Law School, 192-194
　see Citizens United v. FEC
Scholarships, 92, 201, 214, 216. *See also* ALEC

Scholarships, *cont.*
　Freedom Reader's Scholarship Group, 201
　tax credit, 163
　talent pipeline, 192
School Choice, ix, 17, 19-20, 28, 269, 236. *See also* Free market; School vouchers
　Libertarian Party on, 22
　Democratic Party, 23
　Bradley Foundation, 46-47
　faith-based funding for, 47, 242
　Heritage Foundation and, 69
　Ravitch, Diane, 70-71
　conservative think tanks, 77. *See also* ALEC; CER
School Turnaround and Leadership Development Act, 164
Schools,
　charter, 16-17, 23, 27-28, 47, 52, 69, 100
　　Charter School Resource Center, 69
　　Georgia Public Policy Foundation, 77
　　Donors Trust, 108-109
　　Center for Education Reform (CER), 148. *See also* ALEC
　education reforms, 237, 243
　growth of, 245
　myth of failing, 18, 163, 94, 109, 237, 264
　private, 17, 57, 68-69, 94, 242
　　Philanthropy Roundtable, 100. *See also* Vouchers
　public (public education), 16, 23, 25, 237
　　Chodorov on, 57
　　Heritage, 68
　　privatization of, 140,165. *See also* segregation
　　reform, 241-243, 248, 260
　　DeVos, Betsy on, 253
　　role of media, 263, 265-268
　　opinions on, 264, 266

Scott, Rick, 203
Searle Freedom Trust, 145
Segregation, 185-186, 243-244
  Brown v. Board, 187
Sinclair Broadcast Group (SBG)
  Trump, Donald 270
  consolidation and propaganda, 275, 277
Smith Richardson Foundation (H. Smith Richardson Foundation), 38, 41, 53. *See also* Four Sisters;
  Vicks VapoRub grants, 52
  public policy spending, 63
Stand Your Ground law, 147
State-by-state strategy, 141
State Policy Network (SPN), 53, 92, 146, 168, 301
  about, 73-74
  philanthropist funding, 74
  Georgia Public Policy Foundation, 76-78
  James Madison Institute, 202-203
Stokes, Garnett, 203
Stowers, Ryan, 175, 182
Strings attached, ix, 194, 196
  FSU and Koch, 197-198
  resist the gift, 300
Student Future's Program Act, 164
Students for Education Reform (SFER), 248, 250, 252-253
Students in Free Enterprise Club, 201. *See also* Enactus
Super PACs, 133, 299
Suffolk University, 178, 180, 219, 229,
Sydnor, Eugene B., Jr., 33, 173, 219

Taft Hartley Act, 116
Teach For America (TFA), 244-252, 274
Teacher Quality Assurance Act, 164
Tillman Act, 116, 124
Trigger laws, 142-143, 252
Trump, Donald, 9, 14, 240
  and DeVos, Betsy, 17, 253
  and Bossie, David, 118-119

Trump, Donald, *cont.*
  ties to media, 270-273
  TPUSA, 274
Turning Point USA (TPUSA), 274
  mission statement, 273
Twitter, 270, 271

UnKoch My Campus, 194-195, 198-206
UPS Foundation, 145, 147

Vanguard Charitable Endowment, the, 146-148
Venture Philanthropy, ix, 248, 250-25, 25, 262, 277
  organizations, 252
Viacom, 275
Vicks VapoRub, 51
Voucher, School Voucher, 17, 41, 47, 52, 57
  Pro-voucher groups, 46

Walker, Scott, 160
  Ed Uihlein Foundation, 275
Walmart, 41, 84, 144
Walton Family. *See* Walton Family Foundation
Walton Family Foundation, 41, 70, 101, 108, 142, 148, 201, 250-251
War of ideas, viii, 40, 70, 167, 173, 302. *See also* Powell Memo, the
Washington Policy Center, 142
Wealthy, 32, 69, 93, 95, 115-116, 132-133, 175, 184, 187, 243, 262, 284
  corporations, 121, 127-128, 13,
  factions, 126-127, 130
  philanthropists, vii, 91-92, 94, 220, 230, 267
Western Carolina University (WCU), ix, 178, 180-181, 206-220, 229, 231,
  BB&T Foundation, 206, 214-216
  Koch funding, 181, 208-211
  Center for Study of Free Enterprise, 208-215

Weyrich, Paul
 American Opportunity Foundation, 49, 64
 ALEC, 144

William and Flora Hewlett Foundation, 142

YouTube, 270, 272